WORK IN BLACK AND WHITE

WORK IN BLACK AND WHITE

STRIVING FOR THE
AMERICAN DREAM

ENOBONG HANNAH BRANCH
AND CAROLINE HANLEY

Russell Sage Foundation • New York

Library of Congress Cataloging-in-Publication Data

Names: Branch, Enobong Hannah, 1983- author. | Hanley, Caroline, author.
Title: Work in black and white : striving for the American dream / Enobong Hannah Branch and Caroline Hanley.
Description: New York : Russell Sage Foundation, [2022] | Includes bibliographical references and index. | Summary: "Black and White Americans have responded to increasing economic insecurity in very different ways, reconciling their economic realities within distinctly racialized conceptions of meritocracy and the American dream. Americans in all racial groups often put faith in education as the key to upward mobility. But as education provides less and less job and financial security, Black and White men and women are forced to navigate a contradictory ideological constellation where education is still seen as the great equalizer and lynchpin of equal opportunity but where evidence shows that education does not ultimately ameliorate the inequalities they are trying to overcome. For historical reasons, Black and White workers respond to the levels of insecurity in their lives in ways that diverge according to their racial group, and the rise of insecure work has also changed the way Black and White men and women draw on conceptions of race and gender—their own, others'—to make sense of who deserves security. This book highlights the divergence in the narratives that Black and White Americans use to explain their misfortunes and those of others, because the stories people tell matter. By shining a light on the way these stories have influenced people's responses to their struggles, this book offers a possibility for change. It shows that the way people interpret insecurity, inequality, and uncertainty is not merely due to economic misfortune but the result of political choices in the face of the legacies of historical inequality"—Provided by publisher.
Identifiers: LCCN 2022021941 (print) | LCCN 2022021942 (ebook) | ISBN 9780871540232 (paperback ; alk. paper) | ISBN 9781610449014 (ebook)
Subjects: LCSH: Working class—United States. | Middle class—United States. | African Americans—Economic conditions. | Minorities—Economic conditions. | American Dream. | United States—Economic conditions—1945- | United States—Social conditions—1945-
Classification: LCC HD8072.5 .B7265 2022 (print) | LCC HD8072.5 (ebook) | DDC 331.0973—dc23/eng/20220505
LC record available at https://lccn.loc.gov/2022021941
LC ebook record available at https://lccn.loc.gov/2022021942

Text design by Genna Patacsil.

RUSSELL SAGE FOUNDATION
112 East 64th Street, New York, New York 10065
10 9 8 7 6 5 4 3 2 1

For our daughters,
Jocelyn, Jasmine, and Thea

Contents

═ Illustrations ═

Figures

Tables

═ About the Authors ═

Enobong Hannah Branch is senior vice president for equity and professor of sociology at Rutgers University.

Caroline Hanley is associate professor of sociology at William & Mary.

$=$ Acknowledgments $=$

Thank you does not seem like nearly enough to say to the many people and institutions that made this book possible. The book spans three institutions. First, the University of Massachusetts–Amherst, where our fruitful collaboration got its start. We are deeply indebted to Joya Misra and Donald Tomaskovic-Devey, both of whom made it an enriching intellectual environment to begin our academic careers. As we navigated our way through the postdissertation publication haze all those years ago and found our rhythm, their support has been consistent. This book reflects a collaboration that is over ten years long, and Joya and Don have been along for the journey. Reading everything from article drafts to grant submissions and ultimately the book prospectus, they have provided insightful comments and prodding questions that have made our work better, and we are grateful.

Second, William & Mary, where I (Caroline) continued my academic career. Good colleagues make all the difference, and I want to thank my colleagues in the Sociology Department at William & Mary for making Boswell Hall a pleasant place to work and for creating opportunities to build community outside of work. Third, Rutgers University–New Brunswick, where I (Anna) serve in administrative leadership but am able to find space for the intellectual work that I find life-giving. I am deeply indebted to Lajeanesse Harris, Joan Collier, and Jessica Zura, the wonderful folks I have the pleasure of working with every day, for helping to manage my administrative load and hold space so that I can fill my academic cup by ensuring that I find time to write. I owe a special debt to Candace King, my special project and research assistant for the last three years whose analytical brilliance is matched only by her kindness. We would not have been able to complete this book without you.

The research this book shares was supported by a 2014 National Science Foundation grant "The Rise of Insecure Work and Changes in Durable Inequality" (NSF #1424140). Amy Schalet contributed extensively to the qualitative research design as well as the data collection; she and Jackie Stein were members of the intellectual community in which this project was created. We want to acknowledge the many contributions of the research team that supported Anna in the qualitative data analysis. Several graduate students—Armanthia Duncan, Kyla Walters, Lucius Couloute, and Kelly Giles—contributed to the data collection, transcript review, preliminary coding, and early analysis. We also want to thank three undergraduate students—Lajeanesse Harris, Sarah Lilley, and Darriel Alicea—for their extensive support of the qualitative data collection and analysis. We also acknowledge the work of graduate and undergraduate students who supported Caroline's quantitative analysis, including Sharla Alegria and Anthony Rainey, former University of Massachusetts–Amherst graduate students in sociology; and the following William & Mary undergraduate research assistants: Peter Hansen, Bethany Lesser, Kayla Shoemaker, Avanthika Singh, and Emma Schmidt.

There is a reason that Suzanne Nichols at the Russell Sage Foundation is a legend. Her championing of this project from advance contract to serial extensions provided the right mix of pressure and support that kept us on track. If Suzanne was our coach, prodding us to extend an argument here or identify a line of analysis there (for example, Covid-19) to make the project stronger, Chris Lura—developmental editor extraordinaire—was our trainer, going deep into the trenches with us to make sure our argument was clear, concrete, and concise. We would like to thank Joya Misra for her feedback on early drafts of the manuscript and the anonymous reviewers for pushing us to marshal the data we had compiled and refine our story; the final product is infinitely better for your insights.

Although the research leading up to this book began in 2014, most of its writing took place during the Covid-19 pandemic. We produced this book during extended periods of working from home while our spouses worked and our children learned nearby. In this challenging context, more than ever, we are particularly grateful for our families.

I (Caroline Hanley) would like to thank my parents, John and Sandra Hanley, for their boundless love and support and for sparking my interest in work and inequality in our many conversations about good jobs and bad jobs while I was growing up in rural Maine in the 1980s and 1990s. Thanks to my daughter, Thea Stow, who was born in the same year that this project began and whose love of creating art, sharing stories, and playing "the floor is lava" provided many welcome opportunities to put the laptop away during the writing of this book. Throughout the project and long before, my husband, Simon Stow, has never failed to believe in me, to delight with the breadth of his knowledge, to make me laugh, and to see the big picture when I am caught up in the details. Thank you.

I (Anna Branch) am grateful to my husband, Joel Branch. We have been on an incredible ride for many years now. I often say I have two jobs, my administrative role and my academic life, and both spill over well past the day into the night and, at times, the weekend. Joel picks up the slack and shows me some grace. I am grateful to my daughters, Jocelyn and

Jasmine, for ready smiles and distractions, whether I knew I needed them or not. Michelle Stephens, Adia Harvey Wingfield, and Melissa Wooten believed I could do it when, between exhaustion and data overload, I was unsure; they were my cheerleaders, and I am grateful. Finally, I would like to thank my parents, Joseph and Mardette; my sisters, Rachel and Faith; and the extended community I found in Connecticut and New Jersey for believing in me and the countless ways in which they made the material in this book come to life and reinforced the old African proverb, "If you want to go fast, go alone, but if you want to go far, go together." Thank you all for going with me.

Introduction

The Covid-19 pandemic laid bare the inequality of the American labor market. As the economy contracted and unemployment soared in the spring of 2020, commentators noted the racial disparity in who was still going to work. Black and Brown employees were disproportionately represented in traditionally devalued segments of the labor force that were newly considered essential. These jobs were characterized by low wages and uncertainty; though some could be considered full-time, almost none paid a living wage. The jobs that enabled some Americans to stay at home required the exposure and vulnerability of other Americans, and that divide fell often along racial lines. According to one estimate, 80 percent of Black Americans worked in jobs that could not be performed from home.[1]

For the first time in recent history, Americans were forced to see what had previously been rendered invisible—the racial fractures of the labor market. While Black poverty and urban inequality have historically been framed as the result of individual choices and the lack of personal responsibility, the world watched as largely Black and Brown workers stood close together on subway platforms, trains, and buses in New York City, unable to observe social distancing as they headed to work.[2] We witnessed the resulting impact of exposure: mounting fatalities in poorer communities as those workers returned home and brought Covid-19 with them.[3]

Nationwide, Black Americans make up 12.4 percent of the population, but they made up 21.5 percent of the Covid-19 deaths in April 2020.[4] Although comorbidities were a factor, this disparity had everything to do with labor market inequality.[5] If, under the most hazardous conditions, Black Americans risked it all by continuing to work, perhaps the United States is finally ready to collectively grapple with the fact that Black poverty was never about individual choices and personal responsibility. Furthermore, even as it laid bare these deep racial inequalities in the labor market, the pandemic also crushed job opportunities for White Americans, who found themselves in a labor market with unemployment reaching Great Depression levels. It's time we recognize the fact that personal effort alone is insufficient to improve one's occupational or financial situation in the face of vast structural limitations to opportunity.

Until the mid-1970s and 1980s, White male workers, both skilled and unskilled, often took for granted the availability of secure work paying a decent wage that allowed them to support themselves and their families. Black workers were accustomed, historically, to unevenness in opportunity. Their access to jobs was conditioned by market whims and needs. Gender differences in opportunity also relegated Black women to marginalized, uncertain, and poorly paid work.[6] Title VII of the Civil Rights Act of 1964 and the Equal Employment Opportunity Act of 1972 were passed in order to address some of these disparities by prohibiting discrimination based on race, gender, and other protected statuses, with the goal of creating equal opportunity in the labor market. But around the same time antidiscrimination became the law of the land and minorities (and women) began to gain access to jobs with decent wages, those jobs were also becoming more insecure, owing to employers' increasing reliance on technology and outsourcing to manage their labor needs as well as a combination of macroeconomic trends and policy choices. These political and economic changes encouraged employers to approach labor as a cost to be managed and minimized rather than a resource to be developed and invested in. As a result, since the 1970s, economic inequality has risen dramatically in the United States. For Americans, the expectation of working for one employer, attaining a comfortable and stable standard of living, and then retiring has become obsolete.

The ability to achieve economic security through hard work is the central tenet of the American Dream. In the post–World War II period, for example, workers—White males in particular—could gain access to the middle class through well-paying, skilled and unskilled blue-collar jobs, and the American Dream was a plausible aspiration for many people. Institutional protections, such as unions and collective bargaining, created and preserved these well-paying jobs and helped fuel growth in the American middle class in the decades following the war.

Today, however, unions have long been on the decline and the good jobs of the postwar period are gone. Getting a good education—a college degree or even an advanced degree—is increasingly seen as a requirement to be considered for a good job. Although higher education continues to give people advantages in the labor market compared to those without postsecondary education, many people are finding that obtaining an education is not an effective insurance policy against insecurity or a substitute for strong institutional protections and a favorable structure of opportunity (that is, a ready availability of good jobs). Yet as this book makes clear, among Americans across racial categories, the belief that hard work and education will help them achieve prosperity and will deliver security endures, despite evidence that the path to security is less straightforward today, even for those racial and gender groups with more privileged access in the past.

Black and White Americans have responded to increasing economic insecurity in very different ways, reconciling their economic realities within distinctly racialized conceptions of meritocracy and the American Dream. Americans in all racial groups often put their faith in education as the most important key to upward mobility. But as education provides less and less job and financial security in an era of outsourcing, technological transformation, and other macroeconomic changes, Blacks and Whites, men and women, are forced to navigate a contradictory ideological constellation: education is still seen as the great equalizer and lynchpin of equal opportunity, but evidence shows that education does not ultimately ameliorate the inequalities they are trying to overcome. Today all workers are negotiating vulnerability and uncertainty in the labor market. Educated workers in particular increasingly find that their credentials do not provide job security, and educated non-White workers also find that racial inequality continues to block access to work. As we show in this book, White and Black Americans, influenced by the stories that American culture has historically told about the American Dream and about who should have access to it and who should not, are grappling with whom to blame when striving is not enough.

For historical reasons that we lay out here, Black and White workers respond to the economic insecurity in their lives in divergent ways. White workers, having been forced to develop coping mechanisms to manage mounting insecurity and make sense of why their personal efforts have not led to the secure life they grew up believing they would have, are more likely to feel pessimistic and to claim that the American Dream is increasingly out of reach. Black workers, on the other hand, with their historical experience of lack of access to the American Dream, explain their struggle with insecurity differently. They tend to see the lack of opportunities and expanding insecurity in the U.S. labor market as a continuation of systemic inequality, and some connect it to the legacy of structural racism. Although their labor and economic insecurities remain, on average, more significant than those of their White counterparts, they have a different set of coping mechanisms, born of familiarity with insecurity, and they tell different stories about what the promise of education and the American Dream mean in their lives.

The rise of insecure work has also changed the way Blacks and Whites, women and men, draw on conceptions of race and gender—their own and others'—to make sense of who deserves security. Because the stories that people tell matter, we highlight the divergence in the narratives that Black and White Americans use to explain their misfortunes and those of others. These narratives construct the status quo, revealing how evolving ideas about race and gender—alongside ideas about inequality and meritocracy—influence how people cope in insecure labor markets. Stories have the power to make inequality seem legitimate (or not) and to shape action, both in and outside the labor market. Ultimately, as this book shows, how people manage insecurity is determined by their understanding of the status quo—including their expectations and power within that status quo. Most importantly, by shining a light on the influence of these stories on people's responses to their struggles, this book also points to possibilities for change by showing that how people interpret insecurity, inequality, and uncertainty is due to not merely economic misfortune but also political choices in the face of the legacies of historical inequality.

Why Study the Black/White Binary?

Since the 1970s in the United States, we have become much more acquainted with economic insecurity than with economic security. The shift toward insecurity in this socioeconomic moment, however, is determined not just by one's income level or family wealth. Today even those who are wealthy and appear objectively "secure" often articulate feelings of risk and economic insecurity.[7] Indeed, as other scholars have observed, economic security derives from more than just a high annual income, or stable employment relations, or a comfortable standard of living, although these are important. It also requires a deeper feeling of confidence in not being at risk of a hardship-causing economic loss.[8] Hence, access to economic security in the United States begins but does not end with the labor market; to navigate the uncertainties of employment, one must have resources and stability beyond a job itself. As this book discusses, because of America's long history of exploiting and unequally rewarding Black labor, access to economic security has evolved in ways that are highly stratified by race and gender. Although the desire for economic security is universal, the means to realize it are not. In the United States, this is the reality of "work in Black and White."

The sociologist Charles Tilly urges the study of categorical inequalities that do not fluctuate, change, or disappear in social relations and interactions. Black and White labor market inequality deserves special attention because of its durability—its persistence "over whole careers, lifetimes, and organization histories."[9] The power of what Tilly calls "bounded categories," such as Black/White and female/male, lies in the aura of naturalness they take on for most casual observers; they thus become almost invisible as causal forces shaping opportunity. Yet bounded categories are sharply recognized in the resulting economic inequality. The "now you see it, now you don't" nature of bounded categories enables them to do important work in the maintenance of hierarchies. Not all categories are created equal: in a country whose economic foundations were determined according to principles of White supremacy and male privilege, bounded categories such as Black/White and male/female were imbued with power and reinforced by social stratification systems, such as slavery and patriarchy, that led to economic inequality. Today, despite the enduring nature of these categorical inequalities, the differences that persist between these groups are often attributed to individual variation in talent or effort. For example, we often hear the familiar story that if Black Americans took personal responsibility, the economic conditions in Black communities in the United States would improve—a story that ignores the fact that *opportunities for White workers were historically defined by the exclusion of Black workers.*

Race is arguably one of the most durable forms of categorical inequality in the United States, and its intersection with gender in shaping access to occupational opportunity is well established.[10] Although the racial diversity of the U.S. labor market has broadened significantly since 1960, the Black/White binary has remained a key American idea and continues to influence how people understand inequality and access to economic opportunity. This is how bounded categories function: they enable people to rationalize and reconcile contradictions, such as the contradictions between American ideals (of meritocracy and equal opportunity) and tremendous and persistent racial economic inequality. As Tilly notes: "Complex categorical systems involving multiple religions or various races typically resolve into bounded pairs relating just two categories at a time ... with each pair having its own distinct set of boundary relations."[11] In the United States, the salience of the Black/White binary emerged as a justification for slavery, and it was also the bedrock for the legalization of racial segregation to crush the brief American experiment with integration during Reconstruction. The importance of preserving the distinction between the bounded categories of Black and White created and maintained economic and labor inequalities from the end of Reconstruction until the civil rights movement. These unequal labor relationships produced specific racialized and gendered notions of appropriate work that remain relevant today.[12]

Though it may seem limiting to focus on Black and White workers exclusively given the racial and ethnic diversity of the contemporary U.S. labor market, the American labor market story is predominantly a Black/White story. In both 1960 and 1970, over 95 percent of the American labor force was either non-Hispanic Black or non-Hispanic White. By 1980, the non-Hispanic Black and White share of the American labor force was 92.1 percent (see figure I.1). Asian and Asian American, Hispanic and Latino/a, and American Indian, Alaskan Native, Native Hawaiian, and Pacific Islander workers represented larger portions of regional U.S. labor markets in the postwar period and before, but they did not combine to make up more than 10 percent of the overall national labor market until after 1980.[13] By 2015, non-Hispanic Black and White workers' share of the U.S. labor market was 75 percent.

We focus on Black men, White men, Black women, and White women because, despite formal prohibitions against discrimination, racism expressed through the racial preferences of employers in allocating workers to jobs

Figure I.1   Black and White Share of the American Labor Force, 1960–2015

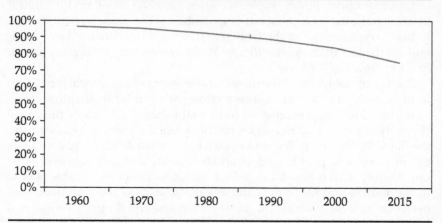

Source: Authors' analysis of data from Integrated Public Use Microdata Series, version 7.0.

remains a stubborn obstacle for Black workers. The sociologist Robert Kaufman found a "systematic patterning of the allocation of Blacks and Whites to labor-market positions, net of the influence of their individual work-related characteristics."[14] He finds evidence of racial typing of jobs in the fact that "low-skill work has been labeled as appropriate and high-skill work has been labeled as inappropriate for Blacks by this society in the past."[15] Indeed, in the postwar period, when racial and gender discrimination was the norm, Black workers were limited to jobs that were marginalized, uncertain, and poorly paid, while jobs that were valued, stable, and lucrative were reserved for White workers. This historical fact has left imprints to this day, when ideas about the "suitability" of certain workers for different kinds of work continue to influence employers. The overrepresentation of Black women, for instance, in nonhousehold service work and unskilled blue-collar labor reflects their association with these occupational sectors as a result of severe occupational restriction for nearly one hundred years.[16] Although household domestic work has declined since 1960, the perception of the appropriateness of Black women for service work as it took on institutional forms was well established, with present-day consequences.[17]

In the postindustrial, post–civil rights era, White women and Black men and women face fewer barriers to occupations that were formerly restricted, yet the broad outlines of racial and gender occupational advantage remain intact. Often the analysis of the influence of race and gender in the labor market is simplistic and fails to capture the extent to which the intersection of race and gender shapes the labor market outcomes of all workers. The labor market experience of minority men is taken as representative of the experiences of all minorities. Similarly, the labor market experiences of women are presented without disaggregation by race. These generalizations reflect disagreements among scholars as to the role that race and gender play in the labor market. On the one hand, some scholars argue that gender and race fundamentally structure labor market opportunity, generating inequality, while others argue, on the other hand, that race and gender may be interconnected categories, but they do not definitively impact labor market opportunity in the long term. We adopt an intersectional approach that empirically disaggregates gender and race; observing Black women, White women, Black men, and White men as race-gender groups, we are better able to see how access to good jobs has changed over time and the extent to which it continues to be stratified by gender and race. Importantly, however, we emphasize that, because *the jobs themselves have changed*, even relatively privileged workers in the postindustrial period face heightened economic insecurity.

Americans Dreaming: Aspirations amid Insecurity

For all workers in America today, obtaining job security is more often an ideal than a reality. But there are notable differences in how Black and White Americans grapple with this change in job security. The way people interpret their current opportunities in the labor market—or lack thereof—is directly tied to their racial group's historical inclusion or exclusion from the American cultural imagination and their historical access to the means of achieving the American Dream (a good job). The economic and cultural tenets of the Dream are familiar and, we found, largely racially universal. Henry, for example, a fifty-four-year-old Black technical writer, captured its basic tenets well when he said in his interview: "The American Dream, in my opinion, is to get an education, you know, get a good job that pays a lot of money, buy a house, have 2.5 kids and a dog, with a white picket fence and two cars in the driveway. That's the American Dream." Both Black and White Americans today aspire to this vision of the Dream. As they increasingly struggle in the face of widespread job insecurity, however, they diverge in their opinions about what is getting in the way of achieving it.

One important divergence is that Black Americans, at far higher rates than White Americans, point to structural inequality as an obstacle to achieving the American Dream. This critique was made by Black Americans from a variety of professional backgrounds. Shawn, a fifty-one-year-old Black executive director of a nonprofit, drew a connection between inequality and the legacy of slavery, "the history of this nation . . . the racial structure of the nation. It's been set up so that, you know, one group were able to come here and realize the American Dream a little bit easier than others." Charles, a thirty-nine-year-old Black superintendent, focused his critique on the present day but came to a similar conclusion: "How can the American Dream be something true if we already know statistically everyone can't obtain it for many different reasons?" As mentioned, this critique of structural limitations was predominantly made by Black workers, but a few White workers shared this view. Spencer, a thirty-four-year-old White marketer, was one of the White participants who made this critique and drew a connection between structure and opportunity:

> I think—there's obvious barriers to the American Dream. Most people will put it as a class issue, that the more money you make, the more privilege and opportunities you're going to have for your family, et cetera. I'll say that even if that's true, there are still other issues in the United States that [disallow] people from having that good life and that good job based on who they are, based on even their gender or their ethnicity.

These critiques of the American Dream based on a view of structural inequality, in highlighting how the Dream has always been out of reach for some workers, stand in notable contrast to how many White Americans describe the situation: they cite the increased insecurity they face today as the obstacle they face in achieving the American Dream. That is, although most White Americans are doggedly pursuing the ideal of the Dream, they tend to simultaneously mourn the loss of the job security they had taken for granted. Black Americans, however, cannot mourn something they never had.

Many White Americans' idea of the American Dream takes for granted the fundamental and central assumption that hard work will yield a good job—secure work that pays a living wage. Although, historically, insecurity has always been a lived reality for some Americans—particularly for vast numbers of Black Americans—enough White Americans were able to achieve a level of economic security to sustain the belief that those who do the right things, such as obtaining higher education or working in a particular occupational sector, can avoid hardship and insecurity. Yet economic shifts and eroding labor protections have obliterated this notion for increasing numbers of both Black and White Americans. Higher education is no longer a foolproof insurance policy against job insecurity, which cuts across occupations and industries.

This new reality is being met by White Americans in particular with disbelief. Claire, a forty-one-year-old White nurse, described with some incredulity her partner's struggles to find employment: "He has been [employed]," she said. "He's an adjunct professor. So he was employed until mid-May, and now over the summer he has no work." During his employment gap, she continued, "he did a short-term grading gig in St. Louis, grading AP exams for one week, which is about as fun as it sounds." His discipline, Claire said, was history, and when asked about his level of education, she said with dismay, "He's got a PhD. That someone with such an elite credential would be subject to short-term contract work suggests that it isn't simply low-skill sectors that are affected, but high-skill sectors as well." The disbelief evident in her remarks that "someone with such an elite credential" would be unable to find steady work reflects expectations about the security that her partner's credential would provide.

Claire's comments, in reflecting the expectation of some Americans that the American Dream will work for them, revealed her understanding of the rise of insecurity in American society, particularly how she and those like her make sense of insecurity when it hits home. Her partner had experienced job insecurity amid recent economic changes and broader societal changes that increasingly disconnect educational investments and labor market rewards in the United States, undermining the American Dream.

For the reasons discussed earlier, however, there are divergent trends along racial lines in expectations that the American Dream will work. In this book, we explore how Americans, Blacks and Whites, men and women, are making sense of this shift toward rising economic insecurity. For instance, Charles, whom we met earlier, argued that the American Dream can't be reality because of "statistical" limitations in opportunity. Continuing in that same line of thinking, he called the Dream "BS" and shared his thoughts about hard work and opportunity: "I'm not going to tell my daughter that if you work hard, great things will happen for you. It's nonsense. If you work hard and do the right thing, you'll have better opportunities. That's a whole different story line."

Charles made explicit his expectation that his daughter will struggle to find employment even if she "works hard." His understanding that hard work is only one part of the equation, and no guarantee of security, was in stark contrast to Claire's surprise regarding her partner's struggles to find work. Many Black Americans, like Charles, have perceptions of current employment conditions and prospects for improvement that have been affected by the decidedly limited occupational opportunities that Blacks faced in the past in the United States. For many Blacks, having had less access to good jobs in the past than today, this means that, despite vast job insecurity, things may still be looking up. For many Whites, such as Claire, the opposite is true.

Perceptions of Past and Future Opportunity: The Racial Futures Paradox

Despite being disadvantaged in the contemporary labor market, Black Americans see more reason for optimism today for improving their lives in the current economic context than White Americans do. In 2013, the Associated Press–National Opinion Research Center (AP-NORC) analyzed the General Social Survey (GSS) and found that expressed optimism for an improved life among Black and White Americans was diverging, producing the largest racial gap observed since the survey began in 1972.[18] Most Black Americans (71 percent), compared to just 46 percent of White Americans, thought that "their family has a good chance of improving their living standard given the way things are in America."[19] While the rise of insecure work has made aspects of the American Dream more difficult to achieve for all Americans—arguably driving perceptions of declining mobility among Whites—the American Dream has historically been out of reach for most racial minorities. Hence, the optimism expressed by Black Americans despite the severity of the Great Recession and its aftermath stems from a comparison to a fundamentally different past. When our Black participants reflected on "how things are in America," they perceived an uncertain occupational future, but one over which most believed they could exert some control. Many conceived of the structural inequalities they faced as a game that they could navigate by attaining higher education, building relationships, adapting to cultural norms, and working hard.[20] For Black Americans, despite still having fewer overall opportunities to achieve job security than White Americans, the post-1970 labor market, however problematic, represents the first time that, as Jennifer Hochschild outlined in her book *Facing Up to the American Dream: Race, Class, and the Soul of a Nation*, the cultural components of the American Dream and the economic means to achieve it appear tenable. This era, in other words, represents the first time in history that Black Americans can imagine applying to their lives former president Bill Clinton's memorable words: "If you work hard and play by the rules you should be given the chance to go as far as your God-given ability will take you."[21]

The divergent levels of pessimism and optimism among Black and White Americans amid the broad economic insecurity of the current era reflect what we refer to in this book as the "racial futures paradox." We introduce this term to capture the complex objective and subjective components of economic insecurity and highlight the contradictions inherent in the empirical realities and lived experiences of Black and White individuals who are simultaneously navigating unprecedented opportunity and insecure times. Examining economic insecurity through this historical and race-gender lens helps us understand why White and Black Americans seem to have different perceptions of the present and different levels of optimism for the future, and it helps reshape contemporary debates over economic insecurity.

As the racial futures paradox also makes clear, although objective material conditions concretely inform Black and White Americans' sense of security and belief in the American Dream, at the same time their complicated subjective evaluation of their circumstances is informed by their different racial histories, which lead them to different expectations and individual assessments of the "same" material conditions. Objectively speaking, Black Americans are more economically vulnerable, but they are subjectively more optimistic, though variation in attitudes among Black people is growing, driven by gender, variation in educational attainment, and socioeconomic background.

The greater employment insecurity that all American workers have experienced since the 1970s has coincided with broad social, economic, and occupational changes, including a significant evolution in both the nature of work and conceptions of masculinity and femininity associated with different kinds of labor.[22] For Black and White women, for example, increased employment insecurity in recent years has developed alongside the rise of female-headed households, the economic devaluation of traditional women's occupations, and the growth of nonhousehold service; all of these developments complicate women's experiences of employment insecurity. For both Black and White men, on the other hand, these broader economic and social changes have led to a crisis of masculinity, their conceptions of masculinity having historically been tied to their ability to provide for their family, even as their ability to do so was fundamentally raced and classed.[23] In the face of enduring insecurity in an era when the pooling and maximizing of the resources of all earners in a household is increasingly required to stay afloat, Blacks and Whites, men and women, are all renegotiating gender roles—particularly notions of masculinity and breadwinning—to match their reality.[24] An important factor driving divergent experiences of economic insecurity is the different rate of marriage among White and Black Americans.[25] Although marriage rates in the United States have been declining for decades, historically higher rates of marriage among White Americans relative to rates for Black Americans have created economic circumstances for White women that provide security and preserve their belief in the Dream in ways that are not possible for Black women.[26] This divergence in access both to the institution of marriage and to its economic benefits is directly tied to the history of structural racism in the United States, and it is a good example of the way past access to opportunity and social privilege shapes the impact of insecure work, while also framing how people understand that impact in their lives. This interplay of race, gender, and class directly shapes how Americans are experiencing and responding to increased insecurity and inequality.

Although rising employment insecurity is radically reshaping the American labor market, in this book we highlight an important yet often overlooked fact—*insecurity is not new for everyone*. The postindustrial period has seen not only the rise of insecure work but also the redistribution of insecure work. To understand this shift and its implications, we need to examine employment insecurity in a historical, comparative perspective.

New Scripts and Old Meritocratic Story Lines: What Middle-Aged Workers Had to Say about Insecurity in 2015

This book homes in on the experiences of a pivotal generation of American workers who were born between 1960 and 1980 and who made specific educational investments that they hoped would put them on a path to joining the middle class. However, the structures of economic opportunity began to change for American workers in the 1970s and 1980s, and the subsequent increase in economic insecurity complicated their ability to obtain the fruits of their labor. Because they were raised in households whose economic fortunes were shaped by one era of economic opportunity (the postwar period) but they came of working age in another (the postindustrial period), these White and Black Americans provide powerful examples of the impact of shifting opportunities to achieve economic security in the postindustrial, post–civil rights era on access to, and understanding of, the American Dream. To capture the authentic insights of these individuals, we—a mixed-race interviewing team—conducted seventy-nine largely race-matched in-depth interviews (twenty-three Black women, nineteen White women, twenty Black men, and seventeen White men) in the summer of 2015. The interviews took place in a medium-sized diverse city in New England with a diversified economy anchored in health care and education as well as manufacturing. This city experienced a decline in manufacturing jobs in the 1980s and thereafter, but some job sectors there have experienced growth.

Most of our participants were between the ages of thirty-five and fifty-five. We focused on the middle-aged to investigate the extent to which the rise of insecure work has disrupted or strengthened narratives of privilege and disadvantage in access to work. Having been of working age for at least a full decade, and being at least a decade away from retirement, our interviewees had witnessed changes in the rise of insecure work. Unlike those in their twenties and early thirties, middle-aged Americans are generally expected to have attained stable jobs.[27] An absence of such stability would be likely to elicit concern as well as reflection. Men and women in this group would also be more likely than not to be married, remarried, or divorced, and thus able to reflect on the impact of their experiences with stable and unstable employment on their identities and intimate relationships.

We were especially interested in educated workers; people with just a high school education would have been insecure long before now. The participation of those who had attained education ranging from a minimum of some college to a terminal degree (JD, PhD, MD) would allow us to explore perceptions of insecurity among those whose access to the economic stability at the heart of the American Dream had been most upended. The importance placed on a college education for economic insecurity, both culturally and institutionally, makes this distinction especially important. These educated, middle-aged participants would be workers who thought their education would insulate them against market changes and who had entered a post–civil rights era labor market that promised de jure equality of opportunity. This was a group of largely lower-middle-class and middle-class families for whom the notion and negotiation of insecurity would be most prominent.

We purposefully incorporated a line of interview questioning to elicit a longitudinal perspective. Asking questions about experiences and aspirations over time moved us beyond naturalized cultural differences between groups and enabled us to get a better view of how previous experiences affected the participants' present perspectives and worldviews. The resulting transcripts of the interviews (which ranged from one and a half to three and a half hours) provide a wealth of data from which we interrogated the implications of economic insecurity for the family, access to work, racial inequality, and perceptions of a just society.

Our sample of relatively educated, middle-aged, Black and White men and women is variable along class lines. We required a minimum annual household income of $30,000, but most were much higher, and some exceeded $200,000. Even though most of them had a household income above the median household income of $56,516 in 2015, our participants' perceptions of their economic circumstances reflected anxiety rooted in uncertainty about the future.[28] Economic insecurity resulting from work instability is now an unwelcome but defining feature of the contemporary American labor market.[29] More and more of those who have done the "right" thing face economic circumstances that mirror the circumstances of those who did not. Staking out the moral high ground of working hard and obtaining an education has not, for many, secured the future promised by the American Dream. In this book, we document how Black and White Americans make sense of this reality.

Race and Economic Security

The life stories of the people we discuss in this book capture a unique racial and political moment. The interviews were all conducted prior to the height of the 2016 presidential race—and thus before Donald Trump became the Republican presidential nominee. On the other hand, the majority of interviews were conducted after the church shooting in Charleston, South Carolina, on June 17, 2015. This massacre, in which nine African Americans were killed during a Bible study at the Emanuel African Methodist Episcopal Church, was motivated by the shooter's desire to "save the White race," since, he maintained, "Blacks were taking over the world."[30] The continued and rapidly rising racial tensions evident today are a product of a purposefully divisive political discourse. In the 2016 presidential race, both Democrats and Republicans sought to tap into voters' feelings of economic insecurity, but observers noted the deeply racialized and often gendered nature of the Trump campaign narrative. The call to "Make America Great Again," issued alongside explicitly racist and denigrating views of minorities and immigrants, scapegoated these groups for America's economic decline and framed their restriction as key to a brighter economic future.

In this book, we examine the lived experiences of individuals in the midst of broader structural changes in opportunity. We develop a historical perspective that shows readers both the shared and the divergent experiences of economic insecurity among men and women, and Blacks and Whites. Our comparative analysis of Black women, White women, Black men, and White men sheds crucial light on their lived reality and the trends behind the rhetoric. Our interrogation of the structural determinants of security that are obfuscated by the belief in the American Dream will help the public and experts alike make sense of the intersections of race, gender, and economic insecurity in the United States and, more importantly, suggest what we can do about it.

This book also suggests the policy conditions under which the ideals of the American Dream could be realized. The absence of a comprehensive welfare state, effective employment and labor law protections, and labor market policies designed to make work pay in America forces individuals to fend for themselves in hard times and to internalize their failures without realizing that another way is possible. We highlight the constraint on collective progress imposed by the meritocracy narrative; as long as American workers are focused on their individual efforts—such as obtaining an education as the key to opening the door to the American Dream—the "us" versus "them" competition will continue, even as who is included in "us" shifts.

The early and persistently disparate impact of the coronavirus pandemic, starting in the spring of 2020, joined with the racial reckoning of the summer of 2020 to reveal to many Americans the fundamental reality of systemic racism and the ways it shapes Black life and death. To understand why Black Americans were disproportionately impacted during the pandemic compared to White Americans—even as many White Americans felt more deeply insecure than ever before—we must look backward and unpack how this reality of work in Black and White came to be. The explosion of uncertainty that Black and White Americans experienced during 2020 fit into specific trends of growing uncertainty in the U.S. labor market dating back to the 1970s, when postindustrial economic restructuring ended the postwar American labor contract, effectively removing security from the deal. But because of historical inequalities in the United States, and because Black Americans have never had the security that many White Americans take for granted, Black and White workers have different views of this growing insecurity, and of potential solutions to ameliorate it.

As we reassess the tangled economic and social impact of the pandemic in the years ahead, recognizing these divergent experiences of uncertainty not only illuminates how we got to where we are now—how uncertainty has been integrated into the lives of American workers in different ways along race and gender lines—but also provides important insight into how we might help more workers gain meaningful access to the promise of the American Dream.

An Outline of the Book

Chapter 1, "The Power of the Illusion: The Way We Never Were," challenges the romanticized view of the historical labor market as a time of economic security and low inequality for American workers. Using data from the U.S. Census Integrated Public-Use Microdata Series (IPUMS) to assess economic circumstances around the postwar transition (1960–1980), this chapter shows that, contrary to the romanticized view of the postwar economy and the deep nostalgia for its low inequality and high average wages, the period was marked by intense racial and gender divisions across industries and occupations that preserved labor market privilege for a few and exposed others to insecurity. Then, in the 1970s, the close associations between race and gender, occupational and industrial attainment, and economic security that characterized the postwar period began to unravel. To bring this transition into view, we focus on two middle-aged cohorts—the "postwar cohort" (who were middle-aged in 1980) and the "postindustrial cohort" (who were middle-aged in 2015)—to provide a snapshot of transformational labor market change over a thirty-five-year period. This chapter shows the consequences of the new economic realities that middle-aged workers today face across racial and gender groups compared to the expectations they formed from the experiences of just the previous generation.

Chapter 2, "The Dream Interrupted: Insecurity among the Middle-Aged," argues that although all workers were affected by postindustrial restructuring, which began in the 1970s, these economic shifts radically reshaped the employment trajectory of middle-aged workers. Blacks and Whites, men and women, all encountered new structures of opportunity as the postindustrial period unfolded, but they navigated these changes from very different starting points. Crosscurrents of change related to class, race, and gender intersected to create new realities that Americans today are still trying to make sense of. Both our Black and White participants narrated experiences of economic instability, but they were experiences rooted in different expectations for security that enable Black Americans to be hopeful about the future despite the challenges of the present.

We call this new reality the *racial futures paradox*. To understand the racial futures paradox, and what it means for the American Dream, we look in chapter 2 at a group of Americans that we call the "vanishing middle" and from which our qualitative sample was drawn: middle-aged Black and White men and women with at least some college education and family incomes above the poverty line. As members of the post-industrial cohort introduced in chapter 1, members of the vanishing middle sit squarely amid expectations formed by the postwar past and realities forged in the crucible of the postindustrial present. Yet as educationally advantaged Americans living above the poverty line, the vanishing middle respond to the economic insecurities they experience with disappointment. In this chapter, as our participants describe their expectations with respect to economic security and insecurity and grapple with their experience of insecurity, we highlight these cracks in the ideal of the American Dream.

Chapter 3, "Privileged Expectations and Insecure Realities," explores racialized conceptualizations of meritocracy and details how our participants reconciled them with their economic realities. Education is supposed to equalize what are otherwise the deeply imbalanced socioeconomic circumstances into which people are born. Yet higher education is no longer a foolproof guarantee of job security, whether for White men, White women, Black men, or Black women. In the narratives of our middle-aged participants, there was shock at the level of change in occupational opportunity and economic rewards since 1980, and the disruption in their sense of stability was a recurrent theme. Some were left bereft by the realization that education had done little to insulate them from the impact of change or to provide the protective insurance they had expected. White blue-collar workers stressed education for their kids as a path to preserving job security and a good life.[31] Black workers who attained high levels of education in order to lay claim to good jobs faced resistance and discrimination.[32] Today all workers are negotiating vulnerability and uncertainty in the labor market. But as this chapter shows, educated workers in particular struggle as they discover that their degrees do not provide the economic security they had imagined and that racial inequalities continue to determine access to work.

Chapter 4, "The Myth of Equal Opportunity," explores the persistence of racial inequality in access to good jobs. The stubborn obstacle of inequitable access to opportunity is a reality of the American labor market that hinders Black economic security. Although the postindustrial economy no longer positions workers against each other by race or gender, as it did historically, privileging one and exploiting the other, organizations still engage in hiring practices that enable race to structure access to occupational opportunity. Most of our Black participants were well aware of this, and they articulated clearly how race had restricted their access to labor market opportunity. Our White participants, on the other hand, bemoaned the emphasis on equal opportunity, which, they feared, advantaged Black applicants at their expense. White participants, however, were better able to utilize networks and, when possible, draw on familial resources to minimize their economic vulnerability. Affirmative action cannot combat the racial inequality that persists as a consequence of differences in access to jobs and the ability to remain financially afloat while gaining new skills to get a better job. In this chapter, in which Black and White workers narrate their experience of vulnerability and insecurity—sometimes providing distorted accounts of those experiences to explain them away—we see the impact of race on access to occupational opportunity.

Chapter 5, "Negotiating Uncertainty," focuses on how our Black and White participants explained their economic misfortunes and those of others. This chapter describes the influence of the structural economic changes shown in the preceding chapters on individuals' perception of that structure. White participants explained success as a matter of luck and connected economic security to deservingness; in emphasizing hard work, they sidestepped the reality that many who work hard have little to show for it. Black participants emphasized hard work as well, but spoke also of persistent racial obstacles; they expressed frustration that hard work did not universally pay off.

This chapter discusses the gap between expectations of security and the reality of vulnerability as a source of great anxiety that affects many families. As economic insecurity has grown, men have increasingly experienced significant downward mobility, and more and more women are taking on the breadwinner role. This shift is forcing men and women alike to confront long-held traditional conceptions of masculinity amid the declining ability of men to meet the gendered breadwinner ideal. We show the ways in which the rise of insecure work has changed how women and men conceive of masculinity, and of breadwinning in particular, as they navigate economic insecurity. We also detail the variation along racial lines in their willingness to adapt to changing conceptions of masculinity.

Insecurity must be actively negotiated by everyone it affects; one way our participants grappled with the absence of security was by making sense of who deserves it. But as this chapter also shows, staggering economic inequality and profound uncertainty were leading some of our Black and White participants to question the legitimacy and fairness of the American Dream. With widespread economic insecurity in the U.S. labor market, American workers across racial and gender groups are struggling to understand how to gain access to security. Their struggle, however, also raises fundamental and difficult questions about who deserves access to economic security. Today in the United States, a country that was built on unequal access to opportunity, economic inequality has reached staggering proportions, and American workers across race, class, and gender groups are grappling with the enduring influence of historic racial and gender scripts. Their struggles have led to very different ideas about what the American Dream could or should mean today.

There may be nothing new about economic insecurity, but as chapter 6, "Economic Vulnerability as the New Normal," shows, the pervasiveness of economic insecurity and its ubiquity across the income spectrum is certainly new. In this chapter, we draw on the arguments in the prior chapters to make the case, in light of economic vulnerability being the new normal, for a renewed focus on individuals (embedded in families) who are insecure along multiple dimensions. The compounding insecurity people are facing presents acute challenges and requires policy interventions that can stabilize individuals and families, as most are likely to experience periods of insecurity despite higher educational attainment. We challenge the prevailing conception of education as the exclusive key to achieving the American Dream. Endless wrangling over whether education is worth the cost—and which key will work best to unlock future economic security—dominates the debates over these issues, even as it leaves unexamined the larger question of what has happened to the lock bolting the door to the American Dream for so many. Government intervention through policies that structure the labor market could disrupt the fallacy that individual effort can override structural determinants and challenge the assumption that the negative effects of market forces and global competition are inevitable. Until we recognize that individuals' keys will not work to open structural locks on the American Dream, and that structural interventions are needed to enable those individuals' keys to work, that Dream will remain out of their reach.

= Chapter 1 =

The Power of the Illusion:
The Way We Never Were

The post–World War II period has an almost mythical status in conversations about the American Dream. It is popularly remembered as a time of high living standards, low inequality, and widespread opportunity, but as the historian Stephanie Coontz observes of postwar family life in her book *The Way We Never Were: American Families and the Nostalgia Trap*, the postwar American labor market of our collective memory does not fully align with the realities of that time.[1] And yet the illusion lives on. Equal opportunity has never been a reality in the United States; then as now, some people were much better off than others.

This privilege in opportunity was reserved not just for the super-rich (or the "1 percent," as they are sometimes described today) but also for some regular folks like Joe, who had a union job at the plant, versus Jason, who did not. Neither Joe nor Jason had more than a high school education, and both worked hard, yet the fruits of their labor were uneven because Joe was White and Jason was Black. Race similarly shaped the occupational options of Jane and Jeannette, though options were further limited for both by their gender. Race dictated that for Jane, a White woman, her place would be in the home upon marriage and she would be only temporarily engaged in the labor market prior to that marriage; simultaneously, race dictated that Jeannette, a Black woman, would be obliged to work whether or not she was married or had children. The constraints on Joe, Jason, Jane, and Jeannette reflected the role of race and gender as central organizing features of the American postwar labor market.

Today large swaths of the American population understand economic insecurity in contrast to a nostalgic and romanticized view of the postwar period. Such a view, however, does not capture the lived experiences of large percentages of the American workforce during that time — specifically, workers who were not White men. In this chapter, we make visible the policies that crystallized racial and gender divisions during the postwar era and created White economic security while limiting Black

19

economic security. We also describe the erosion of the postwar labor contract that began in the 1970s, highlighting how postindustrial restructuring around this time, by blurring the labor market divisions that had characterized the postwar period, dissolved advantages and exposed formerly privileged workers to new vulnerabilities. These changes, with their different impacts on American workers' economic security depending on their gender and racial group, have led Black and White workers to notably different understandings of what the American Dream means now.

In this chapter, we revisit the postwar period, when many of the cultural narratives and economic policies that determined how, or whether, people had access to the American Dream took shape. Without an understanding of the policies that created Joe's good job—or Jason's and Jeanette's relegation to bad jobs—we have no shared language for understanding how things are today—and how they could be different tomorrow.

The Postwar Labor Contract: Codifying Racial and Gender Exclusion

As we discussed in the introduction, and as we explore more in later chapters, the labor market inequalities we see in the United States today are rooted in its history of making economic security available to White workers at the expense of Black workers. During the postwar period, access to economic security in the form of the "standard" employment relationship was defined by racial and gender exclusion. The labor and employment laws passed during the New Deal were aimed at providing economic security for American workers; however, they were explicitly shaped to define and constrain which American workers deserved that security. The unequal outcomes we see today were intentionally produced. Labor unions capitalized on the demand for labor created by World War II and postwar economic policies by bargaining for long contract periods with high wages and benefits for skilled blue-collar workers.[2] This organizing, along with the practice of collective bargaining, was enabled by the 1935 National Labor Relations Act (NLRA, also known as the Wagner Act). Its passage reflected a defining moment in the American labor movement following decades of union organizing that had often been met with violent employer resistance.

The Wagner Act codified the right to form a labor union without employer interference and without direct action tactics, compelled employers to bargain collectively with unions chosen by their employees, and established the National Labor Relations Board (NLRB) to conduct impartial union elections and investigate alleged violations of these provisions. The 1937 Fair Labor Standards Act established, among other provisions, a federal minimum wage, the concept of the workweek, and a right to overtime pay for certain types of work. Together these provisions created what has been called the "standard" employment relationship, understood as "the exchange of a worker's labor for monetary compensation from an employer . . . with work done on a fixed schedule—usually full time—at the employer's place of business, under the employer's control, and with the mutual expectation of continued employment."[3] Thus, postwar economic security was closely tied to jobs organized around these expectations.

The employment protections of the New Deal, however, institutionalized racialized and gendered workplace norms; in some cases, they were even explicitly written to differentially affect workers along racial and gender lines. As Rebecca Dixon, the executive director of the National Employment Law Project, testified before Congress in 2021:

> Nearly half of all Black men, Mexican-American men, and Native American men and women, plus significant numbers of Asian American workers were excluded from Social Security, unemployment insurance, and the right to organize in the NLRA. The effects of this exclusion fell most heavily on Black women because of their concentration as agricultural and domestic workers.[4]

The agricultural and domestic service industries in which, as Dixon notes, Black women were concentrated were exempted from New Deal employment legislation to avoid disrupting the racial division of labor in the South.[5] In other industries with large numbers of Black workers, labor strategies were adopted to depress their wages and exclude them from increasing labor protections—for example, the use of tipping and a subminimum wage in the restaurant industry was explicitly aimed at depressing the wages of Black workers.[6] And even as industry norms and public policy were leveraged to maintain low pay and poor working conditions in sectors dominated by Black workers in the postwar period, Black workers' access to skilled craft and other good jobs was contested by unions whose members sought to maintain advantages along color lines.[7]

A central goal of the labor movement in its effort to institutionalize the standard employment relationship was to secure for its members a "family wage"—the income necessary for a male breadwinner to support a family.[8] Yet this push firmly excluded men of color, as gendered notions of work and workers differed along racial and ethnic lines. For both Black and White men, conceptions of masculinity have historically been tied to their ability to provide for their family, although their ability to do so was fundamentally raced and classed. Meanwhile, conceptions of Black and White femininity were defined in opposition to one other, by the expectation that Black women would work and the expectation that White women would care for the family.[9] The union push to secure a family wage—an effort that succeeded in some instances—formally joined racialized and gendered conceptions of work with economic realities in the postwar period: Black women were laborers rather than homemakers, Black men did not require a family wage, and both were excluded from the frame of economic security as a right.[10]

This frame of economic security as a right was central to President Franklin D. Roosevelt's legislative goals. Consider the words he spoke in 1944 when he was promoting an "Economic Bill of Rights" to Congress: "We have come to a clear realization of the fact that true individual freedom cannot exist without economic security and independence. 'Necessitous men are not free men.' People who are hungry and out of a job are the stuff of which dictatorships are made."[11] Roosevelt died in office before he was able to fully realize his legislative vision of making it the policy of the United States to ensure employment opportunities for all Americans who desired them. After his death, Congress failed to include a federal commitment to full employment, which Roosevelt had championed, in the Employment Act of 1946.[12]

The employment protections of the New Deal did extend economic security, however, to a large swath of the American working population during the postwar period. Yet the *standard employment relationship*, which formalized expectations for full-time work and a family wage in the postwar period, defined who benefited from its policies according to specific race- and gender-based exclusions. Black Americans in particular were written out of the legislation by industry exemptions designed to maintain White political power in the South.

In light of this history, we anchor our analysis of labor outcomes in a racial frame, attending to gender differences within racial groups as race joins with gender to shape labor market opportunities. Consequently, as we discuss in this chapter, despite the fact that these laws were aimed at providing labor protections to the American public, in fact those protections served only to deepen inequality along race and gender lines, producing further class divisions.

Race, Gender, and Economic Security in the Postwar Period

We can begin to see the contours of economic security in the postwar period by looking closely at who did what type of work, the extent to which certain types of employment were organized around the security of the standard employment relationship, and group differences in exposure to unemployment. In each of these areas, there was a sharp race-gender division of labor in the postwar period, with large consequences for access to secure employment, compounded by high levels of unemployment for Black men and women.

The perception of the postwar period as the heyday of American labor, whose terms we might wish to re-create today, requires erasing the experiences of non-White workers. The U.S. labor market was organized around a primary market with stable and high-paying jobs and a secondary market that supported it. This split labor market permitted and organized the preservation of economic security for permanent workers and the maintenance of insecurity and poverty for temporary workers.[13] The racial overlay with employment status was stable and unwavering.[14] With few exceptions, permanent work was reserved for White Americans while Black Americans (as well as other minority groups) occupied the secondary labor market with its attendant conditions—unemployment, underemployment, and economic insecurity.[15]

In the years following World War II, White men were concentrated in the best jobs. Then as now, there were good professional jobs that required a college degree. But more often in that era, having a good job—a job that promised economic security in the form of high wages and benefits, job security, and opportunities for advancement—meant working in manufacturing. The best jobs in manufacturing were highly skilled positions, but unionization brought greater pay, security, and opportunities for advancement for all employees in a workplace. This is the image that comes to many of us when we think of employment in the postwar era, made possible by the institutions and norms that created the standard employment relationship. During these years, however, White women, Black men, and Black women were distributed across less desirable positions—less skilled jobs in the manufacturing sector and jobs in less productive industries with greater obstacles to unionization.

During the postwar period, race and gender directly determined access to good jobs. Above and beyond individual attributes, racial and gender inequalities established and reinforced divisions in the American labor market. To understand what this meant in the postwar period and transition (1960 to 1980), it is useful to consider a person's "labor market position," which we define in terms of four industry-occupation groupings to highlight how much industry and occupation mattered for structuring access to good jobs.[16] Figure 1.1 shows each race-gender group's distribution across the industrial-occupational locations that defined the postwar period.[17]

In 1960, more than two decades after the passage of key elements of Roosevelt's New Deal legislation, de jure segregation was still the law of the land. Since the New Deal had established economic protections for American workers along race and gender lines, the labor market remained heavily defined by sharp racial and gender distinctions. Core industries were largely defined as men's work, with racial divisions. Primary occupations within the core—skilled manufacturing positions whose rewards were created by the standard employment relationship and the idea of the family wage—were often reserved for White men, and secondary occupations were a key source of employment for Black men.

Figure 1.1   Industrial-Occupational Location and the Race-Gender Division of Labor for Employed Black and White Workers Ages Twenty-Four to Sixty-Four in the Postwar Transition, 1960–1980

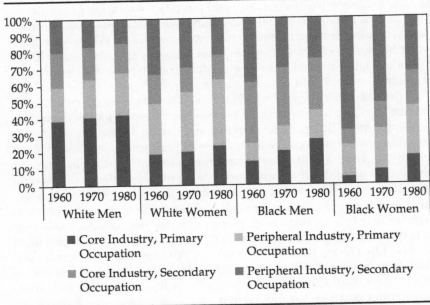

Source: Authors' analysis of data from Integrated Public Use Microdata Series, version 7.0.
Note: Sums to 100 percent within each race-gender group and year.

In 1960, fully 38.7 percent of White men were employed in core-primary jobs (management and skilled work in manufacturing), whereas 35.9 percent of Black men were employed in core-secondary jobs (semiskilled and unskilled work in manufacturing). Nearly one-third (30.6 percent) of White women were employed in peripheral-primary jobs (secretarial and nonmanagerial white-collar) in 1960, while the worst jobs overall in the peripheral-secondary sector (household and nonhousehold service work) were largely held by Black women. The labor market exclusion of Black women from more desirable sectors is evident in their disproportionate representation in this sector: 67.7 percent of Black women worked in these "bad" jobs. The postwar, pre–civil rights era labor market was one of intense racial and ethnic division, and labor market privilege for a few was preserved by a myriad of means both violent and direct ("Negroes need not apply").

Despite the passage of the Civil Rights Act in 1964 and other laws aimed at spurring racial and gender equality in the workplace, the relative stability of the postwar race-gender division of labor continued into the 1970s and 1980s. The civil rights movement and the passage of the Civil Rights Act had aimed to disrupt the persistent labor market segmentation that reserved the best occupational opportunities for White workers. But even though Black men and women expanded their access to good jobs in the 1970s and 1980s, and even as the foundations of postwar security began to unravel in the 1980s, the racial and gender hierarchy remained intact. White men remained highly concentrated in good jobs throughout this period: 40.9 percent of White men worked in core-primary jobs in 1970, and that figure rose to 42.3 percent in 1980. White women's access to core-primary jobs increased from 18.7 percent in 1960 to 20.1 percent in 1970 and 23.3 percent in 1980. Access to good jobs for Black men and women improved by an even greater margin: Black men nearly doubled their concentration in this sector, rising from 13.6 percent in 1960 to 26.5 percent in 1980, and Black women saw a nearly fourfold increase in access to core-primary jobs, from 4.2 percent in 1960 to 16.5 percent in 1980.

And yet, this absolute progress in access to good jobs notwithstanding, the racial and gender hierarchy that determined who dominated or typi- fied each sector was left largely unchanged. The limitations of progress are clear. Though the civil rights movement facilitated transformational social change, the labor story is strikingly consistent. The same broad employment patterns observed in 1960 persisted in 1980. Throughout the period, White men dominated the best jobs of the core industries and primary occupations, White women were particularly concentrated in peripheral industries and in primary occupations, Black men relied heavily on core industries and secondary occupations, and Black women were relegated to peripheral industries and secondary occupations.

As these data indicate, in the postwar period there was a strong correla- tion between a person's gender and race and the nature of the jobs they had access to, and thus the relative security and predictability of their work. What we understand today as secure work was an outcome of the employ- ment protections of the New Deal, which, as noted above, defined the "standard" employment relationship as "the exchange of a worker's labor for monetary compensation from an employer." But workers who were not White males—and who were concentrated in "nonstandard" employ- ment (jobs that deviated from the standard employment relationship)— never experienced or had expectations for secure work.[18] Figure 1.2 shows the distribution of nonstandard employment across industrial-occupational locations. As these data demonstrate, access to core industry and primary occupation jobs mattered; the high degree of variability in exposure to non- standard employment relations across the different types of positions is immediately evident.

From 1960 to 1980, rates of nonstandard employment (part-time, tempo- rary work, and so on) in core industries (such as manufacturing) declined,

Figure 1.2   Nonstandard Employment by Industrial-Occupational Location for Employed Black and White Workers Ages Twenty-Four to Sixty-Four in the Postwar Transition, 1960–1980

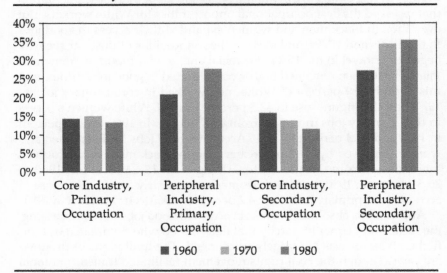

Source: Authors' analysis of data from Integrated Public Use Microdata Series, version 7.0.

while nonstandard employment rates in peripheral industries (such as the service industry) grew. Less than 15 percent of primary jobs in core industries (such as management and skilled labor) were nonstandard throughout the postwar period. There was little nonstandard work even in secondary occupations (such as semi- and unskilled labor) in the core industries throughout the period. As nonstandard employment declined in core industries throughout the period, it grew to 27.6 percent of primary jobs in peripheral industries and 35.4 percent of secondary jobs in peripheral industries by 1980. The race-gender division of labor during the postwar period put the burden of nonstandard work disproportionately on Black workers.

Beyond uneven access to good jobs across industrial-occupational locations, access to employment itself was an important marker of inequality in the postwar period. In figure 1.3, which shows unemployment from 1960 to 1980, we see that race was a consistent and primary vector of difference.[19] In 1960, 3.7 percent of White men were unemployed, compared with 4.3 percent of White women, 7.8 percent of Black men, and 7.5 percent of Black women. Each group had a lower unemployment rate in 1970, with greater percentage-point declines for Black men and women than for White men and women. The variability of Black unemployment

Figure 1.3   Unemployment in the Postwar Transition for Black and White Labor Force Participants Ages Twenty-Four to Sixty-Four, by Race and Gender, 1960–1980

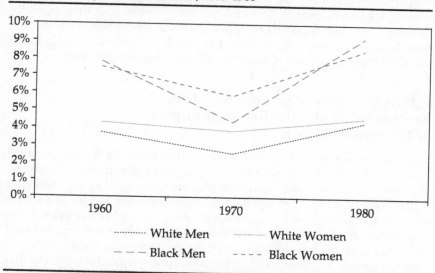

Source: Authors' analysis of data from Integrated Public Use Microdata Series, version 7.0.

illustrates well employers' practice of using Black labor as a source of "flexibility" in responding to market fluctuation. By 1980, the aftermath of a worldwide energy crisis, economic and labor policies based on free market economic ideas, and changing technology and business practices had produced an upswing in unemployment that was especially pronounced for Black men and women: unemployment rates for White men and women were 4.4 percent and 4.6 percent, respectively, while Black unemployment was higher than it had been in 1960, at 9.3 percent for Black men and 8.5 percent for Black women.

The effects of high levels of Black unemployment combined with labor market marginalization were cumulative: employed members of a household were relegated to jobs and industries that were relatively undesirable, and they were also more likely to be at high risk of poverty because they lived in a household where other adults were routinely unemployed. As discussed earlier, vast racial differences in employment in the postwar period were not accidental but intentionally produced and maintained. The close coupling with race and gender of access to good jobs that provided labor protections and expectations of continued employment was a direct function of the way New Deal labor and employment policies were written. In codifying existing racial and gender inequalities in employment, these policies deepened racial and gender inequality in access to good jobs. By 1970, race and gender were so "intertwined with the very fabric of work" that they continued to shape the way workers were selected for jobs even after the racial and gender ideologies that originally sustained unequal employment opportunities abated.[20] Said another way, New Deal employment protections increased the material consequences of employment segregation, cementing Black labor marginalization.

Privilege Interrupted: Postindustrial Restructuring and the Redistribution of Economic Security

Two seismic shifts converged to radically reshape the American labor market following the postwar period. The civil rights movement and its legislative victories ended de jure employment segregation, producing an initial burst of progress in equal employment opportunity for Black men and women during the 1970s. Although the Civil Rights Act helped disrupt the postwar race-gender division of labor, other events and political movements at this time also impacted the privileges that White men had long enjoyed in the labor market. Initially, strong legal challenges to discriminatory practices in the workplace and relatively robust enforcement by the Equal Employment Opportunity Commission (EEOC) opened doors that had been closed to Black workers. This led to labor gains that would continue through 1980.[21] Moreover, the landscape of American labor fundamentally changed with the passage of the Immigration and Naturalization Act of 1968 and the feminist movement. Traditional lines of segregation and competition were challenged when international workers, many of whom were people of color, entered the labor force in growing numbers and women's participation in the labor market skyrocketed.

Despite these initial gains for non-White and female workers, other changes were underway in the American economy that would not only restrict those gains in the years ahead but also introduce more insecurity into the lives of all workers. By fundamentally changing the structure of opportunity in ways that made traditional pathways to economic security less predictable, postindustrial economic restructuring, starting in the 1980s, limited the impact of laws intended to reduce gender and racial inequality in the U.S. labor market. For example, with fewer jobs offering lifelong employment and stable pensions or benefits, workers were forced to compete for less stable jobs more often. These trends, along with the use of "color-blind" methods of maintaining racial and gender labor market privileges, converged to maintain the hierarchy of *relative* advantage (for White men in particular, but also across gender and racial groups) that had become entrenched in the postwar period, while also exposing even the most advantaged workers to new vulnerabilities.[22] To tell this story we need to look at: (1) changes in who does what in the labor market; (2) changes in the rewards that accompany different labor market positions; and (3) how those two processes—matching workers with positions, and matching rewards with positions—converge to create racial and gender differences in economic security.

Who Does What in the Postindustrial Labor Market?

Traditionally, highly skilled and white-collar work was reserved for White men, while White women worked in positions that supported the labor of White men and Black men and women held blue-collar positions.[23] Amid the radical reshaping of the American labor market after 1970, many Black workers gained access to the full range of occupations for the first time, revealing the impact of expanded labor market opportunities for Black people following the 1964 Civil Rights Act. This was also a time when White women began to occupy new kinds of jobs as their labor force participation expanded.

In the period from 1970 to 2015, White men underwent a relatively modest occupational change, shifting away from skilled blue-collar and operative work toward professional and managerial employment and, to a lesser degree, to unskilled labor (figure 1.4). During these years, their employment was scattered across job sectors and no single occupational category accounted for more than one-quarter of White men's employment. On the other hand, White women began the postindustrial labor period (around 1970) highly concentrated in nonmanagerial white-collar (NMWC) jobs (nearly 43 percent), such as retail sales associates or clerical workers. Their reliance on nonmanagerial white-collar work declined in the years ahead, however, as White women moved into professional occupations; by 2015, 36.9 percent of White women were employed in nonmanagerial white-collar jobs (figure 1.4). White women also saw gains in managerial work, and they significantly reduced their representation in operative occupations, which involve operating heavy machinery, including buses. White women's employment in semiskilled and unskilled blue-collar jobs, such as food service and cleaning, shifted the least, decreasing from 16.7 percent in 1970 to 14.4 percent by 2015. Overall, White women remained concentrated in white-collar jobs but moved upward in the distribution of white-collar work, toward higher-skill jobs with greater pay and stability.

For Black men and women, the postindustrial period was similarly a period of occupational upgrading. The shifts for Black men were most evident in their declining reliance on operative work (falling from 30.6 percent to 19.9 percent) and semiskilled and unskilled blue-collar employment (decreasing from 33.5 percent in 1970 to 26.2 percent in 2015). Black men increased their reliance on nonmanagerial white-collar, managerial, and

Figure 1.4   Occupational Attainment in the Postwar and Postindustrial Periods of White Men and Women and of Black Men and Women, by Race and Gender: 1970, 1990, and 2015

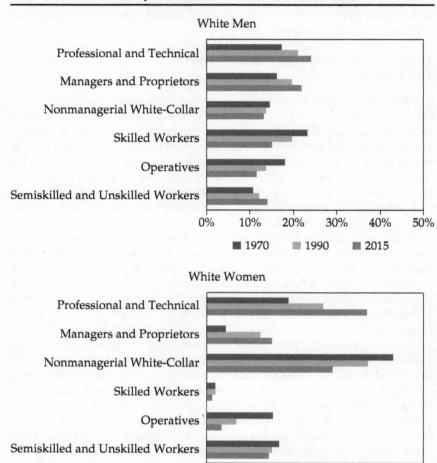

Figure 1.4   Occupational Attainment in the Postwar and Postindustrial Periods of White Men and Women and of Black Men and Women, by Race and Gender: 1970, 1990, and 2015 (*Continued*)

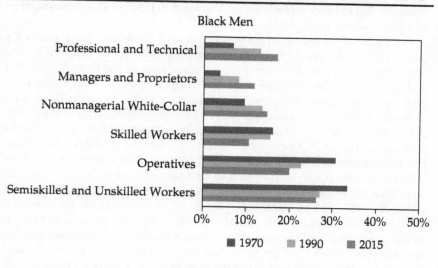

Black Men

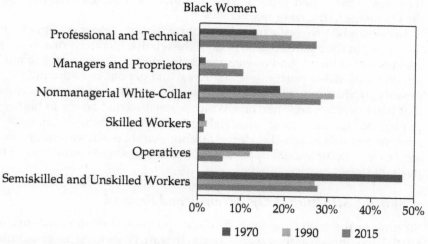

Black Women

Source: Authors' analysis of data from Integrated Public Use Microdata Series, version 7.0.

Note: The percentages sum to 100 percent within each race-gender group and year, affording a clear view of changes in the types of work done by each group.

professional jobs, but their occupational progress was measured: by 2015, those occupations accounted for only 14.6 percent, 11.7 percent, and 16.9 percent of Black men's employment, respectively (figure 1.4). Black men continued to lag behind White men and women in their access to managerial and professional occupations.

For much of American history since the end of slavery, Black women's labor market choices have been significantly restricted.[24] Although new opportunities began to emerge after the passage of the Civil Rights Act and the subsequent enforcement of equal opportunity law, Black women's employment opportunities were still heavily restricted in 1970, as evidenced by their high concentration in semiskilled and unskilled jobs (48.1 percent), and even as late as 2015 their concentration in this sector remained high at 27.7 percent (figure 1.4). From 1970 to 2015, however, Black women made some occupational gains as they moved out of blue-collar positions (including operative and semiskilled and unskilled jobs requiring manual labor) and into white-collar (including nonservice) work. By 2015, 27.1 percent of employed Black women held professional jobs, 10.2 percent held managerial positions, and 28.1 percent held non-managerial white-collar work. Yet among the four race-gender groups we observed, Black women remained the most reliant on the worst jobs throughout the period, reflecting the durability of relative advantage and disadvantage in the labor market.

In sum, while we see a narrowing of racial and gender occupational inequality in the postindustrial period, the relative hierarchy of access to jobs remained intact. And as we show in the rest of the chapter, expanding occupational opportunity along racial and gender lines did not necessarily produce greater access to economic security. At the same time that Black women and men and White women gained access to higher-paying occupations, postindustrial restructuring would dramatically shift the rewards attached to different labor market positions, change the structure of occupational opportunity, and increase the competition for desirable jobs.

A Shifting Structure of Opportunity and Reward

Starting in the 1970s, the foundations of postwar economic stability—partial and uneven as they were—began to shift. Postindustrial economic restructuring led to wide-reaching structural changes in the nature of work, including a reduction in the availability of good jobs that offered access to economic security; as a result, workers in search of the American Dream encountered a fundamentally different structure of opportunity and rewards in the postindustrial period compared with the postwar period. The causes and consequences of postindustrial restructuring went far beyond the turn away from manufacturing as the bedrock of the American economy. Increased competitive pressures associated with globalization resulted in a steep rise in offshoring and outsourcing in the absence of effective policies to limit such outcomes or lessen their impact on those directly affected.[25] New workplace technologies created new types of white-collar work opportunities while automating other jobs, compelling many American workers to forge a new economic path in the absence of active labor market policies.[26] These macroeconomic changes weakened labor unions, undermining their ability to deliver economic security to existing members and to recruit new members.[27] Finally, these structural changes in work were accompanied by the weakening of the social safety net through policies such as the Personal Responsibility and Work Opportunity Reconciliation Act of 1996; aimed at limiting long-term dependence on federal aid, PRWORA increased the vulnerability of low-income families.[28]

Fundamentally, the availability of good jobs that delivered economic security changed after 1970 in the transition from the postwar economy to the postindustrial economy. In the postwar labor market, the close association of standard employment with core industries made it relatively straightforward to assess access to economic security (see figure 1.2). After 1980, however, the foundations of economic security shifted, making the distinctions between core and periphery industries and between primary and secondary occupations less meaningful.[29] With the decline in manufacturing, a large and highly polarized service sector grew and the composition of the American labor market changed; good jobs became less plentiful, and security also became less reliably concentrated in certain types of work. The changes between 1970 and 2015 in three industries— durable manufacturing, retail trade, and professional services—capture this evolution across the postindustrial period in the extent to which jobs delivered economic security (see table 1.1). Most durable manufacturing was considered a core industry in the postwar period, whereas retail trade was exclusively a peripheral industry.[30] Bridging core and peripheral postwar industries and representing a growth area in the postindustrial economy were professional services, which included teaching and health-related fields, engineering, accounting, and public relations. Comparing durable manufacturing, retail trade, and professional services industries allows us to see how the structure of opportunity shifted with postindustrial restructuring and the change in both the composition of American jobs and the rewards they offered.

During the postindustrial period, as table 1.1 shows, the relative size of durable manufacturing in the U.S. economy shrank considerably—from 15.6 percent in 1970 to only 6.8 percent in 2015. These lost manufacturing jobs figure so prominently in nostalgia for the postwar period because they were the ones that had delivered solid economic rewards for those who could access them. In 1970, mean annual earnings in durable manufacturing, at about $52,958, were high. These high earnings from manufacturing

Table 1.1   Earnings Variability among All Workers in Selected Industries,
1970, 1990, and 2015

Year	Selected Industries	Share of Total Employment (%)	Mean Annual Earnings (2015 Dollars)	Variation in Earnings[a]
1970	Durable manufacturing	15.6	52,958.07	0.64
	Retail trade	15.1	32,872.76	0.94
	Professional services	17.2	39,643.83	0.85
1990	Durable manufacturing	10.9	53,889.98	0.73
	Retail trade	14.4	31,796.07	1.02
	Professional services	21.9	41,824.67	0.92
2015	Durable manufacturing	6.8	61,820.71	0.94
	Retail trade	15.6	33,104.08	1.26
	Professional services	27.8	51,050.24	1.11

Source: Authors' analysis of data from Integrated Public Use Microdata Series, version 7.0.
[a] Coefficient of variation = standard deviation/mean.

bring into sharp relief the reason Americans have bemoaned the decline of such jobs in the U.S. economy overall. However, under the rising pressures of global economic competition and a long-standing campaign to reduce the power of organized labor, which became more effective following the economic crises of the 1970s, alongside the neoliberal turn in American politics, U.S. manufacturers began trimming costs via layoffs and relocations overseas. Yet there is evidence of increasing insecurity even for the relatively privileged workers who were employed in durable manufacturing when we examine variation in these earnings. While the mean earnings for durable manufacturing workers increased by about 16 percent, from $52,958.07 in 1970 to $61,820.71 in 2015, the variation in earnings also increased by 46 percent. Exposure to significant income variability among workers holding the same kind of job in the same kind of industry or occupation can provoke feelings of economic insecurity among workers, because the risk of changing economic fortunes is more immediate. In the postwar labor market, good jobs were more universally good—that is, incomes were more similar among workers in the same industry and occupation. In the postindustrial period, the connection between holding a job in a particular industry or occupation and a worker's income has frayed.

Rather than signaling an improvement in the odds for security among American workers, the observed earnings in manufacturing reflect a shrinking sector and the relative ease with which employers eliminated workers not covered by union contracts.[31] Increasing earnings variation within durable manufacturing reflects a change in the industry itself (a decline in the uniformity with which it offered economic stability to its workers) and also in the experiences of its workers: increasing earnings variation among workers in the same industry matters for understanding those workers' experiences of economic security. This variation in job quality among workers in the same job category (evidenced by a high degree of earnings variation) speaks to the potential for insecurity among even the highest-paid workers in an industry or occupation, since they may be aware of others performing the same type of work for lower pay. In the postindustrial period, when workers are increasingly unable to see their work as having a defined and fixed (high) value, their economic fortunes become less predictable and thus more insecure.

The notable lack of meaningful economic security for workers in retail trade since 1970, by contrast, tells a story of economic stagnation and worsening conditions, not conditional progress. As the service sector grew to outpace manufacturing in the postindustrial American economy, and as each recession brought painful structural job losses, the newly created jobs were of lower quality than those that were lost.[32] These structural changes are well demonstrated by changes in the retail sector. Table 1.1 shows that while retail trade accounted for a steady 15 percent of U.S. employment in both 1970 and 2015 (dipping very slightly to 14.4 percent in 1990), mean annual earnings in the industry were relatively flat, ranging from $32,872 in 1970 to $33,104 in 2015, and variation in earnings increased by more than one-third.[33]

This kind of earnings variation, and the economic insecurity accompanying it, also increased in the professional services industry. As manufacturing declined in the postindustrial economy, professional services expanded from 17.2 percent of all working-age employment in the United States in 1970 to 27.8 percent by 2015. Within this highly educated sector, average earnings grew by 28 percent, from $39,643 in 1970 to $51,050 in 2015. Yet earnings variation among professional services workers grew as well, by over 30 percent.[34] With rising variation in earnings among workers in durable manufacturing, retail trade, and professional services, those industries were increasingly composed of relative winners and losers; as such, even the winners were exposed to the economic insecurity that comes from fearing a decline in one's material well-being.

One of the most important changes in the postindustrial American labor market has been rising levels of earnings and income inequality. During this period, annual earnings trends highlight a growing advantage to those at the top, but stagnation or decline for everyone else. This is particularly visible when we look at trends in inflation-adjusted earnings percentiles. Figure 1.5 shows that from 1960 to 1970, the last decade of the postwar period, a rising tide continued to lift all boats: earnings at the twenty-fifth, fiftieth, seventy-fifth, and ninetieth percentiles grew.[35] After 1970, however, earnings growth was increasingly reserved for the top 25 percent of earners (those whose annual earnings, or total take-home pay from their main job,

Figure 1.5   Annual Earnings Percentiles for Full- and Part-time Earners, by Year (2015 Dollars)

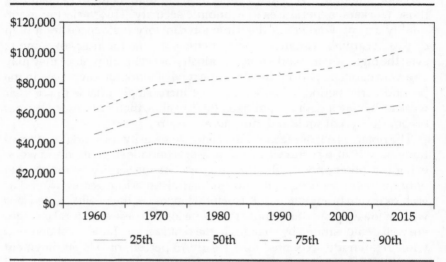

Source: Authors' analysis of data from Integrated Public Use Microdata Series, version 7.0.

placed them at or above the seventy-fifth percentile) while everyone else was treading water.

One way in which occupations (like industries) have become less reliable indicators of job quality in the postindustrial period is that even the most highly skilled occupational groups no longer deliver uniform economic security. Figure 1.6 shows how earnings variation grew within occupations from 1970 to 2015.[36] Relatively advantaged white-collar occupational groups, including professional/technical workers and managers/proprietors, saw sharp growth in earnings variation, complicating the relationship between occupational attainment and economic security. (Earnings variation for professional and technical workers grew by 39 percent, and it grew by 29 percent for managers and proprietors.) Earnings variation among skilled blue-collar workers increased by 47 percent over the postindustrial period. Nonmanagerial white-collar workers—including sales and clerical work—saw a significant jump of 44 percent in earnings variation. Earnings variation among semiskilled and unskilled blue-collar workers increased by 22 percent.[37]

New macroeconomic realities, which were met in the United States with an embrace of the "free market" or neoliberal approach to economic governance and an absence of labor market policies to support new skill development and occupational transitions, brought changes in job stability and compensation that increased inequality both across and within

Figure 1.6   Variation in Mean Annual Earnings within Occupations for All Full- and Part-time Workers in 1970, 1990, and 2015

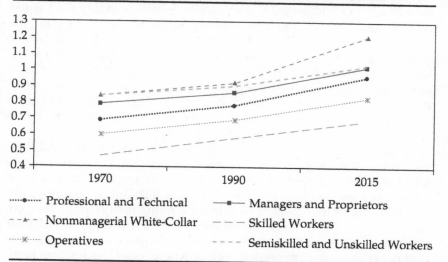

····•···· Professional and Technical   ──■── Managers and Proprietors

── ▲ ── Nonmanagerial White-Collar   ── ── Skilled Workers

····✳···· Operatives   ── ── Semiskilled and Unskilled Workers

Source: Authors' analysis of data from Integrated Public Use Microdata Series, version 7.0.

occupational groups. The close associations between race and gender, occupational and industrial attainment, and economic security that characterized the postwar period unraveled in the postindustrial period. The gap between good jobs and bad jobs grew in the postindustrial economy. It became exceptionally clear that industry and occupation no longer bore a straightforward relationship to economic security.

Postwar and Postindustrial Economic Security among the Middle-Aged

One reason why we see increasing earnings variability within industries and occupational groups is that newly hired workers within a particular field now face very different terms of employment compared to what was offered to those hired in previous years—even when they share the same level of education. Taking a worker's age or birth cohort into account therefore matters immensely when examining shifts in racial and gender inequality in the postwar and postindustrial periods. Black and White workers faced fundamentally different employment conditions, by cohort, as postindustrial restructuring unfolded, and they were therefore differentially impacted by and vulnerable to the broadening of insecurity.[38] Although postindustrial restructuring had a definite impact on all workers, the employment trajectory of middle-aged workers was radically reshaped by the economic shifts described here.

The effects of this postindustrial restructuring on racial and gender inequalities in economic security can be seen by looking at the employment experiences of middle-aged workers (ages thirty-five to fifty-five) across two time periods, 1980 and 2015. The experiences of two age cohorts—the "postwar cohort" (middle-aged in 1980) and the "postindustrial cohort" (middle-aged in 2015)—provide a snapshot of transformational labor market change over a thirty-five-year period, exposing new realities of economic security across racial and gender groups at midlife. We show that while inequalities associated with race and gender at midlife have declined, White men's economic security advantage relative to White women, Black men, and Black women persists.

Postwar middle-aged workers in 1980 were born between 1925 and 1945; they were what scholars today consider "working age" (at least twenty-four years old) during the heyday of the postwar era, from 1949 to 1969. Although these workers lived and worked through the employment restructuring of the 1970s, their relative employment trajectories were heavily shaped by the labor market conditions in which they began their adult working lives. Because these workers began their careers before civil rights and equal opportunity legislation expanded employment pathways for White women and Black men and women, examining patterns of economic security among the middle-aged in 1980 gives us insight into the contours of racial and gender employment inequality during the highly stratified postwar period.

Middle-aged workers in 2015 were born between 1960 and 1980 and reached working age between 1984 and 2004. These workers began their working lives on the heels of an economic recession that was followed by the growth of the service sector and the decline of manufacturing.[39] Their employment trajectories were punctuated by multiple recessions and experiences of economic decline. These workers were particularly attuned to the fleeting and unpredictable nature of opportunity as some became winners while others were losers in the new economy, education and technology created disparities in the quality of new jobs, and outsourcing stoked fears of global competition for American jobs. The retreat from affirmative action, coupled with increasing earnings variation within occupational categories, shaped a complicated picture of racial and gender employment inequality in the postindustrial period, making it increasingly difficult to accurately summarize group economic well-being by referring to labor market position (industry and occupational location). We therefore begin by looking at earnings as a marker of economic security.

Across postwar and postindustrial cohorts, White men's average annual earnings were far higher than those of White women, Black men, and Black women. Table 1.2 shows that White men in the postwar cohort earned an average of $72,053 per year, compared with $30,955 for White

Table 1.2   Annual Earnings Adjusted for Inflation (2015 Dollars) and Earnings Variation among Postwar (1980) and Postindustrial (2015) Middle-Aged Cohorts, by Race and Gender

	Postwar Cohort (1980)	Postindustrial Cohort (2015)	Percentage Change
White Men	$72,053.81	$79,809.82	10.80
	0.614	*0.987*	60.70
White Women	$30,955.83	$50,841.61	64.20
	0.721	*0.991*	37.40
Black Men	$48,171.86	$49,425.63	2.60
	0.604	*0.909*	50.00
Black Women	$31,302.41	$41,025.91	31.10
	0.714	*0.871*	22.00

Source: Authors' analysis of data from Integrated Public Use Microdata Series, version 7.0.
Note: Earnings variation is measured by the coefficient of variation in italics.

women, $48,171 for Black men, and $31,302 for Black women. The gender earnings gap narrowed among members of the postindustrial cohort because of fairly flat earnings growth among men compared with sharp earnings growth among women, but racial gaps among men and women persisted. Black men's inflation-adjusted average earnings increased only by 2.6 percent across cohorts, while Black women's average earnings increased by about 30 percent. Middle-aged White women's earnings increased by 64 percent. Yet White men in the postindustrial cohort continued to out-earn other groups, with mean earnings of $79,809 compared with $50,841 for White women, $49,425 for Black men, and $41,025 for Black women. Earnings variation within racial and gender groups grew significantly across our two cohorts, particularly among men. As figure 1.7 shows, rates of college completion across cohorts far outpaced earnings gains for each racial and gender group. Although the gap between education and earnings was greatest for Black men and women, as we discuss in detail in chapter 3, this gap represented a *new* vulnerability for White men.

Although individual earnings are an important building block of economic security, that security ultimately rests on household living conditions that are shaped by intersecting patterns of individual employment, family structure, and household divisions of labor.[40] Therefore, to see how economic security has evolved in recent decades, we assess two important measures of household income—"working poverty" (an individual's total household income is below the federal poverty line) and "at risk of poverty" (an employed individual's total household income is within 150 percent of the federal poverty line).[41] As discussed later,

Figure 1.7   Rates of College or More Education among Postwar (1980) and Postindustrial (2015) Middle-Aged Cohorts, by Race and Gender

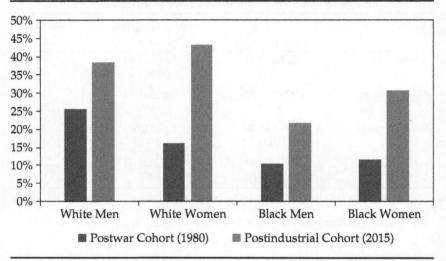

Source: Authors' analysis of data from Integrated Public Use Microdata Series, version 7.0.

both of these measures support our argument that White men hold an economic security advantage relative to White women, Black men, and Black women, even as those gaps have narrowed over time because circumstances have improved for those groups and White men have encountered new vulnerabilities.

Middle-aged White men and women across cohorts experienced fairly low and stable rates of working poverty and risk of poverty, but those figures probably underestimate their experiences of economic insecurity, since most household incomes were a product of significantly more paid labor owing to the rising labor force participation of White women and thus increased household working hours (see figure 1.8).[42] Such shifts in family labor can increase the sense of economic hardship among families struggling to maintain their living standards and can also magnify differences in security across households with different family structures.

Black men's rates of working poverty fell from 9.5 percent in 1980 to 6.6 percent in 2015, while working poverty among middle-aged Black women fell from 13 percent in 1980 to 10.6 percent in 2015. Risk of poverty followed a similar pattern: 6.5 percent of White men in the postindustrial cohort had family incomes below this level, compared with 8.3 percent of White women, 14 percent of Black men, and 20.6 percent of Black women. Group differences in unemployment contributed to these racial and gender gaps in economic security. Unemployment among White men and women in the postwar and postindustrial cohorts hovers around 4 percent, whereas

Figure 1.8   Share of Postwar (1980) and Postindustrial (2015) Middle-Aged
Cohorts Experiencing Working Poverty and at Risk of Poverty,
by Race and Gender

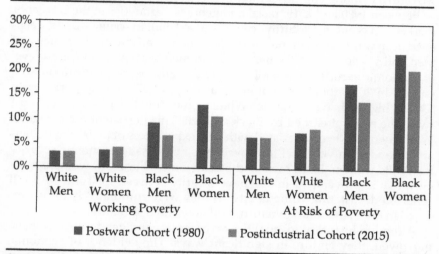

■ Postwar Cohort (1980)   ■ Postindustrial Cohort (2015)

Source: Authors' analysis of data from Integrated Public Use Microdata Series,
version 7.0.

unemployment among Black men and women in the postwar cohort stood
at 7.6 percent and 6.6 percent, respectively, in 1980 compared with 9 percent for Black men and 7.5 percent for Black women in 2015. (For details,
see table B.1 in the appendix.) Although family structure contributes to
the differences in household economic security we have observed—
marriage rates among middle-aged White men, White women, Black
men, and Black women stood at 69.4 percent, 65.7 percent, 51.9 percent,
and 37.8 percent, respectively, in 2015—persistent racial inequality in
earnings and unemployment require that we look at labor market outcomes if we are to understand trends in economic well-being by race and
gender. Said another way, while marriage increases family income and
serves as a buffer against the negative impacts of unemployment, marital
status cannot mitigate fundamentally racially disparate labor market experiences and their hazardous economic consequences.

Overall, individual and household indicators of economic security
point to a complicated pattern of stability and change. As in the postwar period, economic security at midlife in the postindustrial period was
heavily stratified by race and gender, with White men and women
accruing labor market advantages. Gender inequalities across racial
groups declined but did not fully abate over time, and men continued to
be the most economically secure by objective measures. For middle-aged
Black women in particular, the cumulative disadvantages they faced in the
U.S. labor market remained evident, as their modest improvements in

access to economic security reflected a high degree of vulnerability that did not track their steep increases in educational attainment—a theme we return to alongside closer attention to family structure in chapter 3.

Between 1980 and 2015, racial and gender inequalities in the U.S. labor market and economic security were sustained and, in some respects, deepened despite the occupational and income gains made by Black women and men and White women. White men continued to show the greatest level of economic security across all race-gender groups in the postindustrial cohort. In 2015, their mean annual earnings, at $79,809.82, were nearly $30,000 higher than earnings for White women and Black men and almost twice the amount earned by Black women. This persistent advantage of White men, however, coexisted with new experiences of their own vulnerability and with very real improvements in access to economic security for White women, Black men, and Black women. For Black women, however, real improvements in economic security between 1980 and 2015 still reflected devastating vulnerability, as they were cumulatively disadvantaged in both labor market returns and household structure.

Although historical inequalities across racial and gender groups have narrowed, they endure in significant ways. The evidence of economic security must be considered alongside trends in educational attainment to understand what the American Dream means now. Blacks and Whites, men and women, in the postindustrial cohort completed college at roughly double the rates of the postwar cohort, without a proportional improvement in their rates of economic security. This fact is driving new realities among the historically advantaged and the historically disadvantaged as economic security becomes increasingly elusive for all workers despite significant investments. This reality is one reason why people's interpretation of access to the American Dream—which we discussed in the introduction and will discuss more in the next chapters—is so different across racial groups. Their stories are distinctly American: individuals make significant efforts to obtain economic security through historically reliable pathways (educational attainment, occupational choice) but increasingly find that these efforts are not enough. Despite the meritocratic claim that hard work results in economic security and the civil rights movement's push to break the link between racial inequality and occupational opportunity in the United States, racial and gender fractures in the labor market persist. This reality continues to influence how people view their current and future prospects.

Summary

At the beginning of this chapter, we offered a fictional tale to show representative examples of the kinds of life and job situations that four individuals—Joe (a White man), Jason (a Black man), Jane (a White woman), and Jeannette (a Black woman)—would have likely experienced during the postwar period. Revisiting those four individuals' lives in 2015 would reveal something like this scenario: Joe's union job is gone. Jason has probably been unemployed for years or is underemployed. Although both men may be struggling with this newfound reality, statistically speaking, they are differently resourced to survive the economic headwinds. Joe is more likely to be married to Jane, who is White and likely to be employed part-time as she juggles family responsibilities and paid employment. The juggling is sometimes an outright struggle, but Joe and Jane own their home, and by working together and drawing on resources from their family and extended network, they are able to get by.

Jason and Jeanette probably face very different economic circumstances. As a Black man, Jason's odds of being married are less than 50 percent. If he has the good fortune of being married to Jeanette, the hope is that she is employed and contributing to keeping the family afloat. But serial unemployment and underemployment are realities they are both likely to be confronting. Limited working hours, even when they are employed, make achieving economic security a distant dream for Jason and Jeanette as they piece together different part-time occupational opportunities to make it work. They do not own a home, so they cannot draw on equity during periods of unemployment or underemployment, and they are not building wealth. Jason and Jeanette have expanded their notion of kin to survive, a network in which all rely on each other, but with the limited resources of their family and extended network, there is no reserve to tap in hard times.

This fictional tale well illustrates the present-day realities of racial inequality in the United States, and we need to understand what the American Dream means now against the backdrop of those realities. The tale depicts in a simplified way how White men and women, raised on the American Dream that their parents experienced, are confronting a labor market characterized by unexpected and expanding insecurity. It also depicts the experience of Black men and women whose racial status continues to limit their opportunities for economic security, even as their levels of educational attainment climb and their absolute income goes up. These different life stories and opportunities inform their interpretations of the American Dream in their lives today and account for the paradoxical levels of optimism they feel for their future within persistently uncertain economic times. In the next chapter, we explore how middle-aged Black and White Americans understand and account for their experiences and expectations of economic security and insecurity.

= Chapter 2 =

The Dream Interrupted:
Insecurity among the
Middle-Aged

Opportunities for achieving economic security in the United States unfolded on two parallel tracks in the twentieth century. On the one hand, the New Deal created a structure for employment in the postwar era in which racial exclusion was foundational. Opportunity and security for some was predicated on the exclusion of others. The institutional foundations of that employment-based security, however, eroded with postindustrial restructuring starting in the 1970s. On the other hand, the civil rights movement produced landmark legislation in the late 1960s to end housing and employment discrimination, thus granting Black Americans, theoretically at least, access to equal opportunity. When these two tracks converged in the 1970s, good jobs were changing just as the legal barriers to them that Black Americans had faced in the postwar period were being removed. Today even professional and white-collar jobs do not reliably offer economic security, and those with a college education or even advanced degrees find that their prospects for security are by no means assured.

The seventy-nine Black and White Americans we interviewed for this book were all middle-aged in 2015 (between the ages of thirty-five and fifty-five). They came of age during these transitions that upended expectations and realities. Despite living through the same macroeconomic changes, these middle-aged Black and White Americans understood them—and their upending of expectations—differently according to their racial group. In this chapter, we discuss in more detail how many of the men and women in this cohort—specifically those with at least some college education and family incomes above the poverty line—reflect on their economic prospects today. These individuals are part of the generation that experienced the postindustrial period's disruptions that emerged in the 1980s, and they offer insights into the national trends. Although differences in educational attainment between their respective racial groups narrowed during this time, and within-group earnings variation increased, their personal experiences and expectations of economic security and insecurity diverge sharply depending on their racial and gender group. As we discuss in this chapter, these divergent experiences, particularly along racial lines, are shaping their understanding of the past, present, and future in profoundly different ways.

Economic Security among the Vanishing Middle

Americans who were born between 1960 and 1980 and entered the labor force between 1980 and 2000 offer a unique view on the changes in labor market opportunity and its consequences for economic security. They belong to a pivotal generation whose childhoods unfolded during an economic boom that set their expectations for what their life would be and whose entire careers then unfolded in a context of diminishing access to the sense of economic security at the heart of the American Dream, as evidenced by the decline in good jobs, widening earnings inequality, and increasing earnings variability. Among those whose family incomes are above the poverty line and who attained at least some college education, like the people discussed in this chapter, many invested in postsecondary education at a time when it was not a requirement for desirable occupational opportunities, and it gave them a competitive edge as the labor market shifted in the late 1990s.[1] Like our participants, who brought into adulthood the belief that hard work evidenced by obtaining an education would give them a key advantage to compete in the labor market and reap its rewards, these Americans, at middle age, expect a certain degree of middle-class stability and are indeed relatively advantaged compared with the growing number of Americans living at or below the poverty line.

Yet, as a group, they can be described by a single word—anxious. The lived experience produced by the disruptions of the postindustrial period is anxiety. The women and men we spoke with had done all the "right" things—particularly by investing in education—to manage future risk, hedge their bets, and ward off economic insecurity, yet they were economically insecure anyway. In this book, we refer to this group of people as the "vanishing middle." Although their class status is far from uniform, they represent a generation of people whose life choices would have previously put them on the path to the middle class. During the postwar period, this economic status, once achieved, was comparatively predictable and stable. But today the path to middle-class stability is rapidly disappearing. Before the postindustrial disruption, had their lives unfolded as they expected, their educational attainment would have solidified their middle-class status. But as we discuss in this chapter, these individuals have not generally found the middle-class economic security they had hoped to find. Although our participants described barriers to security and dashed expectations that shared common elements, their experiences of these challenges—and their ideas about what these challenges indicated about the future—were strongly shaped by their race and gender. Their stories are part of a complicated American story.

The racial and gender inequalities among the vanishing middle derive from differences in employment security that are magnified by group differences in generational wealth and family structure. These fault lines are clearest when we trace how individual measures of employment security by group (occupation, earnings, unemployment) aggregate into household levels of economic security more broadly conceived.

The people in the vanishing middle are, by definition, educationally advantaged. They typically hold professional and technical or managerial jobs, though White men and women are more likely to hold those desirable positions than are Black men and women (see figure 2.1). There are distinct gender differences in the occupational breakdown, however, for both Black and White workers. In both racial groups, women are more concentrated in professional and technical jobs and men are more concentrated in managerial positions. Nearly half of White women in the vanishing middle, for example, held professional or technical jobs in 2015 (49.3 percent), compared with 35.3 percent of White men. By contrast, 27.9 percent of White men held managerial positions, compared with 16.9 percent of White women. A similar pattern holds among Black men and women: 41.1 percent of Black women and 29.3 percent of Black men held professional jobs in 2015; only 13.9 percent of Black women and 17.6 percent of Black men held managerial positions. Women in the vanishing middle are also highly reliant on nonmanagerial white-collar jobs, which are notoriously uneven in job quality: only about 13 percent of White and Black men held such jobs, compared with 23.7 percent of White women and 25.8 percent of Black women.

Although the gender gap in access to managerial employment is significant, the largest occupational inequalities among the vanishing middle follow racial lines. Much of the unequal access enjoyed by White Americans in the decades following World War II to advantages like homeownership, education, and economic security gave them lasting expectations of good economic prospects. The inequalities connected to this legacy of racial privilege remain highly present among the vanishing middle. For example, within the vanishing middle, White men and women hold a distinct advantage over Black men and women in access to professional, technical, and managerial employment. Among White men, 27.9 percent hold managerial positions compared to only 17.6 percent of Black men. Although White women also hold an advantage relative to Black women

Figure 2.1   Occupational Attainment among the Vanishing Middle, by Race and Gender, 2015

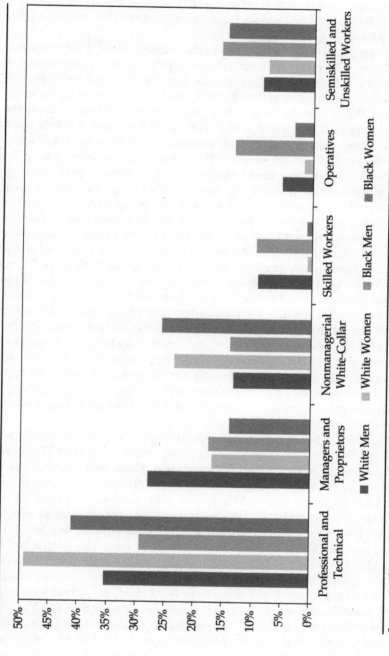

Source: Authors' analysis of data from Integrated Public Use Microdata Series, version 7.0.

in managerial employment, their advantage is even more pronounced in professional and technical occupations: 49.3 percent of White women in the vanishing middle hold such positions, compared to only 41.1 percent of Black women.

Similar gaps along racial lines are also evident in the greater reliance of Black men (13.5 percent) on operative occupations, such as bus drivers and operators of other heavy equipment, compared to other groups. Importantly, Black men and women in the vanishing middle are roughly twice as likely as their White counterparts to hold a semiskilled or unskilled position: in 2015 only 8.9 percent of White men and 7.9 percent of White women held a semiskilled or unskilled job, compared with 16 percent of Black men and 14.9 percent of Black women. The fact that such a large share of Black men and women in the vanishing middle continued to rely on "bad" jobs that mirrored their relegation to undesirable jobs in the postwar period is powerful evidence of persistent racial disadvantage in access to good jobs.

As we discussed in chapter 1, occupation alone tells us less about economic security than it used to, so we draw on measures of earnings and working hours to understand group differences in access to good jobs and thus the different perspectives on what the American Dream means now. Back in the postwar period, the standard employment relationship was central to employment stability, as it created uniformity in the number of hours worked (often full-time) and reduced earnings variation for workers within the same occupation. As the labor market and economic structures shifted in the postindustrial period, this uniformity in job quality changed dramatically, and hours worked and earnings within the same occupation became much more variable. Because of the legacy of structural racism and the labor gender gap, the effects of these changes followed familiar racial and gender lines, even among educationally advantaged middle-aged workers.

Although rates of full-time work among the vanishing middle were high in 2015 for each demographic group—90.3 percent of White men, 77.1 percent of White women, 89.3 percent of Black men, and 87.4 percent of Black women—average pay across these groups was highly uneven (see table 2.1). On average, White men with standard employment relations earned about $101,965 per year, compared with annual earnings of $66,598 per year for Black men, $67,457 for White women, and $54,776 for Black women. Mean hours of work per week varied by group, but not enough to explain the large earnings gap: White men in the vanishing middle with standard employment relations worked only, on average, about two hours more per week than Black men, three hours more per week than White women, and four hours more per week than Black women.

We observed a similar pattern of earnings advantages among those members of the vanishing middle with nonstandard employment relations (part-time, in the temporary service industry, or in unincorporated

Table 2.1   Economic Security among the Vanishing Middle, by Employment Type (Standard and Nonstandard) and Race and Gender, 2015

	White Men	White Women	Black Men	Black Women
Nonstandard employment	9.7%	22.9%	10.7%	12.6%
Mean annual earnings (2015 dollars)	$44,701.81	$27,911.78	$28,991.69	$26,667.15
Variation in annual earnings (coefficient of variation)	1.55	1.14	1.13	1.13
Usual hours worked per week (mean)	37.18	25.72	32.25	27.68
Standard employment	90.3%	77.1%	89.3%	87.4%
Mean annual earnings (2015 dollars)	$101,965.00	$67,457.92	$66,598.80	$54,776.75
Variation in annual earnings (coefficient of variation)	0.91	0.86	0.82	0.72
Usual hours worked per week (mean)	46.6	43.37	44.64	42.23

Source: Authors' analysis of data from Integrated Public Use Microdata Series, version 7.0.

self-employment): White men in nonstandard jobs earned, on average, $44,701 per year compared with $28,991 for Black men, $27,911 for White women, and $26,667 for Black women. White men in nonstandard employment were more likely than other groups to work full-time; thus, they were considered nonstandard employees either because they were self-employed or because they worked in the temporary services industry. Access to working hours among the vanishing middle with nonstandard employment was highly stratified by race and gender: White men in this category worked thirty-seven hours per week on average, compared with thirty-two hours per week for Black men, about twenty-seven hours per week for Black women, and twenty-five hours per week for White women. Finally, unemployment among the vanishing middle was also highly stratified by race: Black men's unemployment rate (4.1 percent) was nearly double that of White men (2.2 percent), and unemployment among Black women outpaced unemployment among White women by about one percentage point (3.6 percent and 2.4 percent, respectively). As discussed in chapter 1 with respect to all Black and White workers, race and gender shape access to good jobs among the vanishing middle in ways that reflect the relative advantages and disadvantages of the postwar period.

These patterns of relative advantage and disadvantage in the work experiences of individuals in the vanishing middle aggregate into household

Figure 2.2   Marital Status of the Vanishing Middle, by Race and Gender, 2015

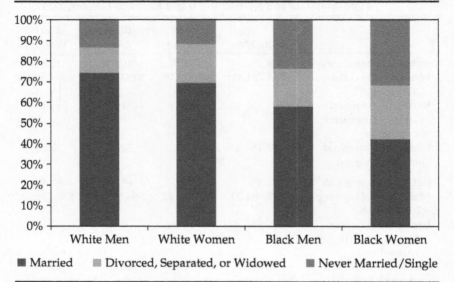

Source: Authors' analysis of data from Integrated Public Use Microdata Series, version 7.0.

differences in ways that deepen inequalities in economic security and well-being, with implications for how these Black and White Americans comprehend their overall economic prospects. Thus, to recognize the impact of household differences between White and Black Americans on their overall perspectives on economic security, we must be attentive to differences in family structure. One important difference is the rate of marriage between Black and White Americans (see figure 2.2). Scholars and policymakers have debated the relationship between economic security and marriage for decades, particularly as part of debates over welfare reform. Some observers argue that low marriage rates cause economic insecurity, and others argue the reverse. As the sociologists Kathryn Edin and Maria Kefalas have shown, White and Black Americans living below the poverty line do not value marriage less than members of the middle class.[2] Across the class structure, Americans are choosing to delay marriage until they achieve economic security; this resolve pushes marriage later into the life cycle for some and delays it indefinitely for others.[3] Because of the significant economic advantages that marriage provides in the United States, however, the notable differences between marriage rates further compound the labor market disadvantages that Black workers already face.

Given the greater levels of objective economic insecurity experienced by Black Americans—including those within the vanishing middle—it is perhaps unsurprising that they marry at lower rates than their White peers. In 2015, 74 percent of White men in the vanishing middle were married, compared with 69 percent of White women, 58 percent of Black men, and only 42.2 percent of Black women. Rates of being divorced, separated, or widowed were higher among women in the vanishing middle, particularly Black women—25.8 percent of Black women compared with 18.2 percent of Black men, 18.9 percent of White women, and 12.7 percent of White men. Nearly one-third of Black women in the vanishing middle had never married (31.9 percent), compared with 23.7 percent of Black men, 13.4 percent of White men, and 12.1 percent of White women.

Because marriage patterns both reflect labor market inequalities and aggregate into larger household differences in economic resources, they are a key influence on middle-aged Black and White Americans' experience of economic security. Following a pattern that has by now become familiar, average household income is highly stratified by race and gender. On average, White men in the vanishing middle lived in households with a total annual income of $151,065, compared with $131,036 for White women. Black men in the vanishing middle had an average annual household income of $115,501, compared with $97,795 for Black women. These are exceptional differences in household income among educated workers: White men in the vanishing middle lived in households with an average annual income that was over $20,000 more than that of White women, over $35,000 more than that of Black men, and over $50,000 more than that of Black women (see table B.2 in the appendix). Behind these numbers, however, are racial differences in household gender roles that shape experiences of economic security. Among married members of the vanishing middle, White women were more likely than Black women to not be employed and therefore to be fully reliant on their spouse's income (19.5 percent and 11.8 percent, respectively, in 2015). Among those married members of the vanishing middle who were employed, Black women's earnings accounted for a larger share of total household income than did White women's earnings (figure 2.3). Although White households in the vanishing middle enjoy a persistent economic advantage, the sharper change in White women's economic roles since 1980 has contributed to racial differences in experiences and perceptions of change in economic security.

Household differences in economic resources across racial and gender groups aggregate intergenerationally as well, producing a large racial wealth gap that affects the perceptions of the American Dream of everyone in the vanishing middle—Blacks and Whites, men and women—and in particular the ability to own one's home. In the United States, homeownership has long been an important marker of economic security and a resource for managing job loss or change. But opportunities for homeownership are highly stratified by race within the vanishing middle. About 80 percent of White men and women in this group own

Figure 2.3   Individual Earnings of Employed Married Women in the Vanishing Middle as a Share of Household Income, 1980 and 2015

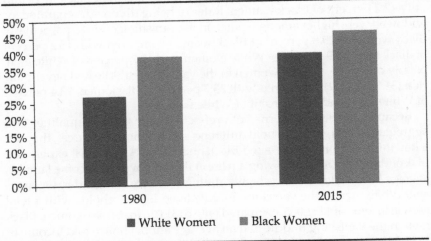

Source: Authors' analysis of data from Integrated Public Use Microdata Series, version 7.0.

their own homes, compared with 59 percent of Black men and 57.4 percent of Black women (see table B.2 in the appendix). The vanishing middle is the generation whose parents were of an age to benefit from the 1944 GI Bill, which supported two defining elements of the American Dream—homeownership and postsecondary education. Homeownership is more than a financial asset: although it serves as a vehicle for transferring generational wealth, the home itself is also evocative of the lifestyle elements of the American Dream. The intent of the GI Bill was to improve access to education, which was seen as the key to gaining access to the good jobs that enabled homeownership and its cultural benefits.

Those who have achieved homeownership—which, among the vanishing middle, is predominantly White men and women, as the numbers cited earlier indicate—have also gained access to broader cultural and lifestyle elements of the American Dream. Homeownership in the context of employment or earnings instability, however, can become a source of financial peril, as was made clear in the mass foreclosures and rising numbers of Americans "underwater" on their mortgages (owing more than the assessed value of the property) during the Great Recession of 2008–2009.

As we saw with access to good jobs, access to homeownership remains racially stratified for reasons that are rooted in the past but reproduced in current practice. Aside from setting aside resources to enable veterans to realize the Dream, the GI Bill, in delineating who had access to the Dream, ensured that Black Americans did not. The GI Bill defined a generation and was racially discriminatory by design to accommodate Jim Crow laws and permit the restriction of benefits to White Americans, and it enabled the intentional and, at times, violent exclusion of Black Americans from homeownership. The virulent racism faced by Black veterans when they returned from fighting overseas in World War II is well known; from lynching veterans for wearing the uniform to restricting them to menial labor, the reinforcement of the racial order was unwavering.[4] It was not until the Civil Rights Act of 1964 that the legal restrictions prohibiting Black Americans from accessing the elements of the Dream were lifted. At that point, White people had a twenty-year federally financed head start in pursuing the Dream that built generational wealth and enabled a level of security that Black people were denied.

The legacy of structural racism dating back to the postwar period has maintained White economic advantage and Black economic disadvantage among the vanishing middle. Advantages accorded to White Americans in the postwar era—in access to secure employment, homeownership, and higher education—continue to shape racial and gender differences in objective economic security today. Yet, despite being more economically insecure, Black Americans are more optimistic about the future. In the next section, we explore why, and we show how both Black and White Americans are using the past to make sense of the present and build hopes for the future.

Race, Gender, and Economic Expectations: The Racial Futures Paradox

As discussed in chapter 1, despite increased access to desirable employment and growing household incomes that have narrowed economic security gaps between White men, White women, Black men, and Black women, economic insecurity continues to manifest along racial and gender lines. Middle-aged White men and women who are members of the post-industrial cohort have had to work harder than the postwar cohort—as measured in educational attainment and family working hours—to maintain similar levels of economic security. Although their levels of working poverty, risk of poverty, and unemployment are similar to those of middle-aged White men and women in the postwar generation, they do not reflect the decrease we would expect given their level of educational gains and increased household working hours (see table B.1 in the appendix). In other words, White men and women are working harder just to hold their ground in the face of sweeping changes in access to economic security.

Middle-aged White men and women, however, remain more economically secure than middle-aged Black men and women, whose educational investments and increasing access to skilled white-collar work have yielded even less security. The economic security of middle-aged Black men and women in the postindustrial period improved compared to Black men and women in the postwar period, but compared to their White counterparts, Black workers' economic gains have occurred alongside ongoing and harrowing levels of unemployment, working poverty, and risk of poverty, despite their similarly steep investments in education. As we have shown in this chapter, the broad patterns of racial and gender inequality in access to economic security that we documented among the middle-aged in 2015 apply even to the educationally advantaged vanishing middle. These patterns of relative advantage and disadvantage today sit in a wider context of growing inequality and instability in economic opportunities, a fact that can make even those in relatively secure circumstances uneasy in their success.

The comparison between those who were middle-aged in 1980 (postwar cohort) and those who were middle-aged in 2015 (postindustrial cohort) underscores the fact that White and Black Americans are drawing on very different historical points of reference as they formulate their views on what economic security means to them now and the extent to which they expect economic security in the future. Economic security and conceptions of the American Dream are contextual. How a person experiences their economic conditions or reflects on the salience of the American Dream in their life depends on a complex constellation of issues that are not fully captured by objective measures alone. An individual's economic security involves very personal assessments of relative well-being coupled with assessments of whether their quality of life is likely to change. In 2013, the Associated Press–National Opinion Research Center found that the expressed optimism of an improved life was diverging for Blacks and Whites, producing the largest recorded racial gap in perceptions of current employment conditions and future prospects for improvement.[5] To gain further insight into how Black and White American workers view their current economic conditions, their future prospects, and their overall subjective sense of economic security, we examined responses to survey questions from the General Social Survey that were focused on these issues, comparing responses to questions from the 1994 GSS survey to responses from the 2016 GSS survey.[6]

Because economic security is a relative measure, how a person views changes in their economic condition over time provides important insight into their sense of economic security. In the GSS survey, several questions were aimed at this particular issue. For example, one question asked: "During the last few years, has your financial situation been getting better, worse, or has it stayed the same?" In figure 2.4, we show responses to this question in 1994 and 2016 broken out by race and gender. As these responses show, Americans' sense of economic well-being was stratified

Figure 2.4   Subjective Indicator of Economic Security Relative to the Past among Middle-Aged Workers, by Race and Gender, 2016

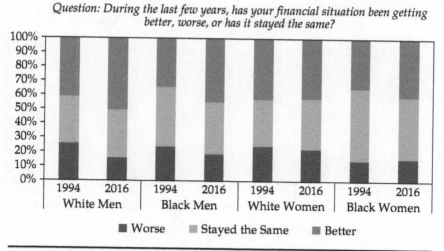

Question: During the last few years, has your financial situation been getting better, worse, or has it stayed the same?

■ Worse   ▨ Stayed the Same   ■ Better

Source: Authors' analysis of General Social Survey Data.
Note: Sums to 100 percent of valid responses within racial and gender groups.

by race and gender. Among the middle-aged in 1994, White respondents had been more likely than Black respondents to report that things were getting worse, with men reporting worsening conditions more often than women: around one-quarter of White men and women reported worsening finances in 1994, compared with about 23 percent of Black men and 14 percent of Black women. At 23 and 24 percent, respectively, Black and White men's 1994 rates were similar, but their dramatic differences in objective material circumstances, combined with similar subjective statistics, suggest a different relationship to those disparate material conditions. By 2016, White women were most likely to report worsening finances: nearly 22 percent of White women reported that things were getting worse in recent years, compared with about 18 percent of Black men and 15.9 percent of both Black women and White men. Black women were the only group more likely to report worsening finances in 2016 (15.9 percent) than in 1994 (14.3 percent). These rankings align with the longer trend in relative security observed in chapter 1, where we showed that long-standing patterns of relative advantage coexist with new vulnerabilities.

What do Americans' different experiences of economic security in the present mean for their expectations of the future? In figure 2.5 we show people's responses in 1994 and 2016 to the GSS question: "'The way things are in America, people like me and my family have a good chance of improving our standard of living'—do you agree or disagree?"

Figure 2.5   Subjective Indicator of Future Economic Security among Middle-Aged Workers, by Race and Gender, 2016

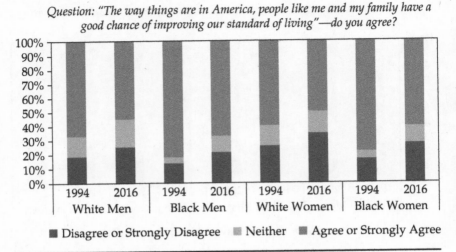

Question: *"The way things are in America, people like me and my family have a good chance of improving our standard of living"—do you agree?*

■ Disagree or Strongly Disagree   ■ Neither   ■ Agree or Strongly Agree

Source: Authors' analysis of General Social Survey Data.
Note: Sums to 100 percent of valid responses within racial and gender groups.

Black men and women were much more likely to agree with this statement than White men and women: they expressed greater levels of optimism despite the strong and persistent racial divide in objective indicators of economic security. In 2016, about 67 percent of Black men and 60 percent of Black women agreed that they had a good chance of improving their standard of living, compared with 54 percent of White men and 50 percent of White women. But the trend of declining optimism for the future held across all groups, as more respondents, Blacks and Whites, men and women, disagreed in 2016 with the statement that they had a good chance of improving their standard of living in the future than had disagreed in 1994. About 26 percent of White men and 35 percent of White women disagreed with the statement in 2016, up from 19 percent and 26 percent, respectively, in 1994. Black men and women were also more pessimistic in 2016 than 1994: 21 percent of Black men and 28 percent of Black women disagreed with the statement in 2016, compared with 14 percent and 17 percent in 1994, respectively.

As these numbers demonstrate, there is a disconnect in Black and White Americans' experiences of economic insecurity, disaggregated by race and gender. Although each group expressed lower average levels of optimism for the future in 2016 than they did in 1994, in both 1994 and 2016 Black respondents nevertheless held comparatively higher expectations than White respondents that things had a good chance of improving in their lives. And yet this comparative optimism in 1994 and in 2016 did not correspond with differences in objective indicators of economic security between White and Black Americans. White respondents who were relatively less optimistic deviated from their comparatively favorable objective conditions, while Black respondents were comparatively optimistic despite their more insecure circumstances. We refer to these dueling realities, which suggest differing assessments of the "same" material conditions, as the "racial futures paradox."

To understand the racial futures paradox, we need to reflect again on the crosscurrents of change that the middle-aged are making sense of. This is a group that was raised during the postwar period with expectations for their own lives that were shaped by their parents' expectations and opportunities. But when they themselves entered the labor market sometime between 1980 and 2000, the labor market their parents had known had been transformed. For White Americans, the primary transformation they grappled with in the years that followed was postindustrial restructuring, which made the connections between education, access to a good job, and economic security less predictable. Black Americans encountered those same changes, but more vivid for them was the added reality that de jure employment discrimination was no longer the law of the land. The civil rights movement affected White Americans too, of course, by limiting their ability to retain preferential access to the best jobs on the basis of race and creating more employment opportunities for White women. But White people's access to economic security was more directly upended by the new and unfolding realities of the postindustrial American labor market. Expectations about the role of women in society were changing too; new patterns in labor force participation and family formation unfolded as women more often worked full-time outside the home and contributed to household income. Again, these changes were not racially uniform, as the gendered expectations shaping the labor force experiences of White and Black women—and the challenges and opportunities they faced— were racially specific.

All of the men and women—both Black and White—of this generation have encountered these new structures of opportunity as the postindustrial period progressed, but they have navigated these changes from very different starting points. The crosscurrents of change—which all tie into race, class, and gender—created the conditions for the racial futures paradox. White Americans are now mourning the loss of widespread economic security, while Black Americans are feeling relatively more optimistic, as they cannot mourn something they never had. Black respondents' optimism for the future, despite the insecurities of the present, is based on how they view their own racially distinctive past.

As this book shows, race and gender intersect in powerful ways to inform both objective material security among the vanishing middle and their subjective evaluation of those conditions. As members of the postindustrial cohort, the vanishing middle sits squarely amid expectations formed by the postwar past and realities forged in the crucible of the postindustrial present. Yet as educationally advantaged Americans living above the poverty line, they respond to the economic insecurities they experience with disappointment: something unexpected happened on the road to middle-class stability, and they are still trying to understand how their plans were derailed. In a nation in which the poor often internalize their own educational and occupational "failures," reproducing the narrative that working hard and doing the right thing in school will lead to success, how do the educationally advantaged make sense of the economic insecurities they face?

To understand the lived experiences of the racial futures paradox—which speaks to the importance of joining objective and subjective indicators—we turn now to the narratives of our participants. Moving beyond survey research, we will hear, in their own words, how Black and White Americans draw on the past to wrestle with the new realities of the present as they make sense of their complex experiences.

The Past Is Present: The Historical Origins of Expectations in Black and White

The racial group histories of security and exclusion directly shape the way that Black and White Americans understand the present and what they expect for the future. In this section, we show that the past is present as our participants, Blacks and Whites, men and women, compare their economic circumstances to the opportunity structure of the postwar period. Distinctive racialized and gendered histories lead to different evaluations of the present. For Black Americans, the progress made in occupational and educational attainment after 1970 did not neatly translate into improved economic security, yet there is a continued willingness to push on and navigate the challenges of the present moment.

Many of the Black men and women we spoke with recognized the persistence of economic insecurity, but they did not necessarily convey a sense of resignation or regret. They did not long for some time in the past when they had it easier because they could remember no such time. By contrast, many of the White men and women we interviewed conveyed the newness of the economic vulnerability they were confronting; for them, the realization that things were now uncertain was unsettling. They expressed a clear nostalgia for a more secure time when employees were taken care of by employers and their well-being was factored into business decisions, when labor was not simply a cost to be managed but a resource to be invested in, and when companies were connected to the community and cared about more than profit maximization for shareholders' benefit.

These differences are noticeable when we compare our Black and White participants' descriptions of the past. Many White participants viewed the societal loss of the more secure jobs they imagined were present in the past as a personal loss, and one that had affected their well-being in the present. Black participants, on the other hand, more often described the loss of these kinds of secure jobs in the abstract, as part of a larger social change, but without mentioning that they are worse off because of it. Consider the different ways that Henry, the Black technical writer we met earlier, and Drew, a forty-three-year-old White salesman, described this larger social change. Henry did not draw attention to his personal loss but instead offered a broader critical description of today's super-rich compared to the innovators of the past:

> You know, look at it this way, you know, as bad as working conditions were in the '30s, the '40s, '50s, whatever, the super-rich people of that era, they made things, they built things. Andrew Carnegie, steel plants, Henry Ford, Ford Motor Company, you know, General Motors—you know, all of these places, they were innovators, they created a company that built things, that employed people, that people could pay taxes, and they could receive health care. It was a mutually beneficial loop.

Henry's comments on the postwar structure of opportunities in the abstract reflected his knowledge that in those days access to these occupational opportunities and the economic security they enabled was reserved for White Americans. Yet note his choice of words: he said that "a company that built things, that employed people, that people could pay taxes, and they could receive health care," was how it *used* to be, but he did not add that this was his expectation of what it *would* be for him.

Compare his comments to Drew's statement: while critiquing his present insecurity, Drew articulated an expectation that a better employment relationship should be available to him:

> I think there is way too much emphasis put on at-will employment as opposed to companies investing in their employees. You see a lot of companies, in this day and age, where a lot of things that I was doing to further my education for that company, I was having to pay for it. That's fine if you reimburse me like a college education program, but more times than not, I just see where companies view way too many employees as expendable instead of a value.

Unlike Henry, Drew saw the new reality as not just a change in the opportunity structure, but a change that took something from him. It's almost as if Henry and Drew were navigating two entirely different labor markets, since they certainly had differing approaches and expectations. Both had less than a bachelor's degree, Drew had an associate's degree, while Henry had completed some college but did not obtain a credential. Both held a position that fit within the professional services industry. But they had very different economic realities: Henry earned less than $40,000 a year, while Drew's income sometimes reached six figures.

Henry and Drew narrated differing expectations and realities of economic insecurity. Their views are instructive in showing how Black and White Americans compare their situation to the past to assess and understand their present reality. Drew's narration of what had been lost in the present laid claim to something that was owed but not delivered, whereas Henry's account made no such claim.

We see a similar distinction in the observations of other members of the vanishing middle. Phoebe, a fifty-four-year-old White city clerk, commented on the good jobs of the past and said that there were not as many of those anymore. In those jobs, she said, "[you can get] a decent salary," and though no one ever got rich in those positions, she continued, "you can have a nice house and be there from the cradle [to] the grave, maybe thirty, thirty-five years. . . . There's none of those jobs right now. Those jobs are not here." Phoebe's choice of words revealed that the lack of good jobs felt like a personal loss for her. Betsy, a forty-four-year-old White nurse, went further in diagnosing the source of the problem. She was critical of "the big companies" for just "looking out for themselves." In her view, employers now feel "they have to protect their own progress and their own ability to have their own business." If they think, she continued, that "paying employees that they don't necessarily need is holding them back, then they're going to let them go." Despite being college educated and earning over $200,000 a year, Betsy conveyed in this account a clear recognition of her vulnerability to labor market change.

> You know it's about staying afloat. Many people lost their jobs [when the company was bought out] because they didn't need extra people doing jobs they were already paying other people to do, and maybe somebody else was doing it better and they were there longer. So they have more seniority, and so if you're not the senior person . . . that's why I'm always hesitant to even change jobs. I've been there twenty-five years. I think it's a bonus I have that longevity there.

Steve, a fifty-five-year-old White school counselor, bemoaned the loss of broad-based security: "I think that there's less protections even though the economy is more stable. The individual worker has less protections than they've ever had." These White workers' sentiments reflected unmet expectations of the labor market. They conveyed frustration with the loss of economic security and the ease with which employers could disregard the needs of employees and not be invested in their welfare. In many ways, White participants projected aspirations consistent with the postwar labor contract. They seemed surprised to have learned that the foundations of postwar security were gone. It is almost as if they thought that the postwar labor contract was still in force and were angry that those terms of employment were not being upheld.

Black participants, on the other hand, knew that Black Americans had been explicitly excluded from the postwar labor contract: the formulation of policy, from the minimum wage to fair labor standards, included discriminatory concessions to preserve the racial order. Their parents had navigated the labor market in the period that preceded the Civil Rights Act, a time when the postwar labor contract had not applied to their parents. Consequently, our Black participants carried no expectation that it would apply to them today, even as they aspired to the same desirable terms of employment. They wanted a good job at the plant, but it was never their expectation that they would have it. It was a goal to work toward, to get that good job and lead that good life, to live the American Dream. Reality for many Black workers, however, persistently and stubbornly belied this aspiration. Black workers' connection to the good jobs of the past was always aspirational; it was about striving for a good job, not about expecting to have one, or remembering a time when good jobs were widely available. This experience of the past led our Black participants to narrate employment struggles from the perspective of a puzzle to be figured out. Where, they asked themselves, can I find opportunity?

For example, Vanessa, a thirty-year-old Black policy analyst, thought that there were good jobs to be had in health care and information technology.

> Well, the thing is, we're getting into a mechanized society, so we have to look at the people that are creating the mechanisms to make it. That's like where the industry is going. It's like when I think of what I want my kid to do, you need to be an engineer, mechanical, electrical, something, you need to have the mind to build something. You don't need to be the guy, like I feel like my dad's generation, you need them to be the guy to build it. For my sons' generation, you need to have the mind to know how to build it. I think that's where the change is in society.

Vanessa's view of industrial change is grounded, at least in part, in the realization that the United States has moved away from a job market that required physical labor for making things to one that relies more on intellectual or cognitive labor. So, in her view, rather than reflect on and mourn the jobs and protections of the past, she needed to prepare herself and her children for the jobs of the future.

Jordan, a forty-five-year-old Black physician's assistant, took a different approach to economic instability than that taken by many of the White respondents. He said, "I'm pretty straight at this particular moment. Will it be that way next year, next month? Who knows? I swim with sharks, and sometimes you get bit." There is a recognition and an acceptance of instability in Jordan's words, with no conception of blame or longing for an alternative past. Neither did Jordan long for a more secure future; he simply saw the future as his to create and prepare for:

> I could do what I'm doing for maybe, like, the next ten, fifteen years or so, but right now I'm in school, I'm getting an MBA. Will I use it? I don't know. But I like to have that in my arsenal in case I need to. I mean, something could happen next year, and I may not have the job that I have now.

Jordan's remarks reflected a sentiment similar to Vanessa's; both of these Black participants were keeping an eye on where the labor market was heading in order to take advantage of opportunity in the future. Their views were representative of how many Black men and women see their present situation compared to the past. On the other hand, our White participants tended to focus on the personal loss and struggle they had experienced as a result of recent economic shifts. We see in these narratives two very different expectations of the American labor market, rooted in racially distinctive group experiences in the past. On the one hand, Black Americans cannot mourn what they never had, their access in the past to good jobs and economic security having been constrained by their racial group membership. By contrast, White Americans, their racial group membership having enabled near-exclusive access to good jobs in the past, struggle with the loss of a security that they took for granted.

The Game Has Changed, but Education Is Still the Key: Making Sense of the Dream

The racial futures paradox underscores that expectations for the future are racialized, in that, even under the "same" material conditions, those expectations are rooted in assessments of different historical realities. The education-security mismatch for the middle-aged does, however, produce racially shared disillusionment, as it is an outcome of their generational assumptions about what their investments in education would produce not being matched by their lived realities. Even those whose lives match their expectations at present fear that they will not be able to hold on to their present lifestyle and are aware that others who invested as they did have much less to show for it. Our participants' lived experiences shed light on how contemporary employment restructuring rests on racial, gender, and class narratives that legitimize insecurity.

Despite clear evidence that public policies related to employment, housing, and education have created or blocked people's access to economic security in both the postwar and postindustrial periods, our Black and White participants continued to see themselves within individualist narratives that located responsibility for success or failure in their own efforts. This perspective focuses on individual hard work and determination—especially in the form of educational attainment—as the key to taking advantage of opportunities, a logic that is in turn used to justify who deserves security and who does not. But as insecurity spreads in the postindustrial era, people are finding that the rewards of hard work and higher levels of education are less than in the past. Although there were notable differences between the objective results of their hard work and their education, the anxiety and frustration expressed by our participants cut across racial groups.

Darius, for example, a fifty-one-year-old Black corrections officer, recalled that his parents made less money than he did, but he suggested that their money went further than his did today. "I knew what they [his parents] made at one point, and I wonder how we did some of the things we did. Like, my father would take us on vacation. . . . Most summers, we went somewhere for a week." Going on a one-week vacation may seem like a minor expenditure, but it was significant for Darius because he couldn't afford to take a vacation right now. He offered a particularly concrete description of his struggle to reconcile his past and present economic limitations.

> I made way more than what they made at my job, but yet I was struggling to survive at times, and I'm going, how did they do it, but yet I'm making probably double what they made, but yet I can't, and I'm looking, and I said, well, one, I know the times are different and things cost a lot more, you know, but somehow they were able to make it, you know, where— some of the comparisons, like, certain things—I make more, but it didn't go as far as like, it did for them, and I still—I talk to my mother sometimes and say, "I don't know how you and Dad did it, you know, but—I make more, but it didn't go as far as what you all did, you know?" And they had a house and all that other stuff, you know, but they were able to make it work, and we could do a lot of things. Where for me, you know, me and my wife, we're like, okay, we can't take a vacation this year because of this, so everything keeps rising and rising.

Darius's reflection was clearly more than just a passing reference to how things used to be. He was genuinely puzzled as to why he couldn't do what his parents did, despite objectively earning more than his parents did. The luxuries of life were just out of reach for him. This bothered Darius so much, he shared, that he still talked to his mother about it.

Like Darius, many of our other respondents, across racial groups, also noted that they were unable to take a vacation. It was striking how many people made the connection between having a good job, economic security, and the ability to take a vacation. Sophia, a forty-eight-year-old White account clerk who described her household as upper-middle-class, expressed frustration about not being able to take a vacation: "We haven't done that in a while, though, because like I said, I haven't been steadily working . . . although we are going in the fall finally." The American Dream promises a good life, one in which hard work is rewarded and children do better than their parents. After owning a home, the ability to take a vacation may be one of the most recognizable indicators of having achieved the American Dream. For Americans, it is evidence that they are able to live, if just for a week, the good life—that they have been able to meet their needs and have something left over for their wants. However, many of those who earn good money, like Darius, struggle to understand the disconnect in their lives: Why aren't their economic means meeting their expectations? How is it that they worked hard and have good incomes, but still feel economically constrained?

Trisha, a forty-two-year-old Black administrative assistant, also referred to the ability to take a vacation as an indicator of financial well-being, but she took it a step further. When asked to talk about the image she had when she was younger of what a good life and a good job would look like, she started by saying, "Being able to support myself," but segued quickly to a different criterion for the good life: being able to take a vacation. "Going on vacation was not something I thought of. It was just something we did." For Trisha, the assumption was that "we could always do that." It was a wake-up call for her and her husband when, despite earning "decent money," they couldn't afford to buy a house or take a vacation. They moved to a more affordable area as a result. She concluded by saying, "I think the good life is being able to go and be on vacation, be able to support yourself and eat. Have a kid or two." All of our participants, across racial and gender groups, made it clear that, in their opinion, the good life was nearly impossible to achieve without a good job, and those were increasingly scarce. This sentiment fueled fears and anxieties among the middle-aged across racial groups about economic insecurity. Indeed, even Black participants, despite the history of Blacks having less access to higher-paying occupations and economic security than White participants, could still point to examples of economic security in their parents' lives that now seemed to have disappeared. Henry, the Black technical writer quoted earlier, provided an apt description of the economy as it used to be for many male workers. "There were jobs that literally, when you got out of high school, if you didn't go to college, you literally put on your clothes and went to work with your father." While nostalgia for the predictability of the jobs in the postwar era was more common among White men, both Black and White men referenced these kinds of past jobs to explain the anxiety-producing instability of jobs in the present.

Jordan, the Black physician's assistant, described his view on working in the postindustrial economy by summarily pointing out that there were "no good enough jobs." Although older generations might have memories of better jobs, the fact that people coming of working age today have never experienced those good jobs should be the reference point. Only those who were middle-aged or older today, he argued, could complain about it. He continued, addressing younger people:

> Well, your grandfather and your father probably can because they remember that they lived that. But young people should not be sitting around saying, there ain't no good jobs, because what the hell do you base that on? That's not your life. You're living in the here and now. There never was any good jobs for you, so what the hell are you saying (*laughs*).

Jordon's comment was a comical delivery of a disheartening truth about the contemporary labor market.

All of our interviewees were part of the generation of workers who began their working lives in the postindustrial economy but came of age in families whose economic conditions were a product of the postwar labor market. Their frustration and anxiety at the lack of "good jobs" in the postindustrial era—a shared anxiety that is nevertheless underpinned by significantly diverging objective financial circumstances according to their racial and gender group—offer valuable insight into the meaning of economic insecurity in the contemporary era. They also revealed the important role of the legacy of racial inequality in determining Americans' subjective understandings of their current economic prospects. Having been of working age for at least a full decade, and being at least a decade away from retirement, our interviewees had witnessed a period of economic change when insecure work increased for all racial groups. They were among those whose access to the economic stability at the heart of the American Dream had been most disrupted by recent restructuring trends. By investing in a college education, the vanishing middle had taken steps they hoped would ensure a secure future, but with mixed results. These were workers who thought that their education would insulate them against market changes, but they could not have conceived of the scope of market transformation that unfolded during their lifetime.

Although some changes were welcome, such as the eroding connection between race and occupational opportunity, the economic transformation of the postindustrial period also eroded job quality and made occupation alone an increasingly unreliable indicator of economic security. As the economy began to shift, workers believed that getting an education demonstrated worthiness and increased their odds of obtaining economic security. The belief in the American Dream among this generation of workers, including the belief that any person can pull themselves up by their bootstraps, despite challenging economic times, has endured. Despite the reality of rising economic insecurity—which impacts people differently according to race and gender—individualist narratives of success persist among middle-aged Americans today. However, cracks in the Dream are showing.

Cracks in the Dream

The disconnect between expectations of security given investments in education and the reality of uncertainty made many of our participants anxious about their ability to achieve economic stability, work toward upward mobility, and guide their children toward a better future. At a time when people can no longer rely on the availability of good factory jobs, widespread unionization, or lifelong increases in pay, many contrast the insecurity of today with the "good times" of yesteryear. Our participants grappled with these economic and labor market shifts. They reflected on their lives and those of their parents but did so in the context of distinct racial realities.

White Americans feel this economic insecurity personally, and many are struggling to find the right way to cope. In describing this struggle, Gus, a forty-nine-year-old White part-time associate in a big-box store, suggested that the economic insecurity he and his wife were facing was not a good thing for the country or the economy. He used himself as an example of the instability in the economy.

> The inability to recuperate from a lost job quickly. I think that's one of the factors that is weighing heavily on our economy. Because by me not being able to recover quickly, it minimizes our spending and it's a snowball effect. It directly affects the economy. I could do some work on my house, but I'm not, because we don't have the income. No money spent at the store, no fabric or product being built, it's just a snowball effect.

Gus also made it clear that the instability he identified in the larger economy was leading to anxiety about his prospects for improving his economic situation. When asked how he was dealing with the instability, the struggle to cope was evident in his response:

> How am I dealing with it currently? In my downtime I'm putting more applications in, and also applying myself where I can, to create income to supplement along with my wife, and create whatever little savings we have, just keep adding to it so that we have an emergency fund. Keeping that emergency fund separate from every other household expense. I guess that's my primary way of coping with it, knowing that in the event of an emergency we have money set aside to handle something. Sheltering, you might say. Not really sheltering, hiding it from the government. I don't keep it in mason jars in my backyard, but that's more the perception, just creating a safety net, so to speak. I guess that's one way of me coping with it, it's being able to put $20 a week or whatever I can into this safety net, in the event of an emergency we have.

Gus's struggle was real, and he clearly articulated the newness of this experience. In his narrative, there was an unstated, but very present, reference to a more secure past that had produced the need to cope with the economic constraints of the present. His economic insecurity was an aberration from what he had expected: having money to do work on the house, or to spend at the store, with all of the positive snowball effects for the economy that such spending would have entailed.

Gus, however, like most White Americans encountering economic decline for the first time, had simply come to experience the labor market as Black Americans—and especially Black women—have experienced it for more than a century.[7] He was both grappling with his new reality and holding out hope that it was temporary. In a way, Gus's story reflects what a belief in the American Dream looks like for White people in his age group: the belief persists, but it feels increasingly out of reach.

Blake, a thirty-one-year-old White fitness trainer, was rigidly holding on to one of the core tenets of the American Dream—pulling yourself up by your bootstraps. Hard work, in his view, would be his salvation.

> Yeah, I'm a worker like there's nothing. I don't know, it's just that everything I do I work hard at. I work to be the best. I put a lot into it and I'm always busy. I'm always on the go. I have my hands in a lot of different pots. So if you were to ask anybody about me, like, what is—give me one trait or something to describe me most, they'd say hard worker. . . . I don't think it's up to America to do that.

In Blake's narrative, it was clear that to him hard work is essential for success. Implicit in his narrative, however, was the idea that if you work hard and stay busy, you'll be okay. For Blake, there was an unstated connection between hard work and good outcomes; as he added, "I don't think it's up to America to do that." Blake's worldview did not account for those who work hard and still struggle. The experiences of Gus and the millions of Americans like him struggling to rebound were absent in Blake's narrative of hard work.

Todd, a forty-eight-year-old White business executive, offered a more complicated perspective on the role of hard work, which he recognized as only part of the equation: "I mean, yes, do I work hard? Yes. But a lot of people work hard and don't get things, so it's just a reality of life. Sometimes, I've been fortunate to have opportunities just kind of fall into my lap."

Derrick, a forty-five-year-old Black truck driver, offered a middle ground of sorts when he described hard work as how a person meets opportunity.

> Don't let nobody fool you. You know, all they say, "I'm self-made." Yes. Somebody helped you make it. Somebody along the way, somebody helped in some small way, shape, form, or fashion, everybody gets help sometimes. Working is how you plug in. I mean, we as a people, irrespective of race, we're like, a communal people, right, we need each other to survive and thrive.

None of the things we have is accomplished by one man or one woman. It's like, people coming together and—so I think work is kind of like a social glue. You've got to be able to plug in. You just can't take from the system and not give anything back.

American individualism is classically reflected in the different weights given to hard work by Blake, Todd, and Derrick in explaining success. Americans, especially White Americans, have tended to explain success, failure, and inequality in individualistic terms, relying on conceptions of individuals as masters of their destinies.[8] Black Americans, who have always encountered structural barriers to success, have developed cultural narratives—about discrimination, for instance—that account for those barriers, as well as strategies to navigate them.[9]

Derrick's abstract critique of individualism pointed out that people are "communal" and "need each other to survive and thrive." Alexandria, a forty-eight-year-old Black clinical services assistant, took that idea even further in rejecting individualism wholeheartedly.

No, I don't do anything on my own. You know, the old proverb, it takes a village to raise a child? These folks out here help me with my kids—with my son. The woman from DCF, which is Department of Children Services— I'm a single mother, so I'm using this as an example. I have to work, so when my son takes the bus home, he knows how to come in the house. If something's not right, these people know me, and they all know us. We're family in this little community here. So we share our food when we cook out. If someone dies, we go down to the next block. If someone is out of a job and they're really going through it financially, why not share your resources or share your connects? Yeah, I have a friend that's actually the VP of HR. I'm going to give her a call and see if she can work something out. So I don't look at that—we all need help. I need you; you need me. So I'm not one of those people, you know, like, a peacock, I did it all on my own, I got here. No, I got here with the support of my family, friends, and people that believed in me, whether it was cooking a dish when I was too tired to come home because I had a paper to do, whatever the case may be, everyone has contributed, you know, that was a positive that has actually contributed to my success, and I have to, you know, pay it forward and give it back, and pull somebody else up.

Alexandria described "those people" who subscribe to the ideal of American individualism and claim to do it all on their own as being "a peacock." She explained her own success as an outcome of being deeply connected to her community, where people supported each other and enabled each other to sustain themselves when they experienced hardship, because they were all in this together. Unlike Derrick, who referred in passing to people being "communal," the "village" was literal for Alexandria: a supportive community taking care of its members was how she has survived.

Figure 2.6   **Mean Annual Earnings (2015 Dollars) among Full- and Part-time Employed Adults, by Education, 1960–2015**

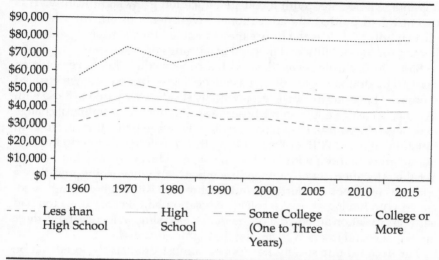

Source: Authors' analysis of data from Integrated Public Use Microdata Series, version 7.0.

The American Dream is a powerful illusion that calls on all workers, regardless of their lived reality, to aspire and work harder for a better life with the promise that, if they do, they can achieve it—and the warning that, if they don't, they are personally responsible for their failure. The Dream calls us to imagine the triumph of hard work—not harder work and fewer rewards. It makes no allowance for persistent labor market marginality due to racism, or a fall from grace due to economic shifts that eliminated workers' jobs. The Dream assumes that there is opportunity to be found and the individual must work for it. The fraying of the connection between hard work—often evidenced by education—and economic rewards weighed heavily on our participants, who were raised with assurances that the hard work of their educational investments would pay off. Many longed for predictability in the rewards for hard work, which they found increasingly hard to come by. Education had offered the promise of a sure thing when today's middle-aged were in their youth—indeed, many of our respondents held a deep, almost religious, belief in the power of education—and this unmet expectation was a source of frustration.

As all of our interviewees were well aware, college education has long provided wage advantages (see figure 2.6). Even in 1960, during the postwar period, college-degree holders' earnings were nearly double those of individuals with less than a high school education on average. In 1970, wages increased across the board, but this moment was an economic blip.

The economic recession of the early 1980s saw declining wages for all. Beginning in the 1990s and continuing into the 2000s, however, the wage advantage associated with a college education grew significantly. This promise had guided the educational investments of our middle-aged participants. This was the future they imagined for themselves, and they longed for the stability and increasing earnings of yesteryear.

Since 2000, earnings for those with a college education have not been marked by dramatic growth, but a college degree has on average enabled those who have one to remain economically steady. Compared to those with less than a college education, whose wages did not see meaningful change over several decades, they have retained the wage gains they accrued in inflation-adjusted 2015 dollars. During this transformative period of economic growth, those with less than a college education were left behind. Yet the educationally advantaged members of the vanishing middle we spoke to were not comfortable and celebrating. Although earnings associated with having at least a college education had increased, so too had earnings variation among degree holders.[10] Said simply, increasingly, there are winners and losers even among the highly educated.

For decades our society has looked almost exclusively to education to reduce inequalities while allowing robust labor market regulation, enforcement of employment rights and antidiscrimination law, and the social safety net to atrophy.[11] Education and schools as a social institution do not shape the structure of opportunity in a society. Educational attainment, a property of individuals, simply provides the tools that individuals can use in the competition for access to good jobs. Educational attainment cannot determine how many good jobs are available, or what kinds of social supports exist alongside paid employment. Although we can see the impact of educational attainment clearly in shaping earnings inequality, the policy choices that structure the labor market, producing earnings advantages and vulnerabilities, are rendered invisible by our almost singular focus on education. In the quest to understand who gets what and why, our participants could point only to their own efforts, which were coming up short. They used education as leverage to access opportunity in hopes of achieving economic security, but their worry that the American Dream would not actually deliver on its promise of hard work leading to a better future only deepened.

Summary

Our examination of economic security among the contemporary vanishing middle exposed new forms of racial and gender inequality experienced by this segment of American workers. More fine-grained measures of standard (full-time) and nonstandard employment enabled us to parse areas of similarity and difference in contemporary economic security for

Blacks and Whites and for men and women. White and Black Americans are drawing on different points of reference as they formulate their views on what economic security means and consider their prospects for security in the future. Conceptions of the American Dream are contextual. Many respondents reflected on how much harder it had been to seek and find employment at middle age compared to when they were young. This difficulty was not just in their imagination. In previous decades, an older worker, particularly a White man, with limited skills could still secure a job relatively easily, since many jobs required little more than a high school degree but still offered a solid income and benefits (like pensions and health care).

These good jobs of the past resulting from the postwar capital-labor accord, and accessible almost exclusively to White workers, were taken for granted as normal. Today, however, middle-aged Americans' expectations do not seem suited to the contemporary labor market, where employment insecurity is the product of intentional economic strategies designed to reduce the cost of labor. This is one reason why we call these Americans the "vanishing middle": they represent and reflect a rapidly disappearing past. Our participants were highly critical of these changes in the American economy as they detailed the deleterious effects on themselves and their families. Some felt hopeless about their ability to realize the labor market rewards enjoyed by workers in previous decades. Black and White Americans, however, did not have the same perceptions of the past and critiques of the present. In the next chapter, we delve further into the reasons for these different perceptions, and the implications for the future of the American Dream.

= Chapter 3 =

Privileged Expectations
and Insecure Realities

On November 7, 2020, the lines dividing two Americas seemed to dissolve in Wilmington, Delaware, when Joe Biden and Kamala Harris emerged as the victors in a contentious presidential race. That night the two Democrats broke the glass ceiling in multiple arenas: the defining moment at the ballot box marked the first time that a woman or person of color was elected to the second-highest office in the land, as well as the first time since 1984 that a non-Ivy-League-educated pair made up the Democratic ticket. This historic election demonstrated that even Americans who attended public universities could ascend to the Oval Office. The president-elect received his bachelor's degree from the University of Delaware and his law degree from Syracuse University. The vice president-elect was a graduate of Howard University, one of the historically Black colleges and universities, before receiving her law degree from the University of California's Hastings College of Law.

In race, gender, and class, Biden and Harris represent different cross-sections of America, but through education and the opportunities it enabled, both made their way to the White House. For many Americans, this feat symbolizes the prized tenet of the American Dream that hard work and the relentless pursuit of higher education can make success not only possible but inevitable. Education is supposed to equalize what are otherwise the deeply imbalanced socioeconomic circumstances into which people are born, such that Americans like Biden, the son of White working-class Americans, and Harris, the daughter of Indian and Jamaican immigrants, can have access to the same opportunity. Yet for every Horatio Alger story that buttresses the "rags-to-riches" narrative of the American Dream, there are legions of Americans who, despite following the rules, lost the game and are living a crushing economic reality.

For so many Americans, a degree has not delivered on the promise of either opportunity or security. Despite middle-aged workers' heavy investments in education as a conduit for success, and despite narrowing racial and gender differences in occupational attainment in the post-industrial period, economic gaps have widened. In the 1970s and 1980s, education was incorporated into the personal responsibility that individuals had to exhibit to lay claim to the Dream. Educational attainment demonstrated that an individual had done the work and was ready to take advantage of opportunity. The twenty-first-century labor market, however, had begun a period of profound change and disruptive inequality. Those changes were evident as early as the 1980s; by 2000, and continuing since, deepening economic inequality, shrinking occupational opportunity, and rising rates of working poverty led even the most optimistic to be less hopeful for a return to the idealized America of yesteryear, when economic prosperity was more equally distributed and the rising tide lifted all boats.

In the stories told by the middle-aged workers in our study, one notably recurring theme was the shock that they felt at the level of change: things seemed to them so different from the past, and their sense of stability had been disrupted. Some were bereft that education did not provide the protective insurance they expected. They had believed hook, line, and sinker in the American Dream, but increasingly the Dream had seemed like an ideal inconsistent with any version of their lived reality. For these middle-aged workers, economic recessions and the labor disruptions that followed had become a regular, albeit unwelcome, occurrence.

From the devastating recession of the early 1980s to the comparatively mild recession of the 1990s, followed by the Great Recession in 2008, which was marked by a very uneven and incomplete recovery, widespread economic uncertainty has become more routine than periods of economic stability. This reality is challenging for most workers, but it is particularly challenging for the middle-aged as they not only grapple with the economic and financial impact of these disruptions but also see their expectations go unmet as a result of the dramatically shifting labor markets in their lifetimes.

For Black Americans, however, even as they confront the economic disruptions of the postindustrial era, there is also continuity. Voting rights activist and politician Stacey Abrams recounts in her autobiography, *Minority Leader: How to Lead from the Outside and Make Real Change,* her parents' experiences coming of age in Mississippi, which, she says, "tried mightily to deny them of futures."

My parents had followed the rules for advancement as they understood them: they finished high school, graduated from college. My mother, one of seven, not only defied family tradition by crossing her high school stage with a diploma, she excelled in college and went on to receive a master's degree in library science. My father, the first man in his family to go to college, did so despite an undiagnosed learning disability. They secured the degrees that should have guaranteed success.[1]

But their investment did not deliver on the promise of the American Dream, she continues in a nuanced view of how her parents bought into and worked toward the Dream and yet stood outside of it.

> My parents, who had marched for civil rights as teenagers, also knew intimately that the end of Jim Crow did not mean the rise of Black prosperity. And they knew the advantages of education provided no security. They worked hard, did everything they were supposed to do—my mom as a librarian, my dad as a shipyard worker—and yet despite following the American prescription for prosperity, they sometimes barely kept their heads above water.[2]

Abrams's retelling of her parents' story—hopeful investment in education resulting in unmet expectations for economic betterment—reminds us that vulnerability despite hard work is not a new experience for Black Americans. Instead, for many, the frustration of the present moment stems from their belief that this time would be different.

This chapter explores racialized conceptualizations of meritocracy and how our participants reconciled them with their economic realities. Meritocracy is an ideology based on the belief that, regardless of an individual's social identity or current economic status, hard work and education can shift or improve the economic realities of anyone who has the desire and follows through by expending the necessary effort.[3] Self-reliance—the willingness to engage in hard work and pull yourself up by your bootstraps—is a core element of the American Dream. In the narrative of the Dream—which was historically accessible only to White people—higher education is a foolproof insurance policy that guarantees job security. Black people, however, both in the past and in the present, have also bought into this belief, even though it never provided them with that kind of foolproof insurance policy. But with increased access to better jobs and educational opportunities in the post–civil rights era, Black Americans hoped that their efforts would translate into increasing access to the American Dream. That did not happen, and many people, especially those who had invested in education hoping for a secure future, were left struggling to make sense of the rise in insecure work and to learn to live with uncertainty.

Is Education Insurance for Hard Times?

Expanding access to higher education in the United States is often promoted with a very straightforward promise: *higher education will lead to greater economic security*. It is widely known that the gap in earnings between Americans with at least a college degree and those without one grew sharply in the final quarter of the twentieth century (figure 2.6). Yet as we show in this book, the pathways that lead from postsecondary education to economic security today are less straightforward and reliable than they were before 1980. This uncertainty represents a very new experience for the economic security expectations of White Americans in particular, even though they remain more economically secure than Black Americans in absolute terms. This now familiar pattern holds even when we look at racial and gender differences in economic security within educational groups.

White men with some college education earn, on average, $65,980 per year, compared with $49,211 for Black men, $42,093 for White women, and $39,731 for Black women. These gaps cannot be fully explained by average hours of work per week (see figure 3.1). Generations of Americans have aspired to a college education in the belief that it represents middle-class status and is a gateway to economic security. Among American workers who were middle-aged in 2015, however, economic security distinctly varies according to race and gender, even among those with the same level of postsecondary education. Figure 3.2 shows that the unemployment rates for Black men (5.0 percent) and Black women (4.4 percent) with some college were more than two percentage points higher in 2015 than they were for White men (2.7 percent) and White women (2.8 percent) with similar levels of education. Further, educational attainment did not flatten the playing field for Black people in terms of unemployment: Black men with a doctoral or professional degree had higher levels of unemployment than White men and women with some college education.

Educational attainment also does not disrupt striking differences in homeownership (see figure 3.3). Among members of the vanishing middle with some college education, about 80 percent of White men and women owned a home compared with 59.2 percent of Black men and 55.6 percent of Black women. This is a sizable racial gap of over twenty percentage points in homeownership for a group (some college) that is similarly educationally disadvantaged. The same pattern of racial advantage among those with some college (but no degree) is evident in annual household income: earnings inequality and differential rates of marriage combined to produce substantial racial differences (see figure 3.4). White men's annual household incomes were, on average, about $4,000 higher than those of White women ($101,520 and $97,159, respectively), but about $18,000 higher than Black men's average household income ($83,370) and over $30,000 more than Black women's ($71,078).

Figure 3.5 shows a high degree of variability in rates of marriage across race-gender groups; Black women had the lowest rates of marriage across the board, but those rates increased with levels of education. White women, in contrast, had high and relatively uniform rates of marriage (approximately 70 percent or higher) regardless of educational status. These differences matter because we see large race-gender group gaps in earnings, income, and homeownership that are rooted in the labor market and magnified by family formation patterns.

Figure 3.1 Mean Annual Earnings (in Thousands of 2015 Dollars) and Working Hours among the Vanishing Middle, by Education, Race, and Gender, 2015

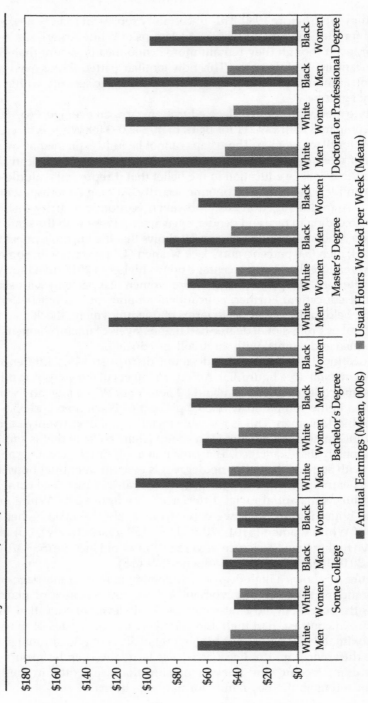

Source: Authors' analysis of data from Integrated Public Use Microdata Series, version 7.0.

Figure 3.2   Unemployment among the Vanishing Middle, by Education, Race, and Gender, 2015

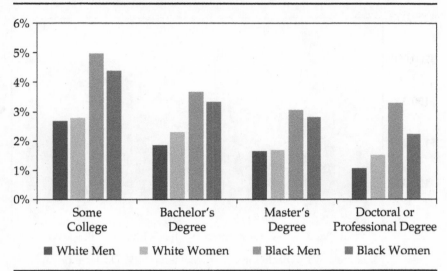

Source: Authors' analysis of data from Integrated Public Use Microdata Series, version 7.0.

Figure 3.3   Homeownership among the Vanishing Middle, by Education, Race, and Gender, 2015

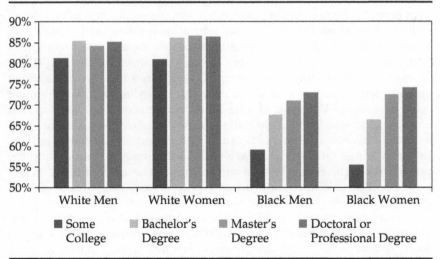

Source: Authors' analysis of data from Integrated Public Use Microdata Series, version 7.0.

Figure 3.4   Mean Household Income (2015 Dollars) among the Vanishing Middle, by Education, Race, and Gender, 2015

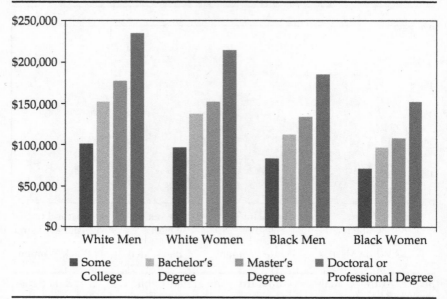

Source: Authors' analysis of data from Integrated Public Use Microdata Series, version 7.0.

White women in each educational grouping had relatively high rates of nonstandard employment (especially part-time work), and those rates of nonstandard work fell with higher educational attainment (figure 3.5). However, their high rates of marriage complicate the interpretation of nonstandard employment as a sign of economic insecurity among White women, who are more likely than Black women to use nonstandard employment as part of a family strategy for balancing paid employment with parenting.[4] Whereas, among Black women, rates of nonstandard employment, which routinely trail those of White women, is more likely to be indicative of economic insecurity in the context of their comparatively lower marriage rates—which have sharply declined over time—and the persistent discrimination against and economic insecurity of Black men.

The pattern of distinct racial advantage observed within the educational group of those with some college was also evident among American workers who were middle-aged in 2015 and had obtained a college degree. For example, while less than 2 percent of White men with a bachelor's degree were jobless in 2015, the unemployment rates among White women, Black men, and Black women were 2.3 percent, 3.7 percent, and 3.3 percent, respectively. Nonstandard employment and usual working hours

Figure 3.5   Rates of Nonstandard Employment and Marriage among the Vanishing Middle, by Education, Race, and Gender, 2015

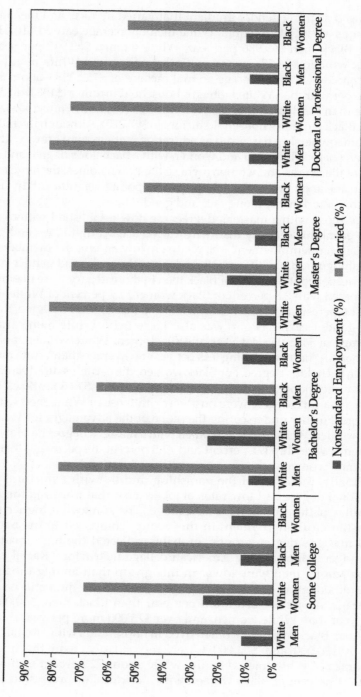

Source: Authors' analysis of data from Integrated Public Use Microdata Series, version 7.0.

followed a strong gender gradient that varied by race, and mean annual earnings are highly unequal: White men on average earned $107,372 per year; Black men $69,986 per year; White women $62,942 per year; and Black women $56,351 per year. College-educated White men lived in households with an average annual income of $152,398—about $14,000 more per year than White women's household incomes ($138,046), $40,000 more than Black men's household incomes ($112,304), and $55,000 more than Black women's household incomes ($97,270). Although the racial gap in homeownership narrowed as educational attainment grew, with about 85 percent of White men and women with a bachelor's degree and 66 percent of Black men and women owning their own homes, the large margins in income and nonstandard employment point to significant divergences in economic security along race and gender lines.

For those with a master's degree, the now-established pattern continued: economic security distinctly varied according to race and gender. Although unemployment was relatively low among the members of the vanishing middle with a master's degree, the racial and gender gradient was steep: about 3 percent of Black men in this category were unemployed, compared with 2.8 percent of Black women, 1.7 percent of White women, and 1.6 percent of White men. For those with a master's degree, the racial and gender earnings gap was also large, with White men earning an average of $125,055 per year and Black men, White women, and Black women, in contrast, earning less per year on average than White men with only a bachelor's degree. For Black women, the earnings disadvantage was even more marked: average annual earnings of $65,865 for Black women with a master's degree were on a par with those of White men with some college. Further underscoring the scope of the advantages for White men and women, Black men and women with a master's degree had lower rates of homeownership (71 percent and 72.5 percent, respectively) than White men and women with only some college education.[5]

Finally, members of the vanishing middle with a doctoral or professional degree had low rates of joblessness that mirrored the by-now familiar pattern of relative advantage. The somewhat higher rates of nonstandard employment in this group, compared to the bachelor's and master's degree groups, probably reflected the high incidence of contingent labor among American college instructors. Racial earnings gaps among men were lower in this group than among those with a master's degree, but at $173,162 per year, White men still earned on average almost $50,000 more per year than Black men, $60,000 more per year than White women, and over $75,000 more per year than Black women. Black men and women lived in households with annual incomes about $50,000 and $82,000 lower, respectively, than the household incomes of White men. Finally, while about 72 percent of Black men and 74 percent of Black women with a doctoral or professional degree owned their own home, they trailed White men and women in this educational group by more than ten percentage points. Within each educational category, White men in the vanishing middle had the highest levels of economic security and Black women the lowest levels.

Although educational attainment affords greater economic security, the fruits of higher education investment were not evenly distributed across racial and gender groups. These trends make crystal clear that race is a particularly salient axis of inequality among the vanishing middle and within educational groups.[6] Inequalities in access to employment, working hours, and annual earnings—which are magnified by, but cannot be reduced to, group differences in family structure—aggregated to produce large differences in household income and homeownership. It is quite striking that Black men and women with a doctoral or professional degree did not achieve the levels of homeownership seen among White men and women with some college education. Owning a home is integral to the American Dream: a home is the image of achievement conjured by many, and owning a home is foundational to wealth building and intergenerational wealth transfer. But the extent of these gaps across race and gender lines among college-educated Americans reinforces what many people like Stacey Abrams and her parents long ago recognized: if education is insurance for hard times, there are gaps in the protection it offers Black Americans.

Returns on Educational Investment in Black and White

During the postindustrial period that began in the 1970s, deep changes in the global economy and in the regulation of the American labor market reshaped the nature of work in the United States. In the 1980s, painful restructuring in the manufacturing sector introduced growing economic insecurity to workers—especially White men, who had previously been shielded from widespread economic uncertainty and hardship. Job growth in the service sector followed a polarized trajectory in which, at least through the early part of the twenty-first century, college-educated workers enjoyed rising security and standards of living—even if at unequal rates when viewed across race and gender—while both blue- and white-collar workers without a college education experienced stagnation or declining fortunes. As the new century unfolded, even college-educated workers experienced uneven protection from economic insecurity. These converging trends reshaped the American labor market and are the context within which we must understand contemporary racial and gender inequality as well as Americans' experiences and perceptions of economic security.

Today Americans avoid explicit references to race and instead use education as a litmus test to distinguish between the deserving—those who have done the hard work and should have access to the dream of economic security—and the undeserving—those whom society can leave behind. In the past, White blue-collar workers stressed education for their kids as a path to preserving job security and a good life, and Black workers attained high levels of education in hopes that it would enable them to lay claim to the good jobs from which they had historically been excluded.[7] Both Black and White workers were preparing themselves for a future that would break with the traditions of the past.

There has unquestionably been progress toward meritocracy in the United States. Today skills, as signaled by educational attainment, help determine access to particular jobs, whereas historically it was not skills but an individual's racial group that determined access to employment, especially access to desirable jobs.[8] However, this progress is incomplete. The racial discrimination that defined the past lingers in the present and is evident in the labor market experiences of Black and White Americans. For example Phoebe, the White city clerk we met in chapter 2, bemoaned the loss of the good jobs of the past when she suggested that a person could earn a decent salary, have a nice house, and be steadily employed for thirty to thirty-five years. But this history, however longingly recalled today by many people like Phoebe, was not a racially neutral history.

Instead, the history that Phoebe recounted was one that captured the experiences and expectations of White Americans. Phoebe was laid off after her company downsized, but she was not worried about job loss: "It never affected me financially. Because I didn't have my college degree. At the time I was making about $87,000. . . . So it never really bothered me. I never needed it. It was never required." Phoebe's seemingly cavalier attitude despite losing a high-paying job reflected her expectations. Although she did not have a college degree, she had reached a position of seniority in her national sales organization and felt fairly secure. When her company downsized after it was acquired by a global firm, she felt that she would land on her feet. "Then the bottom fell out of our market," she said. "All of a sudden it was a whole lot of us that were like, 'Holy crap, we don't have college degrees. We now can't get jobs in our own field without traveling really far.'"

Phoebe's story reflects the labor market expectations of many of our White participants without college degrees who thought that they would be able to maintain their privileged economic positions, which they had so often gained through networks and had not lost, despite labor market shifts, because of their work experience. After all, this was how the American labor market functioned routinely. Although they anticipated labor market shifts and urged their children to be prepared, they were caught off guard by the impact of the labor market shifts in the postindustrial period. Yet not all hope was lost for Phoebe and her colleagues, by her account: they could still get jobs in their field but would just have to travel further to do so. This hopefulness reflected privileged expectations despite an increasingly insecure reality.

Contrast Phoebe's labor market experiences with those of Alexandria, the Black clinical services assistant. Sharing her economic frustration, Alexandria said, "What single mother wants to work three jobs with a master's degree?" At the time of her interview, Alexandria, who described herself as "all over the place," was back in school pursuing another program that her job in health care was paying for. Why would a middle-aged Black woman who already had a college degree and an advanced degree pursue another credential? Alexandria's answer reflected her expectation of the privilege she believed her education would have afforded her by getting her to that desired "workplace" and allowing her to advance professionally, but that didn't happen: "You think after you've gone to school and you've achieved a certain level of education . . . you've been there for a while, and your experience . . . still with the education, I haven't advanced like my counterparts. My counterparts could be individuals of a different race or gender, if that makes sense."

Alexandria was very cautiously raising the idea that, despite her educational attainment and experience, her race and gender had gotten in the way. She described the push among "inner-city African American families" to get an education, but her frustration was evident when she said, "So what I see now is we're getting this education, and we're achieving this, and we still—our hands are tied." When the promise of security that education was supposed to bring goes unrealized, cynicism about change sets in, Alexandria concluded. "Yeah, get those degrees. Get those degrees, even though you're not going to advance. You're really not going to do anything with them. We're really not going to allow you to advance like you should, like your counterpart. Now, that's what I see." Alexandria's frustration was not isolated: her experiences mirrored those of Blacks nationwide who are experiencing a disconnect between their expectations of economic security resulting from higher education and their economic realities (see figure 3.1).

Alexandria and Phoebe represent two opposite ends of privileged expectations. Alexandria invested in education and had the debt to match but not the reward. Her labor market experiences in a growth industry—health care—did not match what she had expected her education to provide: a job, yes, but also the opportunity to advance within it. She was also clear in her belief that she was being held back unfairly owing to her gender and race, a sentiment common among many of our educated Black participants who were frustrated about unmet expectations. Alexandria could not imagine Phoebe's world, where job loss did not produce worry and education was not required to obtain a high-paying job. And Phoebe could not imagine the plight of educational attainment

Table 3.1   Educational Attainment of the Vanishing Middle:
Interviewees by Race and Gender

	Some College	Bachelor's Degree	Master's Degree	Doctoral or Professional Degree	Total
Black women	5 (22%)	6 (26%)	11 (48%)	1 (4%)	23
White women	7 (37%)	4 (21%)	6 (32%)	2 (10%)	19
Black men	7 (37%)	6 (32%)	5 (26%)	1 (5%)	19
White men	7 (41%)	5 (29%)	2 (12%)	3 (18%)	17
	26	21	24	7	78

Source: Authors' analysis of data from Integrated Public Use Microdata Series, version 7.0.
Note: We included in our study one Black man who had only a high school degree, so the total qualitative sample breakdown by education of seventy-eight does not match the full sample of seventy-nine participants.

in Alexandria's world, where education did not translate into sustainable economic rewards.

The uneven value of education in today's American labor market raises many questions for which there are no fixed answers: What does an education mean? Who needs to get an education? What can an individual with a college degree expect from having it? The variability in the opportunities that education appears to offer is the source of much heartache and economic anxiety across and within racial groups. The middle-aged are especially anxious and desperate to figure out for themselves and for their children: What do we need to do to secure the American Dream now?

National trends are reflected in the deep investments in education made by many of the people we interviewed, in the belief that education would be a path to economic security. The vast majority of the people we interviewed—fifty-two out of seventy-nine participants—held a college degree or more. In fact, more than one-third had a master's degree or higher (see table 3.1). The educational attainment of our interviewees far outpaced that of middle-aged Americans overall (see figure 3.6). Our interviewees were a highly educated group across race and gender, and as is true of the national trend, the women in this group had higher levels of educational attainment than the men. Fifty-two percent of Black women held a master's degree or higher, compared to 31 percent of Black men, and 42 percent of White women held a master's degree or higher, compared to 30 percent of White men. As explained earlier, we describe our interviewees as the "vanishing middle" because they reflected the demographic characteristics (education, occupation, age) that would have resulted in middle-class stability had the conditions of the postwar economic structure persisted. Instead, in the postindustrial economy, their investments had continually fallen short.

Figure 3.6   Comparing the Educational Attainment (College or More Only) of the Vanishing Middle to That of All Middle-Aged Americans, by Race and Gender, 2015

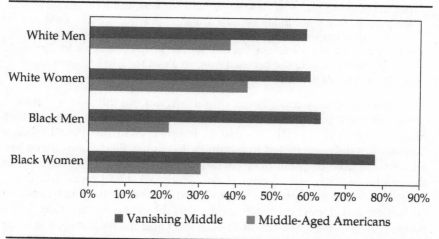

Source: Authors' analysis of data from Integrated Public Use Microdata Series, version 7.0.

Given the high educational attainment of our sample, we might expect them to have felt less anxiety and more confidence about the future. But this was not the case. Instead, their narratives illustrated the way Black and White Americans are being forced to negotiate vulnerability and uncertainty in the labor market today. Clinging to their faith in education as *the* vehicle for upward mobility, their stories revealed the divergent ways in which Blacks and Whites, men and women, are navigating this contradictory ideological constellation: education is still seen as the great equalizer and lynchpin of equal opportunity, but ultimately it does not ameliorate inequalities.

Old Scripts, New Realities

In today's job market, both Black and White educated workers increasingly find that their educational credentials do not allow them to lay claim to economic security. Additionally, Black workers are finding that, despite their educational credentials, they are still facing racial inequality in access to work. Brenda, a forty-year-old Black social worker, expressed the dissonance created when educational attainment does not lead to opportunity in her account of the emotional challenges her friend experienced when struggling to get a job.

Naturally and internally, we want to believe that we are capable, that we are able to do the things that we set out to do, and that we're just as good.

And then when you hit a wall, or you encounter a situation where you realize that you're being made to feel as though you're not as good, it can be a bit debilitating. It can make you question your abilities. It can make you question whether all that you've worked hard for was worth it. Thankfully, she's not in that place today because she's . . . practicing in her field and successful in her own right. But I believe, as a young African American female coming out of college, initially for her it was a struggle for her to get into her field. And she believed over time that the barriers were based upon the color of her skin.

In describing how educational attainment did not mitigate the impact of race in the labor market for her friend, Brenda gave an account that mirrored Alexandria's. This story had a happy ending, however: Brenda's friend ultimately succeeded in landing a job in her field that utilized her educational investment (a doctoral degree) and enabled her to overcome the mental anguish that rejection in the labor market had generated. But it is worth pausing to unpack the emotional impact of the mismatch between education and opportunity, since for many Black Americans that dissonance between their investment in education and the realities of the labor market is a defining and, for some, a recurring experience.

"Debilitating" means "causing serious impairment of strength or ability to function." This one summative word captures so much of the harm that occurs when educational attainment does not result in expected opportunities and racial obstacles are perceived as the cause, since Blacks were told that they could and *must* get an education to have a seat at the table. Shawn, the Black executive director we met in the introduction, exemplified the focus on education of many Black families. He shared that, although his paternal grandparents were illiterate, "they still talked about education as this medium that you can [use to] move up in life. It's one of the things, despite them not knowing how to truly appropriate it, they always pushed for education." Education was supposed to open doors for their children and grandchildren that had been solidly closed to them, but in reality it did not guarantee a seat at the table or the opportunity to touch the glass ceiling, much less break the concrete wall. Even for those with advanced degrees, race and gender can be persistent stumbling blocks to opportunity.

Experiencing rejection leads many to question whether it was worth it, but not Shawn. He internalized the message from his family and continued to push others to get an education, especially a college education, as a means to create options down the line. He did not believe, however, that college alone would fix everything. As Shawn said: "You go to college to explore different fields and decide whether you want to be in one. You may think you like a particular profession today, and ten years later you want to try something different, but because of that exposure it's easier to transition." Shawn's view of the role of college education was consistent with the liberal arts tradition. That view is not commonly associated with Black Americans, who have been known to take a more vocational or utilitarian approach to education, one with a clearer connection between investing in education and reaping economic rewards—that is, opening up greater occupational and employment options.

Shawn, however, was not like most Black Americans. He was college educated and earned about $200,000 a year in a senior management position. His perspective reflected his occupational and economic achievement, but also his family background and the uniqueness of his lived experience. He offered a clarifying take on the American Dream and a nuanced description of how education works to facilitate it.

> Because of the history of this nation, because of the racial structure of the nation. It's been set up so that one group were able to come here and recognize the American Dream a little bit easier than others. I'm not saying that White folks have it easy here, there is unfair treatment of poor White people also in this country, but I do think having lived in spaces where you have trailer parks . . . in the Midwest, the kids in the trailer park, they go to the same school as the kids whose parents are upper management in big companies in the area. When I lived in Brooklyn, the school that I went to was for a particular socioeconomic class, a particular race. I had no White students in my school. Diversity was kids who had parents from Trinidad or from Saint Lucia, that was our diversity. When you're in spaces like that, there is less of a chance for you to benefit from an education because you don't have parents who understand what a good education is supposed to be like . . . so they just assume you're getting a good education because you're going to school. I think, based on the two or three places I've lived in the U.S., I've noticed that is something that you have in areas that are more rural and White as opposed to more urban and Black.

For Shawn, not all education is equal, but a good education is a tool to enable Black people to navigate inequality in access to the American Dream and adjust to changing circumstances in order to have a chance to succeed. This is critical, Shawn said, "because the days of someone picking up a widget and putting it into another widget are slowly [going away]. . . . The American economy cannot afford to have individuals like that again." Making sure all Americans have a chance to succeed in the new economy is the role of education for Shawn.

He concluded his thoughts on education by taking a more traditionally Black approach: advocating for the role of tertiary or postsecondary education (any level of education pursued beyond high school, including certificates, diplomas, and academic degrees). "They need to do more of what they're doing now," he said, "making tertiary education more accessible to people so that they're not that debt laden when they come out of college." In all, despite recognizing the challenges of education, Shawn believed that it is key to accessing the American dream.

Gus, the White part-time associate in a big-box store, agreed. Despite his economic instability as he desperately tried to rebound from job loss, he talked about how important it was that his three children were going to college and "doing the right thing." The most important thing to him, he said, was "just to keep them on track." Given his struggles even with an associate's degree, we asked him, "Why is college the right thing?" He answered:

> Probably more so for the education aspect. To have yourself at a different level, rather than being uneducated and doing the same thing every day. If you have the opportunity to educate yourself and move forward, then that's what you need to do. Education itself may not be the answer. Maybe just focus on one area and move yourself ahead.

While Shawn and Gus acknowledged that the college degree itself might have limitations, they endorsed getting one because, as they both recognized, it opens the door to another world, thus enabling those who achieve it to go further, despite setbacks.

Janelle, a thirty-five-year-old Black office manager, disagreed: "I think education is a sham." She clarified this provocative statement: although she felt that "it's good to be educated for the knowledge," she was critical of the promises made about the value of education.

> At the end of the day, I feel like it's an institution that is pushed on young people with the belief that after they gain all this education, go into all this debt, that it's guaranteed that they're going to have this picket white fence, two and a half kids, a husband, you know what I'm saying, the career, and it really isn't that way. Like, a lot of times it's the opposite.

For Janelle, the gap between investment and reward was striking. It was not simply that education is no guarantee of a job in an individual's chosen field, or any job at all. She went directly after the promise of education not living up to its idealized connection to the American Dream. Without naming the Dream explicitly, she called out its tenets and said that reality does not work that way. Her view that "it's the opposite" is backed by research and comes up in the national conversation about the impact of college debt on declining marriage and birth rates, as well as on home-ownership rates among young people.[9] This challenge is even more pronounced for Black women, owing to the growing educational gap between them and Black men.[10]

More than an abstract critique of education for the young, Janelle's comments were rooted in her own labor market experience of finding that her college degree was not the golden ticket to job security. "My education has not helped me, and that's what annoys me, because they're like, oh, get an education, things will get better, and I'm like, okay, I've been going to school for ten years, hello, when is it going to get better? To me, I had a better job when I had no education, and now I have all this education and still nobody wants to hire me."

Our Black participants struggled to reconcile old scripts about the value of education as the path to opportunity with the reality of unequal access, despite investment, in the larger context of persistent Black poverty. None of our White participants said that, for them, obtaining an education had not led to opportunity.

Although many of our Black participants had advanced degrees and were high earners, they were highly critical of education as the means to mitigate or ameliorate Black poverty. This frustration was brought into sharp relief by Charles, the Black superintendent we met earlier and the holder of two master's degrees.

> When people say all poor people or Black and Brown people can get great educations and they can all go to college—let's do the mathematics behind this. If every Black and Brown person in this country went to college, there wouldn't be some seats for a lot of other people. There are not enough seats in college for everybody to go. When people raise that argument, it's false. It's baseless, and it doesn't make any sense. I'm going to stick by what I know is true. I didn't work any harder than anyone else. There was just this small window of opportunity for me as a Black man, and I was in the right place at the right time, period. I could have easily missed that opportunity and never had it.

For Charles there were only small windows of opportunity to achieve the American Dream. Although he believed that education matters, when examined purely as a numbers game, he pointed out, the claim for education as *the* path out of poverty is untenable on its face because there are not enough seats at the table for everyone.

Building on this argument, Charles pointed to the way our country and economy are organized: "If you have a society built on capitalism, that means you have winners and losers, so somebody has to lose, and it's a very small space at the top for the winners." In this critical view, the relationship between education and opportunity to achieve the American Dream can be thought of as a game of musical chairs: education is the song sung to all, but only the winners get a seat and are able to take advantage of the opportunity when the music stops. Then the losers must grapple with this fact. Again, there is no accountability in the promise of the American Dream. In our national folklore, it is up to individuals to be ready for opportunity, and education is how they will show that they are ready. Even Charles, in his cynicism, bought into this notion as he maintained that education is "key" to having access to the dream.

> It's a key. It's not the key. It's a key. It's probably the most important key, because without it you just won't have any access. Like I said, the other problems still make it even difficult with an education to kind of get access. You know racism, being the number [one] problem. But without education, you're not even on first base. You can't score, you're not even in the game.

He offered a more complex view of education than simply aspiring to go to college. Like Shawn, he brought up the idea of tertiary education as a route to achieving the American Dream:

> I'm not talking about college. I'm talking about education . . . education is number one. Everyone has some type of passion, whatever [it] is. Education is the piece that makes you the master of that passion. You can do something that you're passionate about, but mastering it is more important. . . . It's just one of the keys, but you can't even get in the game without it. And that goes for people who don't want to go to college. Get a certificate in whatever it is. If you want to be a mechanic, go get whatever you need to be that best mechanic so you can master that. To be able to be in the game you got to educate yourself.

Charles and other Black participants offered a broad view of education as essential to being in the game, but they were struggling to close the gap between investment and reward and keep pushing toward the American Dream. They had seen the cracks in the Dream and recognized that it was not working.

Brandon, a thirty-six-year-old Black design engineer, described education as "power," as an asset that can't be taken away from a person. In the same breath, however, he moved into a critique of Black lifestyle choices and of those Black Americans who "spend every penny they got just for a slim hope. If they put that money aside, you don't have to live that way." Education for him was about learning to "live within your means," and he was critical of people who didn't do that: "There's an illusion of flash and cash that we have in society now." He returned to the need for people to live within their means before circling back to college in a puzzling way. "You can live within your means. Don't overextend yourself. Think [about] the next step. You got to crawl before you can walk. A lot of people think they can start out the gate running. In my college, you know how many college people I've seen working at McDonald's? Something's wrong. Something's wrong."

Brandon was struggling in this conversation to make a connection between education and the ability to lay claim to the American Dream, contorting his argument in the process. He argued for the need to take personal responsibility—to live within one's means, to crawl before walking—in one breath, then recognized that people in college were working at McDonald's in the next. He concluded by saying that something was wrong.

This sense that something was wrong haunted Black participants, yet the only narrative they had at hand was the narrative about continuing to strive. How did they compare to White participants, like Phoebe, who were able to lay claim to the good life and historically had been able to get good jobs without an education? Are White Americans also struggling to reconcile educational investment and opportunity, since all workers today are managing unmet labor market expectations of job security, negotiating vulnerability, and living with uncertainty? The short answer is no, and in the next section we unpack why.

Is Hard Work Enough?

Scott, a fifty-four-year-old White pastor, described his father's humble beginnings. "My dad came from dirt poverty, one of six children, worked his way through night school to get a doctorate degree in banking." For Scott, his father's story served as evidence of the power of education and hard work to transform an individual's life circumstances. Scott's story is one of educational triumph across generations. He had urged his two children to follow their grandfather's example, and both were on their way to achieving advanced degrees as well. Scott's family demonstrated that the tenets of the American Dream are intact: We can go far by applying ourselves and working hard. Education is a vehicle to take us further.

But as discussed earlier, and as many of the people we interviewed have seen in their own lives, education in fact enables some people to increase their economic security, while increased economic security is blocked for others because of unequal access along racial and gender lines. Shena, a thirty-eight-year-old Black financial consultant, shared that her friend with a PhD, a Black man, was unemployed and found that a hard pill to swallow, since he felt that he had invested in the degree to become "legitimately middle class." Shena summed up his frustration as "What kind of mess is this?" Contrast the hopefulness of Scott's family with the unmet expectations of Shena's friend, whose educational investment did not have the transformative impact he had hoped for. This contrast between the different economic outcomes achieved by Black and White Americans with the same levels of education mirrors the "mess"—as Shena put it—that we are in. College degrees today do not protect Americans, Black or White, from the realities of employment insecurity; nor do degrees guarantee that they will not experience unemployment or hardship. Nevertheless, White participants rarely brought up the education-security mismatch.

Sophia, a forty-eight-year-old White account clerk with an associate's degree, insisted that she was not seeking an executive position, but acknowledged that "some people have a hard time even with a bachelor's degree. It's like you need a master's degree. But that's in the real higher-up jobs." Although Sophia thought that college was "ridiculous" and "way too expensive," she also said that everyone must "do their part," such as "trying to go to college or something and better themselves in any way, learning things, becoming more employable." After all, she concluded, "a lot of it is the individual."

Both White and Black participants drew on the language of hard work and personal responsibility to pursue the American Dream. Shena offered a similar portrait of individualism. Although her friend with a PhD was still unable to find work, she said that achieving a good life is a personal responsibility. "I feel like it's definitely something that I can own and something that I can accomplish," she said, "but I need to do some things and I need to do the work. And I also think the harder you work, the more reward you're going to see." Black and White Americans are deeply invested in maintaining meritocratic ideals despite rising insecurity and, for Blacks, persistent poverty.

Tanesha, a forty-year-old Black teacher, stressed completing an education as a path out of the projects. "Some people have made it out," she said, "but again, that's through education and determination." She continued:

> You have to be determined to make it out of those projects. I have to be determined and make it out as working class, but that's depending on my self-control with my money. [Being] self-controlled with saving and putting my money in investments, and I have to be taught. You can live in the projects and work your way up. You have to have determination. . . . It's a lot easier for me to go sit in a classroom, a diverse classroom. I can go to college. I have that free will now.

White participants shared this hopeful vision of the future in which education enables Black people to overcome the racial barriers of the past. Kelly, a forty-seven-year-old White medical assistant, believed that there are more educational opportunities now, opening more occupational pathways. "Maybe years ago, it wasn't diverse, but now I think it's diverse," she said. "We're globally integrated more. I mean, a lot of [Black people] have college educations, they're successful. I think it's open more for them. For everybody." Spencer, the White marketer we met in the introduction, backed up Kelly's point of view: "With the right education, you can make anything happen. But all along they were showing us that anything can happen when you put your mind to it, when you really want it."

Both White and Black participants drew on the language of hard work and personal responsibility to pursue the American Dream. Drawing on these traditional scripts, Black participants were more critical of routes to opportunity as unequal. They acknowledged to varying degrees the structural and economic hurdles that perpetuate inequality. Yet ultimately many subscribed to the refrain that the key to achieving the American Dream lies within the dreamers themselves. White participants often insisted on, and were heavily invested in, the frame of equality of opportunity, with education serving as the means through which opportunity is met. Yet many of our Black participants bemoaned having nothing to show for their heavy investment in getting an education.

For example, Betsy, the White nurse we met in chapter 2, believed that "everybody, regardless of what their background is, has this exact same opportunity. And especially if they put the work in." Success, for Betsy, was "just a matter of deciding to do it." Leslie, a forty-year-old White retail clerk, offered the most vigorous defense of equal opportunity and the American Dream:

> I think that people hold themselves back. You know, you have Black people who talk about slavery and they're not treated well, but yet they live in America and I think they have the same opportunity. They might not have it in their community, but if somebody really wants something, they'll go after it. You know? . . . I have a hard time with people saying that Blacks are treated poorly and Whites are treated better, the whole White privilege thing. I don't understand that, because I think we all have the same. We might be on a different footing, like the Black people and the Black communities might be poorer than I am, but it's America, and we still all can be somebody and do something with ourselves because America allows that to happen.

This is a fascinating account because, while Leslie could acknowledge and point to differences in the economic circumstances of Black and White communities, she insisted that the United States is a country that allows anyone to overcome hardship and find success. Black people who didn't succeed were playing "the race card," in her opinion, and weren't willing to take advantage of opportunities.

Kelly, the White medical assistant, echoed this sentiment: "Both of them [Black and Whites] are human. . . . It's just whoever wants to work and go get it. Who wants to run for it and go get it." All of these perspectives on opportunities to succeed rested on an assumption that people have the same access, and so it is a willingness to work hard that sets individuals apart. Leslie, Kelly, and Betsy were not alone; many of our White participants chalked up racial differences in labor market success to hard work. They did not "see" differences in opportunity. From this point of view, the American Dream provides the opportunity, and it is individuals' responsibility to work hard to achieve it. In Leslie's formulation, because America allows success to happen, failure is a personal responsibility.

But not all of our White participants took this view. Valerie, a thirty-five-year-old preschool teacher, started to make a very similar argument when she said that anyone "who works hard enough to get where they want to be, deserves to be there." Yet she grappled with the issue of inequality in access to education as the interview went on:

> I feel like, if I was an African American woman with a master's, I feel like I'd still be able to get a good job. . . . I might be in a bubble thinking that, I don't know, but I think there's less of an opportunity for me to have my master's if I was African American. . . . But I think if I had my master's and I was able to get my education, I feel like then I would still be able to get a good job, but the likelihood of me getting my master's, I feel like would be lower than as a White woman.

Valerie's racially neutral perspective that hard work alone is enough to achieve success did not hold up to her own assessment of access to education. She believed that a Black woman with an education could get a good job, but that belief did not match the experiences of our Black participants. Her perspective, however, represented some degree of progress from the simplistic frame that everyone has opportunity and those who fail simply did not work hard to achieve it.

White participants pointed to the gap between the educational levels of Black and White Americans, particularly in advanced degrees, as an explanation for labor market inequality. To them, the gap was evidence of equality: Black people could succeed if they did the hard work of advancing their educational levels. Callie, a fifty-year-old White social worker, reflecting on jobs in her employment sector, remarked, "There aren't as many Black applicants applying for the same jobs that I'm applying for because they don't have a master's degree, you know, that's the reality of the circumstances." Callie recognized the competitive edge that her degree offered her, and she was not the only one. Steve, the White school counselor we met in chapter 2, went back to school in his thirties to complete his undergraduate degree and do graduate work. Furthering his education was incredibly important to him, he explained, because higher educational credentials were required for him to be successful.

> I think that there's different levels of material success that's cast upon each ethnic group. Like, for a White man to be considered successful, I do believe that that's a different standard. This is one of the negative things about our society, even though they claim equality to be available. . . . What's equal—and if you considered stature financially—is totally reversed, right? You wouldn't expect just in terms of having an education, many people that

I know, Whites would say, look, he's Hispanic with a degree, he's Black with a degree, they've made it, and they would cast different levels of—or measurements to success based on race.

Following Steve's line of thinking, he had to go back to school and earn his degrees to be successful as a White man because he would be held to a different and implied higher standard than a Black or Hispanic man. Missing from such a narrative, however, is the reality of struggle and educational mismatch that was so clearly communicated in the narratives of our Black participants across educational levels. Instead, White women offered several accounts of not working that hard and being okay.

Callie said, "I aspired to mediocrity. . . . I had a good life, and I didn't necessarily want a better one than the one I had. I lack the kind of ambition necessary." Across the seventy-nine people we spoke with for this book, the educational level of the Black women exceeded that of White women, but the White women were almost universally more economically comfortable and secure. Many White women were married and contributed to their household income, but often their husband was the dominant earner. For Black women, the opposite was true; many were single, and when partnered, their incomes sometimes exceeded or matched those of their partners. One explanation for the markedly different narratives of Black and White women on the role of education is that the language and logics of economic security for Black and White women are shaped by marital status in ways that seem to limit White women's ability to reflect on the role of educational investment, ambition, and hard work. Their experiences reflect marital partnerships that have reduced their economic vulnerability.

Not all White women, however, held a simplistic view of hard work being essential for Black success. Susan, a thirty-nine-year-old White clinical psychologist, spoke to her privilege specifically when she said, "We weren't wealthy, but we never struggled." She was crystal clear on two counts: she had to work hard to earn her professional position, and a lot was provided that enabled her to do so. "Both are true," she said, but the willingness she showed to hold the tension between hard work and structural limitation was not common. Susan spoke to this tension directly:

I get really mad at my cousin. He's a libertarian, and he believes that if people aren't successful, it's exclusively because they didn't work hard enough. I get mad at that mentality because some people work really hard but they're in a disadvantaged situation. That no matter how hard they work, they can't just overcome that. I was lucky enough to not be in that kind of situation, so therefore the hard work that I did could get me to where I am. I guess that's sort of the way I see it. I feel like I worked hard and earned what I have, but I had some privilege and advantage to be able to do that from the get-go.

Even Steve, the White school counselor who bemoaned differences in the levels of success expected of different racial groups, could clearly articulate structural gaps in opportunity:

> The differences between opportunities between particularly White males and Black males has changed, so that there are structures in place that make it sometimes impossible for Black males to stay in school, go to school, work within the dominant paradigm of you have to get your degree to get the good job, have the family and the house, and you have to hand this legacy down to your children. It's disproportionally more difficult for Black males than it is for White males in this country.

Both our Black and White participants recognized that zip codes determine the quality of educational experiences and that creating equality of opportunity requires investing in education well before students arrive at the college doors. Jenee, a thirty-eight-year-old Black part-time professor, pointed to the "socioeconomic class that you're born into," stressing that it "makes a big difference from the start." But most of our participants rarely spoke of the structural factors that create inequality from birth and make it hard for some to move up. And when participants did acknowledge that structural factors can enable or limit individual effort, the structure they pointed to was still education. Our participants relied heavily on education as *the key*.

Despite the struggles our participants had experienced and observed, they, like most Americans, held on to meritocracy as a frame and implored everyone to work hard, as if that was enough. But as discussed in the next chapter, American meritocracy is an ideology, not a reality. Belief in it preserves the American Dream and ensures that individuals will internalize failure and struggle as the lack of opportunity draws boundaries between themselves and others, but also that they will stop short of questioning the system and the unfairness of it all. Belief in the American Dream— holding on to meritocracy and continual investment in education to secure a better future—is how Americans, both Black and White, exert some control over the opportunities in their lives and attempt to understand their struggles within an unequal labor market.

Summary

Despite staggering inequality across race-gender groups, due in part to family structure, the differences observed in household income cannot be explained solely by differential marriage rates. Black and White Americans receive different returns on their investments in education. With the onset of the Covid-19 pandemic, the value of higher education once again was highlighted. While unemployment rates skyrocketed in

2020, the rates remained less than 10 percent for college graduates over twenty-five years old—in sharp contrast to rates for those who held only a high school diploma.[11] If the economic recovery is going to look anything like it did in 2016, then Americans with a college degree will fare much better in the labor market than those without one. In 2016, graduate, bachelor's, and associate's degree holders gained over three million jobs, compared to less than 100,000 gained by those without a degree.[12] When our participants spoke about the need for the "piece of paper," this is what they meant. Yet getting that piece of paper is not enough; as competition for good jobs increases, having a network that can be leveraged to get access to opportunity is essential. In the next chapter, we explore how this key difference drove inequality between our Black and White participants.

=== Chapter 4 ===

The Myth of Equal Opportunity

Most middle-aged American workers in 2015 did not have a higher education credential. Historically, a college degree was not a precondition of employment, as there were enough desirable jobs available in the American economy without this credential. Hence, those who did have a degree saw themselves as a cut above the rest. Among the Black and White middle-aged workers we spoke to for this book, all of whom had at least some college and many of whom had more than one degree, most were steadfast in their belief in the importance of education, even if obtaining a college degree had not exempted them from struggles and experiences of inequity in economic security. Most of their generation lacked a college degree, and so they saw education as a means to set themselves apart, to show that they had done the hard work and were ready to meet opportunity. Both our Black and White participants agreed on this score—the bedrock belief in the American Dream was intact. As discussed in the previous chapters, however, achieving the Dream has always depended on access to desirable opportunity, and in America such access has historically been profoundly unequal by race.

The stubborn obstacle of inequitable access to opportunity is the reality of the American labor market that hinders Black economic security. Alongside enduring inequality is the absence of solidarity. Black and White workers continue to see their access to opportunities through the lens of their racial group. The rise of insecure work has not led Black and White Americans to reimagine the distinctions between racial groups and their respective access to jobs. Instead, workers continue to draw on conceptions of race—their own race and that of others—to make sense of who deserves opportunity and a chance at security. The greatest fear of workers, even high-income earners, is unemployment and instability, so they are constantly attuned in their day-to-day interactions to potential contacts as future resources in getting a job.[1] As many as 70 percent of jobs are not posted publicly online, and upward of 80 percent of jobs are filled through networking.[2] As we highlight in this chapter, these organizational practices play a key role in today's labor market in enabling race to structure access to occupational opportunity. In the face of the racial structuring of opportunity, both Black and White workers have developed specific ways of narrating vulnerability and insecurity, at times providing contorted explanations for the impact of race on access to occupational opportunity. We discuss affirmative action as an important remedy, particularly when, as this chapter explains, White workers continue to use racial group membership to manage and compensate for their own increasing vulnerability in the postindustrial economy, a strategy that not only is unavailable to Black workers but restricts their opportunities by race.

Organizational Practices and the Maintenance of Unequal Opportunity

An extensive body of research points to the tendency of management to hire people who are "of their own kind" rather than people who are "different"—a practice known as "homosocial reproduction."[3] Within corporations, there is tremendous pressure to act and make decisions in ways that conform to the status quo; if left uninterrupted, this pressure shapes the demographic composition of organizations, limiting the opportunity of those who are dissimilar. The sociologists James Elliot and Ryan Smith found in their 2004 study that "most groups attain [workplace] power through homosocial reproduction, but what differs is the opportunity to engage in such reproduction." While White men excelled, women and minorities did not.[4]

This has everything to do with racial and gender differences in management and authority. Two other sociologists, Kevin Stainback and Donald Tomaskovic-Devey, found that the racial composition of employees constrains who the manager will be, but that this impact does not limit the occupational opportunities of White men.[5] Their 2009 study of long-term trends in managerial representation found that White men managed men and women of all races, White women managed women of all races, and Black men managed Black men and women, but the only constituency Black women managed was themselves. In *Opportunity Denied: Limiting Black Women to Devalued Work*, Branch argues that "hierarchical relationships of power based on race and gender map directly onto formal authority structures within organizations," with implications for who is likely or unlikely to enter management and who is likely or unlikely to be hired.[6]

This pattern of race limiting opportunity has been observed not only in managerial positions but also in job screening for entry-level positions. Consider the field experiment conducted by Marianne Bertrand and Sendhil Mullainathan: to test for labor market discrimination, they sent résumés with either Black- or White-sounding names in response to advertised jobs in Chicago and Boston. They found a 50 percent gap between the callback rates for Black and White names, and White-sounding names needed to send approximately ten résumés to receive a callback, compared to the fifteen résumés required for Black-sounding names.[7] Similarly, the sociologist Devah Pager conducted an audit study and found that White résumés with criminal records were more employable than Black non-offenders.[8] These studies and many others that focus on the actions of employers to document the extent of employment discrimination at early stages in the hiring process have gained widespread attention, even in the popular media.

Given the increasing recognition of racial discrimination in the labor market at the level of job screening, more and more young job seekers are taking steps to mitigate against the impact of race in the hiring process. A recent 2016 study by Sonia Kang, Katherine DeCelles, András Tilcsika, and Sora Jun examined racial minority (Black and Asian) university students' use of résumé whitening—concealing or downplaying racial cues in their job applications—to avoid anticipated discrimination in labor markets.[9] From altering their names to modifying the description of their extra-professional activities (such as volunteer work), 31 percent of Black interviewees and 40 percent of Asian interviewees, they found, had engaged in résumé whitening. Even among those who rejected the practice, awareness of it as a strategy was common; "two-thirds of all interviewees reported knowing others (typically friends or family members) who whitened their job application materials." The universal motivation for whitening was to mitigate against discrimination and "pass as white at the résumé-screening stage of the process."[10] A Black law student explained:

> If I have an African name, or if I'm, like, president of the African American Society or something, if that's on my résumé, they automatically know my ethnicity. And because of that, if I have the same credentials as someone of another race, let's say a white person, then they would get a callback over me. So if from the beginning they don't know my race . . . then I'm more likely to get a callback.[11]

To generalize beyond their interview findings, Kang and her colleagues conducted a randomized résumé audit study akin to those carried out by Bertrand and Mullainathan and by Pager, but measuring the degree of whitening in the résumés: no whitening, whitened first name, whitened experience, or whitened first name and whitened experience. Their findings were consistent with their interviews: "whitened résumés led to more callbacks than unwhitened résumés."[12] Only 10 percent of Black unwhitened résumés (ones that included, for example, "Lamar J. Smith," "Aspiring African American Business Leaders," and "Black Students' Association") received callbacks, compared to 25 percent of Black résumés with whitened first names and whitened experiences (ones that included, for example, "L. James Smith," "Aspiring Business Leaders," and "University

Student Association"). This Black callback gap, a ratio of 2.5 to 1, was much larger than the Asian callback gap of 1.8 to 1.

As these examples show, from screening for entry-level jobs to selection for managerial positions, Black workers face an uphill battle in the American labor market. Most White workers we spoke with, however, were hesitant to acknowledge the racial hurdles that perpetuate economic inequality; instead, they relied on individualistic narratives as shaping success and failure. This belief underpins White Americans' enduring faith in the American Dream, including their pessimism about it in the current era of economic insecurity. Their cries of reverse discrimination allege that the road to opportunity is smoothly paved for Black Americans, creating a shortage of good opportunities for White Americans. Yet the organizational practices experienced by Black job seekers as limiting their opportunities have been critical to sustaining opportunities for White job seekers in ways that enable them to maintain their belief in individual agency while benefiting from organizational patterns of racial exclusion. By contrast, Black job seekers, aware of discriminatory hiring practices, maintain optimism in the face of these restrictions by strategizing on how best to manage them. These contradictory orientations to the labor market induce very different expectations among Black and White Americans as they grapple with inequality of opportunity and its impact on their economic prospects.

In the next section, we discuss our participants' experiences of job seeking while Black and show the impact of their experiences in the job market on their perceptions of access or exclusion from opportunity.

Black-Out: Racial Guessing, Job Screening, and the Creation of Unequal Opportunity

The multitude of experiences that our participants had while seeking jobs and navigating the labor market reveal significant differences in the way Black and White Americans are treated in the labor market. More importantly, their experiences reveal a large divergence between racial groups in awareness of this differential treatment as a factor shaping occupational opportunity. Take Jim, a fifty-year-old White mail carrier, who explained that race should have no impact on occupational opportunity. "It's an individual thing. It's all up to you," he said. Jim, who described his upbringing as very diverse, believed that education makes the path to success color-blind: "Because it's not the color of your skin, it's what's in your head, how you go about learning and doing things. There's many, many White people that are millionaires; many, many Black people that are millionaires. Either way, you can get there. You could be any nationality. It doesn't matter. That's how I feel."

Jim justified this assertion that "what's in your head" matters more than the color of a person's skin by pointing to the fact that "many, many black people are millionaires." Yet, as he continued to discuss the relationship between race, education, and occupational opportunity, he observed, "There could be ten White people that all went to Yale, okay? There could be one Black guy that didn't go to Yale, but that one Black guy knew somebody who owned a business, and he got a job over the ten graduates from Yale." Set aside for a moment the fact that Ivy League schools such as Yale boast well-connected and high-profile alumni who are more likely to own the businesses and create the opportunities that Jim posited in his fictional example that aimed to illustrate Black labor market advantage. Focus instead on the shift in Jim's frame from "what's in your head" to who is in your network as a strategy to affirm his belief that opportunity is color-blind.

Now contrast Jim's point of view with the more circumspect view on the relationship between race, education, and occupational opportunity offered by Tony, a forty-eight-year-old Black bus driver and paraprofessional educator: "If you come from a certain public school or district, you're not going to have the same chance as the kid who did the same exact work as you that came out of the private school with a good network behind him. I'm sorry—that's your fate in life." Like Jim, Tony pointed explicitly to networks as the means through which educational achievement is converted into occupational opportunity. He did not, however, convey his fatalistic critique in racial terms; instead, he pointed to public versus private schools and the "good network behind him" as the vector for success. "The kid who did the exact same work," in Tony's view, doesn't have a chance. Both Jim and Tony were reflecting on how access to occupational opportunity is shaped by the networks a person has access too. Jim relied on education, Tony pointed to class, and both squarely downplayed race as shaping occupational opportunity.

Yet, as the literature reviewed here makes clear, race has everything to do with occupational opportunity in the United States, as was very clear to some of our participants. Henry, the technical writer we met in chapter 2, spoke of the "good ole days" when getting a job meant being able to graduate from high school one day and, if you didn't go to college, walk into the factory where your dad worked and have a job the next day. Although he criticized the capitalist structure of American society and openly admitted to giving "rich people a hard time," he was resigned to the reality that the wealthy are just following the model that they have been given. He said, "If the idea is that this country is built on a capitalist society, a capitalist model for economics, and the idea is to make as much money as possible, that's really the idea." When discussing the hiring process, Henry's views on race took the notion of capitalism a bit further. He insisted, "I honestly think that with all other things being equal, they will hire the person they most relate to, that looks like their uncle Joe or their nephew Jim, because they trust them. Why wouldn't they trust them? They trust what they see in the mirror."

Desmond, a thirty-three-year-old Black security guard, put it another, perhaps more devastating way: "Black is looked at as kind of negative. So just when you see someone of Caucasian descent, you just feel like you got somebody pure, reliable, a good worker. I just feel like you are already selling it once you said White." Henry perceived racial preferences as being about comfort and trust, whereas Desmond saw race as being used to construct entire character profiles and determine eligibility for job positions. Casting personal characteristics and educational achievement aside, Desmond's and Henry's intuition about how race functions in the labor market is backed, unfortunately, by extensive research. They were attesting to an empirical reality.

Despite acknowledging the systemic racial preferences that determine hiring trends, Henry, like most Black participants we heard from in the previous chapter, found relief in the role of meritocracy and his ability to distance himself from unambiguous Blackness in the screening stage of the hiring process. He confessed:

> You never know what goes on after you have an interview, or after people see you. But I'm a meticulous speller, for instance. You're not going to see my résumé and see a bunch of mistakes on it. . . . So the only thing you're going to be able to gather from my résumé is there's a person here of reasonable intelligence who doesn't make mistakes on their résumé, so now I know I can trust them to fill out stuff in my job or whatever. That's all you're going to get from me. Now, if you talk to me and you see [I'm Black], I can't tell you what happens after that. I know I present well, so I guess if you're asking me if I think I ever didn't get a job because I was Black, I just don't have any knowledge of that. I don't have any knowledge of that. Like, I would have to be able to reflect back on a time when someone was obviously hostile to me. I can't reflect back on that. I can't say that. It's just been my personal experience. But again, for instance, my name—my name, in particular, carries no ethnic feel to it. So you can't look at a résumé and know who I am by my name. Someone might pick out a Tyrone or a Laquisha or a this or that. I think there's too many factors that go into that for me to determine if I've been excluded from a job because of it. I've never felt that way.

Henry's response demonstrates how some Black participants strive to evade economic vulnerability by being not only good enough but twice as good. He segued quickly and easily from describing racial preferences in the job market and White supervisors' (implicit) desire to hire someone who looks like them to, in the next breath, relishing his linguistic talents as key to responding to these preferences. More striking still was his take on the value of not having an ethnic-sounding name. Name discrimination, as we have discussed, is a well-documented form of discrimination in the workplace.

Yet Henry was still unwilling to fully place blame on racial preferences in hiring. After candidly making these statements, he clarified: "Now, see, I'm not willing to go so far as to say that everyone in these positions [is] racist or prejudiced. The reason I can't do that is because there's too many Black people working. The evidence doesn't bear that out." Despite Henry's open acknowledgment of racial preferences and the strategies he deployed to get around them in the screening process, he still had faith in meritocracy—the belief that an impeccably organized résumé and a college degree will get a Black job candidate a seat at the table.

Getting in the Door: Race before the Hire and on the Job

Not all of our Black participants were as willing as Henry to diminish the role that race plays in gaining access to opportunity. Instead, many of the Black workers we spoke with recognized clear racial discrimination in the labor market and told us that racial ambiguity in their names had served them well in that market. For example, Alexandria, the Black clinical services assistant we met in chapter 3, described getting callbacks because of her White-sounding name. "When they called me on the phone, surely, I didn't sound like an Alexandria," she said. "I get that a lot of times." She told us how the conversation sometimes went when an employer called and said, "Can I speak to Alexandria?" She would reply:

"This is Alexandria." "You don't sound like Alexandria." Well, what am I supposed to sound like? Am I not supposed to articulate my words or speak proper, you know, English? So, there's a lot of that going on. So, I said that to say maybe the perception of who they thought I was, I wasn't really that person.

Adève, a thirty-seven-year-old Black financial analyst, had similar job-seeking experiences while Black:

I'm always viewed as Caucasian on paper, because if you look at my résumé, it has Accenture on it, it has JP Morgan on it, and my name is French, they don't know I'm from Ghana. They don't know where I'm from until maybe I open my mouth a little bit. There's a slight lead of accent, but you can't tell where I'm from, right? On paper, it's—I want this girl. I just interviewed today on the phone for a hedge fund. On paper, they don't know who I am until they see me in person, which has happened before at a small law firm, and they're like, they love me, but then it's kind of like, but you're a person of color. So it's not—it has gotten better, but it's still there.

Both Alexandria and Adève saw racial ambiguity as a characteristic that served them in their efforts to find a job. For Alexandria, who had a master's degree in health-care administrative services, racial ambiguity created uncertainty that resulted in more callbacks but also exposed her more often to what she perceived as systemic racial bias against Black candidates. In recounting the following experience, she saw racial bias arising from perceptions of a person's racial identity not just from their name but also from their address. (In cities where racial segregation is pronounced, an applicant's address will give employers some degree of confidence in whom they are calling back.)

> I was surprised that after almost twenty years of applying to the university health system, I got a call that they wanted to have me come in. So I'm thinking, they looked at my name, Alexandria Nash—surely it doesn't sound like a Black woman's name—master's degree, Clive Street, solidly middle-class area, surely she's of a different persuasion. So I was called in. Of course, I interviewed well, because I had friends that were on the inside that I knew, I'm very confident, and I've been in the professional world a lot, so I know how to interview well, so I wasn't concerned about that. But it was interesting—even when I had an inside connection on what to say verbatim, pretty much, I still didn't get the job.

Alexandria's supposition about the reason she did not get the job would have been familiar to many of our other Black participants who talked about how they were perceived and how those perceptions could hold them back.

> Because once they realized who I was—there's a level of intimidation, because we've been looked at as these aggressive people, so now we've been aggressive in the physical aspect, so now they may still think that that aggressiveness can spill over into the professional world. She has her master's degree, oh, I only have my bachelor's degree. She's going to come in here and try—you know, they're headstrong, she's going to come in here and try to take over things. So, you know, and that might be just a little off, but I think that there's a level of intimidation.

For Alexandria, racial discrimination did not end at the screening process—it also impacted hiring decisions. Even when she got a job—the proverbial seat at the table—she learned that her chair was lower than others'. Alexandria spoke at length, and with great frustration, about her White colleagues without a college degree who took home near-six-figure salaries, or the equivalent of a whopping $40,000 difference from her own salary. Even in a booming field like health care, an advanced degree, related credentials, and experience did not translate into security or opportunities for advancement. The costs were both financial and emotional, in that she questioned whether asserting herself in the workplace and utilizing her expertise would result in being misjudged as aggressive.

Adève, who had a bachelor's degree and worked in financial services, also described the emotional toll of seeking a job while Black. For her, the consequence of making it past the racialized screening process and into the job was persistent isolation, which, in her view, had deep racial roots in ideas about who can do what kind of work. She explained:

> The playing field is still not leveled. We're nowhere near there. At Accenture, when I was there . . . I was only one in my group. When I got to Lockheed, I was the only one in my group. When I was in college, I've been the only person in the class. So, financial services, you may not see too many people like me in the hedge fund. And I interviewed for an asset management firm today on the phone. I'll probably be the only one in the office. Police officers, social services, you tend to see more of us, so economically, they, you know, the playing field is kind of level in that way, but then the problem is depending on what you're doing being a social worker, the money is not as much, do you understand? But given the fact that I've worked in the Accentures of the world, the JP Morgans of the world, and some of the financial companies I'm seeing a lack of equality there, but an overflow of us in these other sectors, which is good, because I think there should be more social services programs, but it needs to be all mixed up and jumbled together, it needs to be even. You know, I should want to be a social worker because I want to be a social worker, because I'm passionate about it. And if I want to work at a hedge fund, there should be more of me in a hedge fund as well. It should be all mixed up, and it's not all mixed up. We are here because sometimes that's the job that we can get. It's the social services, it's the police officers, it's the armies, the navy, it's the service to the country or to our people or government. Those are our opportunities. There are certain job opportunities that are available to us, and then there are certain [ones] that are not available to us. Not available.

As Adève shared her striking and complicated experiences in responding to racial preferences in the workplace, we learned that there are two options for Black people like her: the one seat at the table or none at all. The pressures on Black Americans to meet the requirements for that exclusive seat require them to come across as an applicant as close to the unstated but widely known preference as possible. The more an applicant presents like a White man, the higher the chances for a callback. The takeaway from both randomized audit studies of corporate practices and the personal stories of people like our interviewees is consistent: racial preferences limit job prospects for Black people. In America, equal opportunity is an abstract ideal, not a reality.

Despite this employment reality, among the dozens of people we spoke with, our White interviewees rarely recognized inequity in the labor market and its impact on the opportunities available to Black Americans. In one interview question we asked directly, "Do you think that being White is an advantage or disadvantage when it comes to finding a good job?" Black participants overwhelmingly noted the racial inequity in the job market, but with varying caveats that affirmed meritocracy. Henry, for example, said that he had never perceived any racial issues when searching for a job, whereas Alexandria said that race often kept Black applicants from making it past the first round. By contrast, only a few White participants were willing to acknowledge racial bias. One of them was Jared, a thirty-six-year-old White nonprofit administrator, who said that being White was "a definite advantage." He explained:

> People are more likely to think that you're competent and capable and to believe you when you say stuff, which helps. I just think statistically, you're more likely to be employed, so something is going on there certainly. . . . It seems like there is a better chance of getting a job if you're White. People have the really weird perception that the Black mayor only hires Black people and I'm never going to get a job and it's harder now if you're a White man than anybody to make it around—I'm like no, I can't. There are efforts for people to, like, diversify for whatever reason, but I still don't think that results in you having disadvantage as a White person.

Jared offered a transparent assessment of the imperceptible ways in which race privileges White applicants in the labor market that have nothing to do with credentials or experience. Whiteness, in Jared's summary, results in positive determinations about applicants, the implication being that non-Whiteness results in negative assessments of Black applicants as incompetent, incapable, and untrustworthy. Toward the end of his answer, he nodded toward the White anxiety created by the increasing focus on racial diversity in employment but dismissed it out of hand, concluding: "I still don't think that results in you having disadvantage as a White person"—an assessment supported by a large body of sociological and economic research.[13]

Jared's forthrightness was uncommon. White participants were more likely to deflect in their answers and express resentment as well as feelings of being shut out from employment opportunities by affirmative action policies. Lacy, a forty-six-year-old White early childhood educator, argued that attempts to boost employment equality tend to overlook the quality of candidates:

> I think that with affirmative action, you have to meet your quota, I guess. I mean, I don't know, I've never been in human resources, I don't know how it works. But in my mind, you have to have a certain number of African Americans and/or minorities working for you, and it doesn't matter if this person is more qualified, we need to fill the spot. And so, they're going

there. This sounds very crass, and I'm not, I don't mean it this way, but this is the best way to describe it, so they're going to fill those two slots with minorities, but then the rest of them, they can fill it with the best qualified. And one concern with that is if you put people that are not qualified in a job, how does that affect the morale of the rest of the workplace? At my school in North Carolina, it was a predominantly White school, and we got an assistant principal who was African American, and unfortunately, she wasn't very good. And so immediately people are talking about it being affirmative action. Obviously, she's [an] affirmative action hire.

Lacy was uncomfortable with the notion of affirmative action because it is not "merit based." Lacy believed that the integrity and quality of the workplace are diminished in the quest to get certain "slots filled." Although Black participants drew on meritocracy—the promise that hard work and education would overcome racial bias—many of the White participants asserted that meritocracy is now trumped by racial preference. The "best candidate" should get the job, they argued, and a Black candidate gets the job only because of racial preferences and "quotas," not because they are the best candidate.

Phoebe, the White city clerk we met in chapter 3, expressed similar views: "I had a supervisor at one point who was Black who wouldn't have had her job except that she was Black because she had basically told them flat out, 'If you fire me, I'm going to sue you, because I'm a Black woman,' which was really weird because we all loved her." Phoebe's interpretation of the Black supervisor's threat to sue as evidence that she had her job only because she was Black provides a fascinating glimpse of the role of race as an obstacle to solidarity or even mutual understanding in the workplace. Even though Phoebe suggested that everyone "loved" the supervisor, she still took the supervisor's assertion—that firing her would be discriminatory— as a confession confirming her belief that the supervisor had her job owing to affirmative action. This reaction illustrates what Jared observed earlier: that competence, capability, and trustworthiness are associated with White workers, while any evidence of Black workers being challenged on the job is attributed to race. Furthermore, as Jared's point also implied, Black people are seen as lacking the positive characteristics associated with Whiteness—thus, any attempts by Black workers to push back against discriminatory corporate practices is evidence of their undeservingness.

Affirmative Action and the Limits of White Guilt

All of our participants, regardless of race or gender, agreed on the importance of meritocracy in principle. This belief in the value of meritocracy has long been a core element of the American Dream, and even as Black people acknowledge the historical obstacles associated with the Dream for themselves, their shared belief in the connection between "hard work" and "opportunity" has helped maintain the importance of the myth of meritocracy to getting ahead in the United States. Both White and Black Americans vehemently assert that the matching of individuals to occupational opportunity in the labor market should be "fair" and based on their ability. The problem is that *the United States has never been a meritocracy*. The implicit association between "fairness" and meritocracy made by both Black and White workers overlooks several important facts of American history. For generations, Black Americans were systematically excluded from opportunities in the labor market. Despite the civil rights movement and the resulting landmark legislation requiring affirmative action and equal opportunity for all gender and racial groups, the legally sanctioned discrimination of the past clearly continues to have a lasting impact in the American labor market.

Today affirmative action is commonly invoked to account for and assail Black people in the workplace as undeserving or to challenge requirements that minority groups be represented. This development in White people's perception of affirmative action has nourished a belief that the American Dream is being closed to them. From this perspective, they see their economic insecurity as due not only to an increasingly insecure economy but also to Black people being hired for positions that they think they would have been hired for instead in a true meritocracy.

Affirmative action in the United States began when President Lyndon B. Johnson issued Executive Order 11246 on September 24, 1965. This policy built on the Civil Rights Act of 1964 and the Voting Rights Act of 1965, which combated racial discrimination and outlawed discriminatory voting practices, respectively, by establishing a requirement that federal contractors establish nondiscriminatory practices in hiring and employment. Most important, federal contractors were required to take affirmative action to ensure equal opportunity for employment. Section 202 outlines these requirements:

> The contractor will not discriminate against any employee or applicant for employment because of race, color, religion, sex, or national origin. The contractor will take affirmative action to ensure that applicants are employed, and that employees are treated during employment, without regard to their race, color, religion, sex, or national origin. Such action shall include, but not be limited to the following: employment, upgrading, demotion, or transfer; recruitment or recruitment advertising; layoff or termination; rates of pay or other forms of compensation; and selection for training, including apprenticeship.[14]

Affirmative action policy, and in particular enforcement, applied only to federal contractors. There was no coercive pressure for noncontractor establishments.

Initially, as the economist Jonathan S. Leonard has documented, the U.S. Commission on Civil Rights, the U.S. General Accounting Office, and the House and Senate Committees on Labor and Public Welfare shared a relatively widespread sentiment that affirmative action was "ineffective" owing to "weak enforcement and a reluctance to apply sanctions."[15] In the mid to late 1970s, however, enforcement became much more active, and representation rose for protected groups in contractor establishments who were obligated to comply with the policy compared to noncontractor establishments who were not. Then the Ronald Reagan administration tried to dismantle affirmative action altogether. Although it was unable to fully accomplish this, it did succeed in fundamentally changing affirmative action from an active program to a symbolic one, since there was virtually no enforcement after 1980. Further, the economic woes of that decade marked a definite shift in the national climate regarding affirmative action, and the laudability of its goals was brought into question as more and more workers became newly vulnerable. As a result, since the 1970s we have never returned to active enforcement of affirmative action policy.

The sociologist Nancy DiTomaso contends in *The American Non-Dilemma: Racial Inequality without Racism* that the target of affirmative action policy was all wrong:

> Framing the civil rights movement and subsequent legislation only in terms of making it illegal to keep Blacks out therefore ignores the primary process by which racial inequality is reproduced, namely through the help and assistance that Whites give to other Whites.[16]

White resistance to affirmative action is grounded, in her view, in the unwelcome disruption that civil rights and the push for "equal opportunity" imposed on the "unequal opportunity" that White Americans had taken for granted and some had relied on to "access a middle-class lifestyle."[17] Although the White respondents in her study viewed helping one's family and friends as a harmless practice that most people engaged in to "get in the door," they minimized the extent to which the opportunities they wanted to reserve for themselves and share among their networks were procured by a legacy of markedly unequal access to opportunity and were shared almost exclusively among White families. They also minimized the extent to which the state had sanctioned this unequal access—for example, by explicitly limiting the ability of Black families to build social resources that they could then share among themselves.[18]

Nearly all of DiTomaso's 246 respondents had used personal connections (social capital) to find a job; only two (less than 1 percent) did not.[19] Yet very few acknowledged that they had done so. Instead, each respondent treated their own work history as the exception, not as the rule, and minimized the role of the help they received in their success.

"Everyone says they support equal opportunity," DiTomaso writes, "but at the same time, almost everybody instead seeks unequal opportunity (that is, advantage) and relies on special favors for getting ahead—and almost everybody thinks they got ahead through individual effort."[20]

Yet legends about the negative impact of affirmative action on White labor market opportunity live on. Tales of reverse discrimination caused by quotas requiring slots to be held for minority applicants are false. Quotas are illegal. In 1978 the Supreme Court ruled in *University of California v. Bakke* that "public universities (and other government institutions) could not set specific numerical targets based on race for admissions or employment."[21] Affirmative action regulations call for organizations to take affirmative steps to attract and increase the representation of either women or people of color where they are underrepresented, relative to their availability within the workforce, but it is illegal to hire based on race and gender at the expense of merit.[22] There is no law, however, that prohibits hiring based on relationship. Nepotism—the practice of giving jobs or favorable treatment to friends and family members—is not illegal. While discouraged, and in some states prohibited for public officials, it is not illegal to give jobs to friends and family members.

Both White objection to affirmative action and Black acceptance of network reliance as a strategy ignore the fact that even though people share resources within their contact lists across racial groups, the types of resources they have access to vary widely. Black and White racial groups are differently positioned to provide the kind of meaningful help necessary to access occupational opportunity. Across occupations and industries nationwide, White dominance in leadership—and therefore in access to resources and social capital—is unrivaled, to the benefit of White job seekers over Black job seekers. The general trends in the labor market advantages and disadvantages of racial groups constrain job seeking and ultimately employment in the United States. But these trends underpin the narratives of "normalcy" that Black and White Americans maintain as they construct their perceptions of their access to economic security—that is, how they compare their current economic security to that of their parents' generation, and how they imagine their economic prospects for the future.

The more White Americans feel shut out of the kind of secure labor contracts that they perceived their parents as having (particularly their fathers), the less accessible the American Dream feels to them. For Black Americans, as discussed earlier, even as they too remain frustrated in their pursuit of the American Dream by insecure employment and unequal access to jobs, pessimism is tempered by a different historical legacy and a sense of newfound control over the future enabled by the removal of legally sanctioned discrimination. This paradox had led our White participants to stress group harm and our Black participants to stress individuality and self-reliance—both perspectives being based on many misconceptions about access, equality, and affirmative action. The result is widespread resistance, though differently motivated for Black and White Americans, to the development of race-targeted policy to address unequal opportunity.

Even President Barack Obama emphasized universal versus race-specific programs as good policy and politics, rooted explicitly in White discomfort with the centering of Black experiences. In his 2006 book *The Audacity of Hope: Thoughts on Reclaiming the American Dream*, he relates the following story:

> I remember once sitting with one of my Democratic colleagues in the Illinois state senate as we listened to another fellow senator—an African American whom I'll call John Doe who represented a largely inner-city district—launch into a lengthy and passionate peroration on why the elimination of a certain program was a case of blatant racism. After a few minutes, the white senator (who had one of the chamber's more liberal voting records) turned to me and said, "You know what the problem is with John? Whenever I hear him, he makes me feel more white."[23]

In response to the White senator's comment, Obama defended his Black colleague by explaining the difficulty of striking the right tone when "discussing the enormous hardships facing his or her constituents." Yet Obama then describes his White colleague's reaction as "instructive": "Rightly or wrongly, white guilt has largely exhausted itself in America; even the most fair-minded of whites, those who would genuinely like to see racial inequality ended and poverty relieved, tend to push back against suggestions of racial victimization—or race-specific claims based on the history of race discrimination in this country."[24]

Although Obama attributes this White response partly to the race wars and to conservatives' exaggerations of the adverse impact of affirmative action on White people, he concludes, "It's a matter of simple self-interest. Most white Americans figure that they haven't engaged in discrimination themselves and have plenty of their own problems to worry about."[25] "By garnering advantages through favoritism and cronyism, as opposed to racial discrimination," the sociologist Brittany Slatton writes, "whites are able to define themselves as good people who help family members and friends and have nothing to do with racism or racial inequality."[26]

Closed Networks, Back Doors, and Unequal Job Access

In the interviews we conducted for this book with seventy-nine middle-aged Black and White American workers, we were specifically interested in learning whether the rise of insecure work across the labor market has influenced their perception of race and its relevance for access to jobs and economic security. Their responses showed that, despite their enduring belief in "ability" as the essential factor for job opportunity, and even though, again, their perspectives on it continued to diverge according to racial group, both Black and White American workers continue to use race as a central marker for who deserves to have access to jobs. For example, Kelly, a forty-seven-year-old White medical assistant who was struggling to make ends meet, applied for a job, got the job, but then learned that it came with some startling stipulations that mitigated against long-term stability, so she began looking for another job through a revised search strategy. "They said they can hire me as a temporary. . . . Okay, I said yes. Why not? It lasted six months, seven months. The maximum was six months, but it lasted longer because they liked me. But they couldn't hire me." Frustrated with the prospect of instability, Kelly tapped into her network. "You have to jump on the bandwagon and get your résumés all out," she said. "It's tough. You do little things, you start networking. Talk to this person, talk to that person." Kelly's temporary work dilemma was soon eased by her network. With good recommendations under her belt, Kelly was finally hired in another section of the same company. Though her network played a role in her own ability to land the job, she reasoned that hard work and merit should be the markers of job eligibility. She explained:

> I think my philosophy of temp work is trying to find an employee that's good and if you find one that's a temp, hire that person. Just don't keep them in limbo, because when you're a temp worker you don't have benefits. You don't have insurance. Hire them. That way the temp agencies can hire more people and have them hired as permanent workers. But that's not the way business works.

Although Kelly may have excelled at her job, she acknowledged, vaguely, that "that's not the way business works." In the job market where most of our participants were competing, their network determined their net worth and their contact list was a major asset in their arsenal. In other words, to use Kelly's frame, business works according to an individual's network. The importance of a contact list was a persistent stumbling block for our Black participants in their job hunts as many struggled to land jobs they were trained for—and even overqualified for in some cases.

Take Brandon, the Black design engineer who reminded us in chapter 3 that "you got to crawl before you walk" in the job market, because it is a market that dictates that one cannot "start out the gate running." Nevertheless, Brandon maintained a belief in education and its ability to help anyone transcend their economic circumstances. Yet, in a dramatic turn, he dismissed the idea of equal opportunity in job access, saying unequivocally that it is networks that matter: "I've known people who've owned businesses who gave jobs to their family members even though they weren't qualified and passed up the people who are qualified." Despite the "power" of education, Brandon concluded, "it's always going to be who you know. Always, in this country."

Jordan, the Black physician's assistant, took Brandon's observations a step further. It's not only about who you know, he said, but also about "what the faces of those people look like." He clarified:

> It's not one man alone in control, it's actually a network, and who's your network? They're not faces that look like mine and yours. They're not female faces either. They're mostly older white men, so if you look like them, that's, like, a basic animal instinct. They're going to be more accepting to you if you look like them. Of course. You know, if you're my boy and I like you and you like me, I'm going to look out for you. Of course. That's how it's always been since the beginning of time.

Both Jordan and Brandon had concluded that a person's network is key to opening doors and accessing occupational opportunities. For them, despite education and other credentials, who you know usually trumps what you know, and both begrudgingly admitted that race constrains those personal networks.

Yet, despite their recognition of staunch racial preferences in the workplace, Black participants were reserved in their condemnation and instead viewed these preferences as the reality of the status quo. Lloyd, a forty-one-year-old Black sales manager, compared finding a job to finding a plumber: "Everything is a connection today. How do I find my plumber? I ask my neighbor. So I think people realize that, and then you look at things like LinkedIn and all those things to help people get jobs that are all about the connection, so I think it's just what happens once you get the job." Jamal, a forty-one-year-old Black clerical worker, shared Lloyd's point of view, but suggested that Black people need to show more determination on the job market.

> You have to go through so many more avenues and so many more dead ends before a door opens. It seems like it, and you have to be more persistent. We have to be more persistent, and we have to work harder, it seems like, before an opportunity comes our way. It's sad but it's the truth. Because my dad, he got discriminated against. My mom did [too].

Jamal's knowledge of the reality of discrimination and how it limited opportunities for his mom and dad had led him to naturalize that reality. He saw discrimination as a de facto aspect of the hiring process, since discrimination to him was not new. Since it appeared to him to be here to stay, Jamal's logic was to outsmart and outwork it.

Although most Black participants shared job-seeking experiences that highlighted race as a potential limiting factor, if not outright discrimination,

Darius, a fifty-one-year-old Black corrections officer, perceived race as offering an advantage in jobs that called for more diversity. Drawing on his own experiences working in the criminal justice system, Darius explained how this advantage plays out, not only racially but also in terms of gender.

> They might give you a little bit of preference because maybe they're looking for a Black person. And I'll use corrections as a perfect example. When they would sometimes hire supervisors, they would try to keep things balanced. At a particular facility, they might say, "Well, we need a White female supervisor, lieutenant," so that's primarily who they interviewed. I don't have a problem with that, because if you're talking about affirmative action, trying to keep things equal, try to keep them fair, then you have to do that, where a Black person might get mad—oh man, they could make me [supervisor]—no, but you've got to understand, it can't just be all about you. If this is the way it's supposed to work, then it has to be spread out for everybody. So over here, they might want a Black male supervisor, so that's who they're primarily going to interview. It might be here they might want a White male. But you have to give everybody a chance in this—if you're trying to make it be fair and apply the system the way you say it's supposed to be applied. So, you know, you go on interviews—I've gone, I'm sure, on interviews where, okay, he's nice, he's qualified, but we're really looking for someone that's White. That's unfortunately how it goes sometimes. I'm not always going to be happy about it, but sometimes that's the way it goes. It's different if they just don't want to hire me because I'm Black, which you don't really know for sure sometimes, you know, but if we're going on affirmative action and trying to make it equal and give everybody a chance, then sometimes somebody's feelings are going to be hurt in the process.

Like Jamal, Darius acknowledged the perils of preference on the job market and concluded that it's just the way it is.

Darius's response is particularly striking because he conflated discrimination and racial preference, describing the latter incorrectly as affirmative action. On the one hand, he suggested that racial preferences help keep the workplace "equal," but then, on the other hand, he confessed that such preferences make it difficult to ascertain whether he is being passed over for a job because of his race. Instead of interrogating this or considering the systemic impact of racial preferences in limiting Black labor market opportunity, he personalized his observations as "hurt feelings."

Though Jamal and Darius arrived at complicated assessments of racial preference on the job market, they, like Lloyd, believed that networking plays a key role in the path to job security. For our Black participants, the value of networking could not be ignored, but our White participants were not as forthcoming. Recall Susan, the White psychologist we met in chapter 3 who understood that, however hard she had worked to achieve success, "a lot was provided that enabled her to do so." Susan had not considered the role of networking until she was asked about it in our interview. She responded:

> I've never thought about this, but now that you're saying this, it makes sense that it would be right, because if it's like a closed-door network, then it's hard to break through. Then you're kind of, like, keeping it within your own group. Yeah, it seems like it could. For me, it's more of just, like, I was thinking about jobs too, but I never thought about the networking aspect of it. I think about it more like employers. You have a White candidate and a Black candidate that has equal qualifications, but it's going to impact your hiring decision even if you don't realize it. That's more how I thought about it. But the networking part though. Yeah, I never really thought about how that's really fueling it until you brought it up.

Susan's lack of awareness of her racial advantage had let her assume that résumés trump relationships in the job market. Her response extended some of the perspectives offered in chapter 3, where participants described their belief that hard work and education are keys to at least opening the doors to opportunity. It is particularly striking, yet not surprising, that Susan did not think about the role of networking considering that her family network of privilege was second nature to her. Given her parents' economic status, Susan had grown up with a relative sense of comfort and stability. To date, she had never had to worry about economic security because she was confident that her family and friends would provide support during any breaks in her employment. "I wouldn't be just, whoa, woe is me. It's not really in my nature," she shared. "I would definitely get back [on my feet] and not feel sorry for myself. Do whatever I could to makes ends meet. If it was a health thing, I'd be proactive in getting medical attention." Susan could admit that she had some privilege and advantages that could help her navigate employment instability and even get medical attention; for most people, health care is rooted in employment. Her awareness of her network reliance, however, had not extended to the job market.

Our White participants had a notion of community as providing financial security, whereas our Black participants, because community was often unable to offer financial resources, conceptualized security more broadly as social support. Shantelle, a fifty-nine-year-old Black tutor in English as a second language, shared that members of her community checked in on her to make sure she was okay.

> If I'm away, they hear something, or they don't—seriously, when the couple upstairs, when they don't see me or see my car too long, they come knock on the door. "Mrs. Shantelle, you okay?" "I'm good." You know what I mean? But thanks, you know, and love you guys. You know that type of thing. And when she needs something, she will send her kid upstairs, you

know. "Mrs. Shantelle, do you have a can opener?" I said, "Here, you can keep this one. I'll get another one." "Oh, thank you," or whatever. "Do you have a Band-aid? We don't have a Band-aid," and I said, "Oh, no, no, here's a couple," you know? So we take care of each other. We do, you know?

Both our Black and White participants had networks that helped secure their well-being, but the different resources of their networks helped them navigate insecurity and access opportunity in different ways.

Susan's ambivalence about the role of racialized networks in securing opportunity was as clear as any of our White participants were willing to be in acknowledging labor market advantage. Most rejected the idea out of hand. Kate, a fifty-two-year-old White paralegal, asserted that discrimination is a thing of the past and that race has no advantage in the job market. She observed that companies have made an effort to level the playing field through affirmative action efforts. "I know for a fact, just being a paralegal, that most companies are required, especially any manufacturing company," she said, "they're required to have a certain amount of Whites, certain amount of Blacks, certain amount of Hispanics, whatever."

Another White participant, Jim, the mail carrier, summed up his thoughts about discrimination at the workplace as a "huge conspiracy." "It sounds like if you're Black or if you're White, you have two different sets of rules," he said. "These guys, they know people, and they're going to get a shot at a job before these guys because they don't know people, but that's too far-fetched for me to think that."

Remember that, when we met Jim earlier in the chapter, he offered the example of Black labor market advantage—the Black guy who got the job over ten White guys who went to Yale because he knew somebody. Jim's apparent indecisiveness on the impact of networks in shaping access to opportunity and his perspective on discrimination were indicative of his attempt to rationalize the insecurity of the labor market in a way that would encompass his vulnerability—a rationalization common among White workers who were mourning their secure past. When speaking of his experience working at a bakery, Jim lamented that he was the "minority" and "lower than most of the Black guys working there." He said, "It's different for me. It sounds like somebody in the media is making this up and saying that Black people can't get jobs because White people are taking it from them, and I don't know how that could be the case. If you are qualified, you should get the job and that's it. That's how I feel, so I don't know."

However, in periods of insecurity—what Patrick, a thirty-one-year-old White graduate student, describes as "famine times"—people tend to look out for their own. He explained that "race tends to play a large part of it because of the artificial construction of groupings of people. So, in those famine times, you're like, 'Oh I'm only going to help out the White people or the people who look like me,' because I have to make some sort of artificial distinction on which groups are [deserving]." In Patrick's view, this is just the way it is—"just a little bit of our monkey brains working," he said. "We are social animals," he added. In times of plenty, we can share with less regard for identity, but in times of famine, he argued, people "tighten the net of who they consider helping." For Patrick, this is the root of Black labor market exclusion, and the reason for heightened vulnerability in insecure times.

Charles, the Black superintendent, made a similar point:

> I think when the economy is worse off, racism is even more prevalent, and what I mean by that is, when the economy is bad, you have predominantly middle-class White Americans who now blame minorities for taking their jobs or whatever else. Like, I won't even say it becomes—did I say prevalent? Yeah, it does become more prevalent, being it just becomes more open. They've become much more open about it, not that it doesn't exist regardless, but they've just become much more open about it.

Taking Patrick's perspective a step further, Charles was suggesting that not only are racial minorities iced out of the hiring process, but they are also blamed for "taking jobs" from middle-class White Americans.

Rising economic insecurity has not changed the way Black and White Americans view each other and distinguish between themselves. Workers are still drawing on conceptions of race—their own and that of others—to make sense of who deserves opportunity and a chance at security. These enduring conceptions have had devastating consequences for Black workers, who are often excluded from the networks within which desirable occupational opportunity circulates. Nevertheless, the narratives of both Black and White workers about meritocracy and work cast the individual as deserving security if they work for it. These narratives do not speak to the fairness of the system itself or the feasibility of the American Dream, and they have not led to greater economic security for Black workers or helped reduce the difference in levels of access to opportunity, which White workers, particularly White men, continue to enjoy. Indeed, these narratives support an enduring faith in an American Dream that has always been more accessible to White workers than Black workers, while maintaining persistent inequality in the U.S. labor market.

Summary

It is not just the sharing of labor market opportunity among White people that reproduces racial inequality, as DiTomaso asserts, but the active exclusion from access of Black people, whether or not they are cognizant of being excluded. From the screening phase to the hiring phase to the workplace, Black identity is scrutinized and excluded from labor market opportunity. The different ways in which Black and White Americans are unable to see and acknowledge inequality of opportunity have implications for who and what is to blame for insecurity and for imagining solutions. Further, White participants' reliance on networks and the ability of some to draw on familial wealth to replace income during unemployment spells were largely not available to our Black participants. This difference in access to jobs and the ability to remain financially afloat while gaining new skills to get a better job lead to persistent racial inequality that affirmative action cannot combat. Given this fact and worsening economic realities, how do Black and White Americans think about who deserves security as fewer and fewer people have it? We pick up this question in the following chapter.

= Chapter 5 =

Negotiating Uncertainty

In the American postwar economy, which lasted from 1945 into the 1960s, good jobs were largely reserved for White workers and the occupational choices of Black workers were actively constrained. In 1944, the sociologist Gunnar Myrdal predicted in his pathbreaking book *An American Dilemma: The Negro Problem and Modern Democracy* that America's racial problems would be short-lived. "Racial inequality cause[s] a moral dilemma for White Americans," he explained, "because the American creed of 'liberty, equality, justice and fair opportunity' for all was incompatible with the reality of racial inequality."[1] Yet today America's racial problems are perhaps more salient and visible than at any time since the civil rights movement of the 1960s, especially since the racial reckoning of 2020. In the nearly sixty years since then—a period marked by dramatic societal and economic transformations—how has racial progress remained attenuated at best? Perhaps more importantly here, what do Black and White workers' conceptualizations and understandings of this inequality have to do with it?

There are a number of reasons why progress toward racial equality has stalled over the years, but by looking at the way Black and White workers conceptualize inequality, as we do in this book, we can show the influence of inequality on the way people today navigate economic insecurity. We can also illuminate the different rhetorical strategies that Black and White workers have developed to manage inequality, often drawing on the logic of the American Dream to do so, even if the Dream is increasingly unobtainable.

As we have shown in the previous chapters, the erosion of the postwar labor contract exposed formerly privileged workers to vulnerability, creating a paradoxical impact on Black and White Americans' perceptions of economic insecurity. White workers became more pessimistic about the evolution of the American Dream compared to Black workers navigating the same insecurity. But the Black participants in our study did not portray their frustrations as evidence of a lost American Dream, but rather as a continuation of the racial obstacles that Black workers have faced for so long.

Today, as many of the Black workers we interviewed point out (see chapter 4), race is still a factor in workers' economic security, as it continues to shape people's access to labor market opportunity. The role of race can be seen in the way White workers utilize networks that generate racial advantages for them in getting jobs—and in the option for some of drawing on familial resources to minimize their economic vulnerability—while at the same time bemoaning the effects of equal opportunity laws, which they fear advantage Blacks at their expense. *The reality of economic uncertainty, however, haunts both Black and White workers.* These uncertainties have spurred anxiety among all workers. Both the uncertainties and the anxiety they provoke are strongly influenced by changes in the U.S. economic structure since the 1960s, and individuals' perceptions of inequality and their access to the American Dream have evolved alongside those changes.

In this chapter, we describe this anxiety that both Black and White workers are experiencing, but we also explain the differences in how this anxiety is experienced depending on one's racial group. Despite people's broader anxieties, and beyond the racial barriers explicitly described by Black participants, workers have generally not turned to critiquing the economic structures to explain the insecurity and anxiety they face. More often than not, workers instead continue to turn to ideas of meritocracy to discuss their prospects, frequently leaning on the tenets of the American Dream to understand their options in the face of this economic insecurity, even when this logic is contradictory or confusing. For example, White workers have developed rhetorical strategies to explain that, even when family resources gave them a head start in life, their professional or financial success was still the result of "individual hard work." At the same time, Black workers—who are far more likely to begin their educational and professional lives without the kinds of resources available to White workers—rely on different rhetorical strategies that often acknowledge White advantage but still describe their own prospects through individualistic narratives.

This chapter also discusses the notable impact of these recent structural economic changes on traditional, heterosexual gender roles—specifically the struggle among men to affirm their masculinity by being the "breadwinner" as women take on more and more breadwinning responsibilities in their households. As we discuss in this chapter, since Black women have long worked outside their homes to provide income for their family and the "male breadwinner" family structure has historically been reserved for Whites, this shift in gender roles is likely more shocking for White women. As White men increasingly struggle against economic insecurity and White women take on economic responsibilities in addition to domestic work, this shift is likely to play a role in the larger racial futures paradox described earlier in this book: White workers expressing higher levels of pessimism about their future than Black workers, for whom economic insecurity is nothing new.

Navigating Insecurity, Narrating Deservingness

The chance of winning the lottery is remarkably small, yet thousands of Americans line up at their local convenience stores, supermarkets, and gas stations to purchase a ticket with the hope that luck is on their side. Vivid dreams and special prayers aside, most people generally believe that there is no formula to winning the lottery, but they do believe that buying a ticket gives them a chance, even if it is infinitesimal. As jackpots rise, people often buy more tickets to increase their odds, because they believe the game itself is not rigged. The lottery is fair—a pure game of chance—and if they are lucky they can win. But they can't win if they don't play.

As outlined in previous chapters, many of the White workers we spoke with reflected on educational achievements and job seeking in the same way: they suggested that education is a necessary investment to increase the odds of success, but that, ultimately, achieving the American Dream and economic stability is still a game of chance and luck. Maureen, a forty-five-year-old White store clerk, remarked, "Some people have more luck than others. I don't really know what to say. Some people, I don't know, lottery system. They got picked, you know." Kyle, a fifty-eight-year-old White teacher, pointed to the kind of luck that starts at birth. There is a "sort of genetic lottery," he remarked. "America can't control who has a baby, and somehow make that person have genetic material that is going to be successful." He continued that, aside from winning the genetic lottery, the United States could encourage "people to have babies when they're ready for it," through access to health care and contraception, because "unwanted" children have "terrible" outcomes.

Both Kyle and Maureen seemed to suggest that, since no one can choose the family or economic circumstance they are born into, success is the result of chance and individual choices. Kyle, acknowledging that it may seem "eugenicist," referred to himself as being "lucky" because he "won the genetic lottery." He explained:

> I regard it as totally a matter of luck that I was born to an intact, loving family, and I was given an intellect, which I think is a good one. And my parents, through a wonderful rearing of me, gave me a work ethic and a sense of joy about life and community service that has helped me. So I didn't go out and dig a ditch, or, you know, move five billion tons of iron ore. I didn't in any sense deserve that, but I was given that. But then I took those advantages, and they led me maybe naturally to a point where I've been useful and successful, productive. So who knows where the shovel was given? My father

dug with it and worked in a productive way and helped me to get a shovel that was useful to me, that has served me well. . . . So I think that I deserve to have gotten the fruit of other people's, you know, hard work, and continued hard work by me.

Kyle moved semantically from luck and the "genetic lottery" to hard work and deservingness of the advantages he possessed. He recognized that unearned benefits that he "didn't in any sense deserve" had come to him, but insisted that, through hard work, he built on those advantages and was now "successful" and "productive." Kyle explicitly recognized the role of inheritance—which he referred to as "luck"—in enabling his economic stability.

Kyle continued to describe as "luck" the help he received from his parents and four grandparents, as well as the help he received from his wife, who was also helped by her family. Kyle was transparent in his belief that all of this help contributed to his present economic well-being. He said, "I've just been able to take advantage of the financial and other markets that allow for passing resources." From education in private schools to summer vacations, Kyle described the material impact of generational wealth for White Americans. Though his life experiences were in no way representative of White America, they stood in stark contrast to the life experiences of most Black Americans, who are cognizant of the help they did *not* have in pursuing the American Dream.

As Dwayne, a forty-three-year-old Black corrections officer, put it, "Now we're—I don't know, six generations behind. They're six or seven generations ahead of us. To us it's not a small feat for somebody to get a master's, or PhD, or bachelor's, but to them, you go in their house, it's like your grandfather, father, they all had these qualifications, you know what I'm saying?" Although Dwayne's assumption of White wealth does not match the reality (the United States also has a very sizable population of poor Whites), he was nevertheless pointing to the fact that, on average, White families, compared to Black families, have higher rates of generational success that they are able to pass on.

Over the course of the twentieth century, owing to both racism and structural differences in opportunity created by law—such as the GI Bill in 1944—White families accrued cumulative advantages that Black families did not (see chapter 3). Jordan, the Black physician's assistant, emphasized that White Americans are set up to succeed: "You're going to have to work hard not to succeed." White Americans, as he put it, are "meant, you know, to succeed." Both Dwayne and Jordan concluded that the legacy of resources, networks, and supports passed down in White families from generation to generation positions them to "succeed."

Yet the language of legacy and lottery are in opposition. The former recognizes the compounded value of help and connections shared across generations, and the latter is a game of chance. Economic inequality is not the outcome of some people being randomly selected in an economic lottery; instead, it reflects structural, compounded disadvantages stemming from differential economic rewards for Blacks and Whites, not merely for individuals but also throughout the social system.[2] In their classic 1995 book *Black Wealth/White Wealth: A New Perspective on Racial Inequality*, the sociologists Melvin Oliver and Thomas Shapiro examined the racialization of state policy, which, they demonstrated, has simultaneously impaired the ability of Black Americans to accumulate wealth and promoted the accumulation of wealth among White Americans.[3] Thus, White Americans can profess a belief in racial equality and still reap the material benefits of racial group membership.[4] In our interviews with White middle-aged workers, discussion of luck and chance frequently emerged when our White participants accounted for their current economic position. It was a way for them to both acknowledge the advantages they possessed and avoid acknowledging the structural imbalances and their implications for Black communities. By emphasizing luck while also emphasizing their commitment to hard work, they could rhetorically connect their advantaged class status to a belief that they had "earned it," and to the recognition that their success was enabled by their family background.

This rhetorical strategy for describing their economic status was commonly used by the White workers we spoke with, particularly those from higher economic brackets. For example, Drew, the White salesman we met in chapter 2, after describing his upbringing as "not middle-class, but probably upper middle-class," made this same rhetorical conflation. "My father was financially very well off," he said. "But for me and my brothers, we had to earn every single thing we got." This experience, he maintained, inspired him to be "self-sufficient." He certainly worked hard, and that contributed to what he had, but did he earn "every single thing"? He undoubtedly had help. Drew was unable to see—or perhaps, more critically, unwilling to acknowledge—the relationship between his dad being very well off and his ability to be "self-sufficient." Such an acknowledgment would have shattered the illusion that hard work alone facilitated his success and that he had "earned" what he had in life. It would require contending with the fact that other people, including Black Americans, also work hard but do not receive similar fruits from their labor. *Hard work alone does not work for everyone.*

Not all White workers framed the sources of their economic well-being in the same way. However, even when it differed, many still framed that success in somewhat complicated—and contradictory—ways, underscoring the dilemma that financially well-off White workers face in rationalizing their success in a country with a history of profound racial inequality. For example, Phil, a fifty-nine-year-old White salesman, recognized the role that family background played in his success but also spoke of confounding factors. He said, "We all benefit—and are victims of . . . our situation that we started."

> My parents certainly—their hard work in starting something, that business, it was okay. It wasn't actually great when they started, but it was something—a seed that could grow, so, I would never [say it's fair], I don't. I think luck plays a huge role. I think timing plays a huge role. Race and ethnicity—I mean it's easier as a White male, and I certainly know that.

Phil did not try to justify his advantages; he acknowledged that the job market is not fair and that race plays a role in inequality. Voices such as his illustrate the struggle for some of our White participants to reconcile their recognition of being given a head start—at birth and because of ongoing racial privilege—and their belief in the American Dream, whose cardinal premise is that those who work hard can transcend difficult circumstances.

This struggle was illustrated in many different ways by our White participants as they sought to reconcile their faith in the American Dream with the advantages they had been given. Spencer, the thirty-four-year-old White marketer, even as he reflected on inequality, stressed his desire to maintain a belief in America as the land of opportunity. "This is tough," he said. "I don't want to believe that there's a difference. I'd like to believe that everybody has an equal opportunity." For many of the Black workers we spoke with, however, this perspective on the American Dream was simplistic. For Ellis, a forty-two-year-old Black professor, the belief that America is fair and that opportunity is equal was far-fetched and did not describe the world in which he lived. Although he claimed to subscribe to the idea of America as "the land of opportunity and being able to do things and have freedom," pointing out that, "Yes, we do have all these freedoms," he was also clear in his assessment that freedom and fairness are not the same thing. "Think about the housing inequalities and think about the schooling, think about the way schools are funded. No. It's not fair." Ellis contrasted students in suburban schools that have "four classic football fields and AP courses and all that stuff," enabled by high taxes, with schools in the inner city, where tax revenues are low. He said, "They don't have access to that [tax revenue], but we still expect them [the students] to compete for the same positions. No, I don't think that it's fair."

Our White participants were more likely (though not uniformly) to be able to identify with the suburban example Ellis offered and to call going to that kind of school luck. Our Black participants were intermittently able to stand outside of their circumstances and name structural inequality, but they were also invested in the narrative of striving to overcome. Americans celebrate the rags-to-riches story of self-made men or women who have pulled themselves up by their bootstraps. We rarely examine differences in opportunity and its relationship to the means to achieve economic security. We certainly do not acknowledge the lasting impacts of historical exclusion and opportunity hoarding in shaping today's over-whelmingly high racial imbalances in wealth. Instead, we narrate success as a matter of luck and connect conceptions of economic security to deservingness, which absolves structures of any blame for people's eco-nomic insecurity. This willed ignorance of the historical forces shaping economic security is required to sustain the simplistic narrative of the American Dream. Their economic circumstances notwithstanding, the Black and White Americans we spoke to affirmed their belief in American individualism. Yet the gap between their expectations for achieving security and the reality of ongoing vulnerability was causing them much anxiety.

Living with Anxiety

Both Black and White Americans accept that the economy has shifted. In the knowledge economy, success is predicated on what one knows instead of the physical tasks one can perform. This shift is driving high anxiety about the future, fueling fears of jobs lost to automation and globalization. Even jobs that were once good jobs, workers recognize, are increasingly unstable, and that shift from perceiving themselves as having a "good job" at a big company to not being able to count on it has sent many American workers into a tailspin.

Even those without direct experience of a layoff experience anxiety connected to large-scale layoffs. Desmond, the Black security guard we met in chapter 4, expressed disbelief about the scale of the layoffs at a large well-known company (two hundred to three hundred people) that he had recently heard about. This event was particularly remarkable to him because the layoffs were focused on the kinds of jobs that people used to seek out for security. These objectively "good jobs" were lost by people who had been working there for twenty to thirty years. "Twenty or thirty years ago," he said, "they weren't worried about [going to work for that company]. Now you're worried, 'Am I going to have a job?'" His incredu-lity was based on his prior conceptions of the security of being employed at this company, which, he said, "was one of the sturdiest. . . . If you got in . . . you were good for the next thirty years. Now you're like, if I even get past year five, I am doing well in my field."

Phoebe, the White city clerk who spoke in chapter 2 on the good jobs of the past, referenced the same company in her interview with us when she suggested that now even those who have a "good job" there are inse-cure because they live in fear of future layoffs. "It's like, I can't do this because there might be a layoff in six months. . . . So they are always living on that edge, like, oh my God, what's going to happen if there's a layoff?"

Phoebe was also projecting onto these workers her own anxiety as she relived her experiences of being laid off. Her company had downsized after being bought by a global firm, going from 125 to about 30 employees, and "to this day," she remarked, many of the workers who lost their jobs had not been able to find employment at a similar level in the same industry, despite extensive experience.

The larger economic shifts that occurred between the postwar period and the postindustrial period in the 1970s and 1980s significantly changed workers' levels of economic security—specifically in the manufacturing sector—in a relatively short period of time. For White workers in particular there have been major consequences—not just for their economic security but also for their sense of well-being, both physical and mental—as they have lost their privileged access to those jobs and the economic security they once offered. Black workers are also nostalgic for those kinds of jobs, but they are also aware that, just as their access to these jobs was within reach, the meaning and security associated with them shifted. The insecurity of the contemporary job market that both Phoebe and Desmond described has the same consequences across racial lines on physical and mental well-being.

All of these shifts are part of a remarkable change that has taken place within a single generation. Economic uncertainty takes a toll on workers as it shadows their need to continue to show up and work hard. Jamal, the Black clerical worker we met in chapter 4, exemplified this fear: "I used to worry about that when I first started off working. I would think, 'My gosh, I'm just going to lose my job.' It was like an anxiety thing. . . . I used to speak to my therapist about that." Economic anxiety has impacted marriage rates and led to increasing levels of marital dissolution. Commentators and researchers today talk about the impact of student loans on marriage, childbirth, and homeownership rates for young adults. But the pattern is also evident in the trends concerning their middle-aged parents and other family members.[5] "Time," Desmond shared, "is definitely eroding certain things, and the certain things that we need [are] eroding the more important things like stability, cohesiveness, family." The culprit in Desmond's story, however, is not time, but rather anxiety grounded in profound economic instability.

The willingness to work hard does not offer protection from the anxiety of economic uncertainty. Workers both Black and White and across the earnings spectrum expressed anxiety. For instance, Janelle, the Black office manager we met in chapter 3, was not completely satisfied with her current job, but she could not afford, she said, to let it go in this economy. "When the market is down, when you can't find a good job, you just got to take what you got to take so you can survive," she maintained. "Yeah, like my current job is definitely not where I ever imagined myself working, but I'm there five years later."

The fear of job loss was not abstract or imagined for our participants; it was a very real threat that many of them had either lived through or had some direct knowledge of through the experiences of a coworker, family member, or friend. Stories of job loss on any scale stoke fears, but the sense of inevitability due to global competition for jobs that can be outsourced is particularly palpable. Even workers who are relatively insulated from these trends fret over the experience. Claire, the White nurse we met in the introduction, felt despair that her husband did not have a steady job despite having a PhD. Claire shared how she imagined factory workers felt after their jobs were sent overseas. "It's not just you. It's like all fifteen thousand people that worked at your factory who are now out of work. It's not like you all of a sudden all just became lazy and you all deserved it. It's that, you know, the garment worker in Indonesia will make the same thing for like one-twentieth as much as what you were getting paid."

The fear of job loss, expected or unexpected, that Claire described here is particularly dangerous to a person's faith in the American Dream, because there is no room for economic uncertainty in the Dream. It assumes that economic stability can be attained and sustained for anyone who works hard. Black workers also fear this kind of instability, though they are less likely to associate it with a perception of the fading of historical access to economic security. Angelique, a fifty-two-year-old Black school coordinator, captured this fear succinctly: you can work for a company for thirty years, she said, then come to work one day and be told, "We're taking it overseas." She continued: "I think about it all the time because of my age. Because I'm fifty-two. If I lose my job today, I have something that I can go back to, the school system. But what if they don't take me back? . . . What am I going to do? Come work at Panera Bread? Come work at Burger King? So it can happen any day."

There is a particular and profound anxiety for middle-aged Americans in "good jobs." We might think that there would be comfort in having a good job in insecure times, but market instability and layoff fears mark a good job as something to lose, since there are not many jobs like that left. If or when middle-aged Americans lose a "good job," finding another will be nearly impossible. For them, the fear takes on a life of its own.

In all of these accounts, it is very striking that any mention of the lack of availability of good jobs in general—the structure of opportunity itself—was absent. Our participants did not speak to the kinds of jobs that are available and why. Both Black and White workers we spoke with generally did not critique—outside of acknowledging the insecurity they faced—the corporate practices and governmental policies that underpin this insecure labor market. Considering the levels of economic insecurity among both Black and White workers, and the anxiety they all feel from that insecurity, it seems reasonable to wonder why American workers continue to focus on the idea that hard work will help them obtain stability when, as they acknowledge, many jobs that might have offered such security in the past are no longer available for anyone, Black or White, in the labor market. This structural lack of opportunity remains an invisible backdrop against which Black and White workers narrate their struggles to get ahead in an insecure economy and their fears about not being able to do so. It's not that they do not see the impact of these structures on their lives, but that they are unable to account for it in their narration of their own responsibility to work hard. Even when our participants acknowledged that there are not enough good jobs to go around, they often seemed resigned to the inevitability of this kind of economic insecurity; as they understood present conditions compared to a more secure past, new technologies and globalization had changed the game and there was simply no going back.[6] Consider how Patrick, the White graduate student we met in chapter 4, described changes in the economy:

> Yeah. I thought about labor, and I thought about just the sort of classical thing, like in the nineteenth century when everyone had horses and we started developing cars and then two horses are talking about how it's going to be in the future and they're like, "Ooh." You know, they're just going to free up horses to do even better jobs and more interesting jobs and things like that. And then, it just ends up being that there's actually no jobs for horses. So I think that same conversation's going on now, and automation, and things like that, are just going to free up humans to do more interesting jobs, but then it's probably not going to go that way. There's probably going to be less and less jobs, because, you know? General shifting—the economy is going from higher-paying jobs to lower-paying jobs. I think that general trend will continue.

Patrick's abstract take on labor market change was both brilliant and firmly detached. At the time of the interview, he was in grad school, and notably, he did not see these critical shifts as impacting him. He expressed no economic anxiety connected to his understanding that there would be fewer jobs, apparently assuming that he would be able to navigate any complications in the labor market later if he needed to.

By contrast, Adève, the Black financial analyst we discussed in chapter 4, described labor market changes in concrete and deeply personal terms.

> Well, right now, it would be my current situation. It would be what's going to happen a year from now, six months from now. Am I going to lose my job? What about my five-week-old child? How are we going to make ends meet if I do not make this money? How does this work? You know, where do I go from here in terms of opportunities [in this geographic area]? How do I get to a place of relaxation where I don't have to worry about these things? And the answer is, you don't. You always have to hustle, especially as a person of color, unless it's handed to you, you know, because we don't—we just don't have it like that. Yeah, race plays a factor in this, because I sound

like a Black person. I have White friends, and they get laid off and get a job in two months, three months. I get laid off, it takes three years for me to get to a place—I mean, between [my last job], this is my only permanent job since 2009. And now, this company is laying off. It takes longer for us. So I'm thankful that I know what's going on now, so we have to get ahead of the curve.

Adève's anxiety and sense of vulnerability were visceral. There was no abstraction or distance in her narrative. She focused on the impact of racial networks, but the shift in the structure of opportunity itself was invisible to her. Unlike the Israeli workers whom Ofer Sharone describes in *Flawed System/Flawed Self: Job Searching and Unemployment Experiences*, who could clearly articulate structural explanations for their prolonged unemployment, American workers tend to minimize inequality, advantage, and disadvantage in shaping opportunity.[7] Though some Americans do offer these explanations for the U.S. labor market, individualistic explanations have typically prevailed.

For a very long time in the United States, this belief in individuals as masters of their destinies made particular sense for White men, who, until relatively recently, did indeed have far more opportunities than their Black counterparts. Even as those opportunities started to shrink in the 1970s, researchers found that the individual remained central to White Americans' cultural sensibility, as did the belief that they were responsible for their own fate.[8] White Americans tend to view their own accomplishments and those of others as the product of individual effort, and thus they often inadvertently ignore the privileges they have been accorded and the structural barriers encountered by Black Americans.[9] As the labor market has shifted, fracturing the link between effort and success, Black and White Americans are placing their hopes for the future within the context of divergent pasts.

At the same time, a conservative shift among Black Americans since 1980 has led to a convergence with White Americans in person-centered explanations (human capital, motivation) for income inequality, as opposed to structuralist explanations (such as discrimination).[10] Educated Black Americans, many of whom are middle-class workers, are especially prone to drawing on individual strategies to continue believing in meritocratic ideals, even if their efforts to get ahead must be conducted within a context of broad racial inequality. Even though many educated Black workers have reached an income level commensurate with a middle-class lifestyle, many of their attempts to lay claim to good jobs are still met with resistance and discrimination. As discussed in chapter 4, educated Black workers are also navigating a shifting labor market in which education is not the key to security that it was promised to be. This reality is beginning to fracture the resilient ideal of the American Dream by challenging individualistic meritocratic notions. Black and White Americans who did all the right things are increasingly aware of the uncertainty of their future. They are negotiating privileged expectations and insecure realities. In the next section, we unpack the impact of this persistent and growing anxiety on American workers across race and gender, looking specifically at the influence of gender expectations on their thinking, especially around masculinity.

Insecurity and the Family: Who Is Responsible for Bringing Home the Bacon?

The Black and White workers we interviewed were well aware of the economic insecurity in their lives. Many spoke of having to navigate this vulnerability in the past or described living through it in the present. The focus for them, however, was generally on the will to succeed. If they kept getting up and working hard to play the game of the life, they felt, they could win. Blake, the White fitness trainer we met in chapter 2, offered an instructive take on resilience in navigating hard times:

> You're the lowest of lows. Do you stay in that low or do you rise up and move forward and get back up and dust yourself off and figure out another plan and push forward? You do that in football. You got a big lineman that's in front of you that keeps knocking you down every time you go around him or you go to hit him, you know? Are you going to keep doing the same thing, you're going to get the same result or you're going to figure something out and get around him? You're gonna figure something out. So, it's the same idea with the game.

Like many of our male respondents, Blake approached insecurity by attacking it head-on.

Similarly, Henry, the Black technical writer whom we met in prior chapters, took a proactive approach to overcoming insecurity: he went to the library daily to fill out job applications. "If you have the feeling that your next opportunity is right around the corner, you know, all I've got to do is stick with it." But after he received no callbacks for several weeks, he confessed to being discouraged. "You know, my position, I just felt like nobody's going to hire me."

Insecure times, he saw, required that he lower his job expectations and consider taking a job with mediocre pay. "Any job, always on the table with me," he said. "You know, that's another self-responsibility thing. When I hear somebody say that, 'Well, I ain't working for ten dollars an hour,' I want to just slap them. Are you stupid?" For Henry, the realistic comparison of low wages was not with high wages but with unemployment. He jokingly concluded that the $10 an hour on the job you don't want should be compared to "the money that you're making not working."

U.S. popular and political culture of the postwar era romanticized and normalized the expectation that married women would stay home and their husbands would earn enough to care for the family. This vision of the American family was crystallized in the television show *Leave It to Beaver*, which ran from 1950 to 1963. Although some people were able to live out this vision of the American family, it was hardly the universal reality. Since White men, rather than Black men, were the ones with access to the jobs that would permit such a family structure, this vision of the family was within reach for White Americans. Even if that reality was never feasible for everyone — as it was not for most Black families — Americans today continue to be aware of this ideal, and some still aspire to it.

The gendered division of labor that helped set the foundation for this model in the United States arose in the nineteenth century when work was separated into two spheres, a public sphere and a private sphere. With women's labor relegated to the latter, the normative gender ideals of the "male breadwinner" and the "female homemaker" were established. But these ideals were always based on racial ideologies. For example, the "cult of true womanhood" that dominated American culture in the early nineteenth century encouraged White women to tend hearth and home in their "natural" role as mothers and caretakers, while it simultaneously demanded that Black women's own familial needs remain secondary to the demands of their employers.[11] Moreover, with widespread racial discrimination historically limiting Black men's earnings, Black women's need to work after they married and had children made clear the racial dimensions of these "ideal" gender models. Black women forged an alternate model of femininity, a "co-breadwinner" model that aimed to reconcile the constraint of Black men's depressed wages with a valuation of women's contribution to the household and to the community.[12]

The Great Recession of 2008 disrupted on a large scale people's ability to rely on the male breadwinner model.[13] The number of stay-at-home dads, Pew researchers found, "reached its highest point — 2.2 million — in 2010, just after the official end of the recession."[14] Nearly one-quarter of stay-at-home dads reported that they were home because they could not find work. Women, especially White women, responded to the increased economic vulnerability of their families by increasing their financial contribution to the household.[15] The first decade of the century witnessed a dramatic growth in female breadwinners; the Pew Research Center found that, in 2011, "40 percent of all households with children under the age of 18 include mothers who are either the sole or primary source of income for the family," up from 11 percent in 1960.[16] These numbers highlight the significant shift in gender roles in the American labor force since the postwar era; this shift has also precipitated a masculinity crisis for many men, many of whom hold on to the fiction of breadwinning as core to masculinity despite diminishing means of achieving it.

Among American workers, the Great Recession created economic anxiety that accompanied the increasing economic insecurity discussed in earlier chapters. That anxiety has taken a unique toll on men, for whom unemployment and underemployment, in inhibiting their ability to be "real" men, threaten their masculinity. Darius, the Black corrections officer we met in chapter 4, for example, spoke to the emotional impact on men who grapple with the long-term inability to get a job.

> I think it's hard for them to deal with that, because if you are a man who's trying to do the right thing and you get work for six months, a year, and then you lose that job, the company closes or whatever, it makes it very difficult on you, and it makes a lot of stress on you, because you know that you feel like you're letting your family down, and that's one thing—any man who is a real man, who values his family, one thing you don't want to do is let your family down, and when you feel like you're letting your family down, it makes it very hard on you, you know, and then unfortunately, it's going to come out in different ways when dealing with your family members, you know? You might snap at them, because they don't understand, you know, you—they might say, "Oh, it's okay," but for you it's really not okay, because protecting and providing and being a part of helping your family is vital for any real man, you know, so if you—if you've got a job and they move or they close or whatever, that's a—that's a tough blow, because we also define ourselves by our jobs, as men.

Darius, a Black man, shared what in fact is a racially universal sentiment and story of struggle. Claire, the married White nurse whose husband did not have a steady job despite having a PhD, aptly summarized the stranglehold of gender norms:

> Heteronormative masculinity just sucks for everybody. You know? It means that men are supposed to be like macho and manly.... I think that man drag is probably also really hard to wear all the time. You know? And especially if you're in a generation of people for whom you can't find a good job, you can't find a good enough job. You just, like, you suck as a man because you've been unemployed for two years.

At the same time that men find themselves without access to financial affirmation of their masculinity in steady employment, women are also renegotiating their understanding of gender roles—especially the centrality of breadwinning to masculinity in the face of enduring employment insecurity as it is increasingly necessary for a couple to pool and maximize the resources of all available earners to stay afloat.

Our interviews showed us what appears to be a widespread, maybe even universal, renegotiation of gender roles among heterosexual, middle-aged Black and White workers. The "male breadwinner" ideal persists among both White and Black men—and among White and Black women—despite the fact that, for historical reasons, race has largely determined men's ability to achieve this ideal. As discussed earlier, the male breadwinner model was primarily available to White families, though the desire for this ideal form of family support was shared by some Black families, who would go to great lengths enduring financial struggles to achieve it.[17] Hence, though both Black and White women are renegotiating gender expectations, their experiences and expectations are racially divergent: White women are renegotiating a model that had White men serving as sole breadwinners supporting their families, whereas Black women's renegotiation is taking place in the context of the ongoing struggle of Black men to do the same. The result of this expectation-experience paradox is a crisis of masculinity that cuts across racial groups. Additionally, because Black men, unlike White men, have historically struggled to obtain secure employment, the increasingly common need for women to become breadwinners may play a role in the comparatively high levels of pessimism that some White workers feel compared to Black workers about their diminishing access to the American Dream.

Because women's idealized expectations, both stated and unstated, of the relationship between breadwinning and masculinity often shape whether or not men are able to enter into and maintain a heterosexual relationship, women's narratives offer important insights into how the crisis of masculinity is playing out among heterosexual White and Black couples today. Here we highlight many of the narratives that the women we interviewed used to understand men's difficulties in fulfilling a breadwinner role. Although there were differences between how Black women and White women viewed this struggle, it is worth noting that, when women insist on adherence to the male breadwinner role, the cost to men for their inability to meet it remains high.

Among the people we interviewed, there were twenty-three Black women and nineteen White women. The majority of the White women were married (twelve), divorced and cohabiting (two), or otherwise partnered (one); only four out of the nineteen were single and never married.[18] The majority of the Black women were single and never married (eleven), although a substantial number were married (six), partnered (four), or divorced (two). Together the Black and White women we interviewed provided a valuable portrait of the way middle-aged working women with some college education understand the renegotiation of gender roles in this era of increasing economic insecurity and diminished access to the American Dream.

In general, both White women and Black women shared the hope that their male partner would be able to provide for the family—if not as the sole breadwinner, then as a significant contributor to the household's economic stability. Lacy, the White married woman we met in chapter 4, was underemployed by choice at the time of our interview (given her college degree and work experience) because she was frustrated in previous jobs that had matched her skills. Her perspective on male breadwinning focused on the family and men's responsibility. "Well, if the man has a family," she said, "you need to be a provider. You provide safety and security to your family." Her emphasis on provision was how she defined "the job" of manhood: "He is the breadwinner, he is the main support, he is going to be the only supporter of our family." Lacy offered a traditional (White) perspective on male breadwinning defined in stark contrast to women's responsibility. Although she was college-educated and able to earn more money if she could tolerate unfulfilling jobs, she did not have to:

> So, when I come to him and say, "What would you think about me quitting my job? Do you think we could do it?" I'm honestly asking him because I have no idea. In some respects, I feel like that's wrong of me. I think I should be more involved, know more, be a contributor to that. . . . And I don't want to. I don't want to. And I have that freedom because my job pays so much less than his, I have that freedom where he doesn't. And so, he's here, so okay, so a man in America is a provider.

It was her husband's "job" to provide, and her low wages gave Lacy "freedom." Although she expressed some guilt about the burden her choices placed on her husband and even acknowledged that it might be unfair, she did not want to change the situation, because breadwinning was the man's responsibility. For Lacy, the male breadwinner was not just a historical model but also a contemporary requirement. While her view was in some ways unusual, she was not alone. Rhonda, a forty-two-year-old single Black woman, described a good man as a "hard worker" who "wants to provide for his . . . kids or he has a family, this is what your life is." While Rhonda's life did not match the ideal, her perception of what that ideal should be was clear: "You're really trying to work to keep them safe, to keep them happy, to keep them financially stable. All of that. To try and provide a good life for them."

Rhonda, like Lacy, was advocating for a "traditional family ideal" in which the man's responsibility was to provide. The adherence to this ideal of the Black women we spoke with, the majority of whom were single, seemed to contradict their desire for a mate, given Black men's earnings. Ashley, a forty-eight-year-old single Black woman who had never married, said, "Now, to be quite honest with you, I got my girlfriends, and we get together, and we be like, I don't want nobody if he ain't making $100,000"— or 40 percent more than she made. Despite sharing this ideal with her girlfriends, Ashley was more undecided than she appeared. "I can work with a guy that's only bringing $40,000 home and I'm making $80,000. I can work with that. So I'm not one of those, you know, women that [says to men], 'You're the breadwinner.'"

Despite the persistence of the male breadwinner as an ideal to which they aspire, Black and White women know that men are struggling. Black and White women's understanding of the hardship imposed by the breadwinner role often emerged from their reflections on the challenges in their present relationships. Phoebe, the married White woman we met earlier, bluntly described the challenge for men who fall short: "How are you going to be satisfied with your life if you can't at least provide?" She described this need felt by men to provide as "very caveman" and connected to men's "sense of self." "I know it was hard for my husband when I made more money consistently because I was a salaried person," Phoebe recalled. "There was a part of him that was like, 'Wait a minute, I'm supposed to earn more money than you.'"

Claire concurred with Phoebe, observing, "It's been really hard on my husband." She added, "I think that for many men, it's profoundly destabilizing to feel like they're not fulfilling these older ideas about like, (*deepens voice*) 'what it means to be a man.'" The pressures of the breadwinner role are suffocating many men, Black and White women acknowledged. When asked how men are coping with the mounting challenge to provide, Keisha, a fifty-four-year-old Black woman, answered:

> I think they're probably angry. They may, you know, check out, you know? If you're not—you know, if you're not happy in your job, and—or just the pressure, you walk away. You may walk away from your family. You may turn to drugs, turn to alcohol, turn to whatever other things, just because you can't do what you feel you need to do for your family, or other things. You may feel like, "Well, I'm going to get it some kind of way," and then it leads to trouble. So, I think it makes it hard.

Ashley said, "I know it's hard. It's hard, and you know what, I didn't realize that. It's—I think it's extra hard for men than it is for women. Black men more so than Black women. It's very hard." While the breadwinner ideal persisted, most women could and did point to instances where it harmed men themselves or stunted relationships.

There were also differences in the way Black and White women sympathized with the struggles of men—differences that probably drew on their differing access to economic security in the past and, by extension, their view of whether their contribution to the household was required or value added. Some White women harbored expectations of men that conflicted with contemporary economic realities. Black women shared similar expectations for men to serve as breadwinners, but they quickly accounted for the lived reality that it was out of reach in ways that affirmed and did not blame men. Trisha, the married Black woman we met in chapter 2, put the problem succinctly: "Sometimes they have that thought in their head that they have to be the breadwinner, and they can't." Angelique, the single Black woman introduced earlier in this chapter, said, "Actually, they can't deal with it. Most men can't deal with it" (that is, with not being the breadwinner). Black men's inability to cope, in Angelique's view, is tied to their adherence to the breadwinner role despite its infeasibility. Black men, she said, try to figure it out on their own, but they don't have to, she maintained. "I mean, it's sad that we put that limitation on them like that because you have a partner," she said.

Despite the significant overlap in the hopes of the White and Black women we interviewed that their male partners would be breadwinners, the disparate historical experiences of access to secure employment by race probably explains the key differences we observed in the way both women and men made sense of the shift in gender roles in their relationships. Black and White women's narration of their experiences and candid accounts of their struggles to sustain relationships with men at midlife when they were unable to meet the breadwinning ideal offered some insight into the consequences of economic insecurity for family life. Marriage, a crucial part of the conceptual and cultural frame of the American Dream, is an increasingly frequent casualty of insecurity in this complicated and shifting economic context. Many of the key ingredients of economic security that White men and women used to rely on—comparatively high historical marriage rates, the near-exclusive access of White men to "breadwinning" jobs—are disappearing or being diminished as the postindustrial economy evolves. As discussed in chapter 4, as "good" jobs become scarcer and insecurity increases, White workers more often blame affirmative action as a source of their insecurity. Together, these various pressures on gender norms and access to secure jobs have threatened an entire worldview that White Americans used to take for granted.

Both Black and White Americans continue to doggedly pursue the American Dream, including marriage, but as White workers face more and more obstacles to economic security, their pessimism about the achievability of the Dream appears to be growing more quickly than Black workers' pessimism. In particular, because of White men and women's shared historical past—a time when White men were able to meet the breadwinner expectation—White women are unrelenting in their expectations and blame men for falling short. In contrast, Black workers are also pessimistic and frustrated in the face of the insecure postindustrial economy, but their frustration is less often focused on the loss of the American Dream and men's struggle to be breadwinners. For Black workers, this is a familiar and accepted struggle. Instead, they are frustrated with an enduringly unequal playing field that disrupts their ability to achieve security in an unpredictable and insecure job market. Race differently shaped the expectations held by Black and White women for their lives and, by extension, their expectations of men, and those different expectations underlie their flexibility or rigidity about gender roles.[19]

Inequality, Fairness, and Negotiating Uncertainty

We began this chapter by highlighting the differences in Black and White workers' conceptualizations and understandings of the persistence of racial inequality alongside the ideals of equality and meritocracy that drives belief in the American Dream. In the narratives of deservingness, the expressions of anxiety, and the laments over the demise of the "traditional" family due to the increasing inability of men to meet the breadwinner expectation, we see the impact of rising economic insecurity. Across race and gender groups, our participants deployed different rhetorical strategies to negotiate insecurity, often drawing on the logic of the American Dream—even though, for a host of reasons, the Dream was increasingly unobtainable. In the remainder of the chapter, we show that, despite the unequal—though increasingly shared—experience of insecurity, and despite the structural challenge of persistent racial inequality, both Black and White workers continue to see the American Dream as fair and as a legitimate goal.

Some Black Americans, however, tentatively question the fairness of the system. Vanessa, the Black policy analyst we met in chapter 2, stated clearly that "life is unfair." She continued: "There are a lot of people who work hard who will never be able to achieve anything in life just based on the luck of the draw." Like our White participants quoted at the start of the chapter, luck started for Vanessa with being born into a family that valued education. Nevertheless, she was cynical about hard work as a means to guarantee success and economic security.

> At the end of the day, they're going to work hard forever, but unless they create something or own their own business somehow, they probably will not end up being successful. It's just the function of life. I don't really know if there's a way to explain it beyond, like, I don't want to say it's divine, but it's just the way life is, it's tough. Because I think it's just because someone is just going to look at someone White and just think they're smarter. It's just what it is. It's what it is, it's, I don't know, because the world is just the way it is.

In moving from "the luck of the draw" to mentioning the "divine," Vanessa clearly articulated that America is not fair. Nevertheless, she made no effort to assign blame for this lack of fairness or to suggest any illegitimacy to underlying economic and social structures. Instead, she expressed a fatalistic conclusion that racial inequality is "just the way it is."

Other Black participants, however, expressed anger and attributed a basic illegitimacy and unfairness to America itself. They grounded these comments in a critique of historical inequality and one of America's original sins. Chattel slavery, which built the economic might of this nation, provides a shaky and contradictory foundation, they argued, upon which to claim that America is a "fair" nation, especially for Black Americans who were objectified and dehumanized in the past. Henry, the Black technical writer, eviscerated the "heroic" narrative often associated with President Abraham Lincoln: "This great emancipator thing is bullsh—t." He explained angrily, "You call yourself giving us something you never had the f—king right to take in the first place, and you want to pat yourself on the back for it 250 years after the fact." The notion of fairness in America, to Henry, had no value beyond a shiny "design on paper" — referencing the image of President Lincoln on the $5 bill.

Yet this historical critique grounded in centuries of oppression during slavery and the decades of overt discrimination following Emancipation has led some Blacks to celebrate the ideal of fairness and the more equitable opportunity that characterizes the present moment. Consider how Tanesha, the Black teacher we met in chapter 3, explained whether success is predicted by history or determined by effort, concepts she offered in the conversation.

> In the late '50s, '60s, early '70s, I would have said history. We have made great gains, but because of those laws, back then, because our forefathers fought for those laws. That's why it's easy now for it to be determination, because now, okay, I have equal opportunity. There are equal opportunities laws, you know. I have that now. They didn't have that. So now I have to say it's determination. You can live in the projects and work your way up. You have to have determination. Back then, I mean, they had to be determined, but it was more so history holding them back. They were determined, though, to see fit that the future had it a little easier. And I think we do now have it a lot easier. Is there still discrimination? Of course, of course, but it's a lot easier for me to become a teacher and, you know, move up the ranks.

Tanesha was a poster child for the persistence of the American Dream. History may have held her forefathers back, but with "determination," she suggested, moving out of the projects is possible. Discrimination exists "of course," but through hard work she could still "move up." America is fair now because her reference point was the nation's unfairness when historical and violent exclusion of Black workers was the American way. With overt discrimination made illegal, she felt that success is now predicted by a person's determination to get ahead.

Black Americans, despite persistent racial inequality, remain deeply invested in the American Dream and the notion that hard work will yield the good life. The ability to compete in the labor market without overt discrimination is driving an optimism about the future that deviates from the perspectives of our White participants and lies at the heart of the racial futures paradox. Though Black Americans experience more economic insecurity, almost across the board, than White Americans, our participants retained a triumphant belief in the American Dream.

For example, Blake, the White fitness trainer we met earlier, believed that, regardless of personal background, hard work is the main ingredient of success. He explained:

> You got to work for anything you want. Nobody is just going to hand it to you. Anybody that made it in this world, you know, I'm sure that all these multilevel billionaires and all the millionaires and whatever, I mean, there was some point, like, I don't think that it was smooth sailing for them the entire way. They had to work for it. They might have been given a good opportunity, have been born into it, but at some point in time they had to work for what they have. They had to have a new idea or hire the right person to have the right idea for them. You know what I mean? That's the other thing. But there's also a level of work to doing that.

Blake offered billionaires and millionaires as examples of those who worked hard, and he equated "having been given a good opportunity at some point" with "being born into it." Winning the birth lottery, to him, was the same as hard work. Those who make it have simply worked for it, and therefore, with hard work, anyone else can too. In contrast, Renee, a fifty-year-old Black administrative assistant, derided the idea that the wealthy worked for what they have:

> The 1 percent are the Donald Trumps of the world. That's the 1 percent. Those are the people who are entitled, who were born into entitlement, who don't understand that they're born into entitlement and think they've worked their way up when you inherited $40 million from your dad. You really didn't work your way up, like you were given something. And very few people like his dad built himself from nothing. But I feel like very few people build themselves from nothing.

Renee was critical of the idea that the wealthy "worked their way up," and she made a nuanced distinction between working your way up and being "given something" or being "born into entitlement." This distinction is particularly critical, because the American Dream is premised in large part on the ability to build something from nothing by virtue of hard work. If, as Renee suggested, no one can attain security and live the Dream unless they were given something to build with, then we would have to confront the fact that most Black Americans and many White Americans are not given the tools with which to achieve the Dream.

Yet, the reality of persistent inequality, both racial and economic, did not drive dissatisfaction. Instead, many of our participants pointed to the super-rich as evidence that hard work can lead to profound wealth. The continued belief in this core tenet of the American Dream among our respondents—that hard work will lead to economic rewards and stability—in the face of staggering and exponentially rising economic inequality and insecurity suggests that vulnerability itself is not in opposition with the American Dream. Individuals would rather account for their own failure than question their beliefs.

Summary

Economic insecurity has long coexisted with the ability to triumph over it as an acceptable, even celebrated, tenet of the American Dream. Deeply entrenched in this centuries-old meritocratic ideal is the seemingly foolproof notion that hard work and education not only lead to but even guarantee security regardless of a person's past or current economic realities. A goal for the economically striving and a badge of honor for the economically comfortable, the American Dream is powered by the idea that economic insecurity can be a rite of passage on the way to achieving the big house with the white picket fence. But as the cost of living in the land of the free rises with each coming year—and with a stagnant minimum wage that fails to help people confront it—more and more Americans are experiencing economic insecurity. Indeed, it is now quite clear that the vulnerability that Americans faced during the economic shifts at the beginning of the twenty-first century is here to stay.

═ Chapter 6 ═

Economic Vulnerability as the New Normal

"**A**re you better off than you were four years ago?" That was the simple, powerful question that presidential candidate Ronald Reagan asked voters in his televised debate with soon-to-be ex-president Jimmy Carter in October 1980. Voters responded with a resounding "no" that carried Reagan to the White House in a landslide election.

In 1980, the United States was in the midst of a recession that followed almost a decade of bad economic news. The rising inflation, high unemployment, and stagnant wages of the 1970s had marked the end of a long postwar period of widespread economic security. The voters in 1980 could not have known that things would get worse before they got better: over the next two years, earnings inequality spiked to levels not seen since the Great Depression as the rich got richer, the poor got poorer, and everyone else had to work harder to maintain their standard of living. In 1984, when Reagan easily won a second term as president, he campaigned on the hope that things were about to get better with a television advertisement that began:

> It's morning again in America. Today more men and women will go to work than ever before in our country's history. With interest rates at about half the record highs of 1980, nearly two thousand families today will buy new homes, more than at any time in the past four years. This afternoon 6,500 young men and women will be married, and with inflation at less than half of what it was just four years ago, they can look forward with confidence to the future.[1]

A good job. Homeownership. A happy family with high hopes for the future. This was the American Dream.

But the American Dream is also more than that. As Sarah Churchwell explains in her book *Behold, America*, the term "American Dream" was coined by the historian James Truslow Adams in 1931 as he reflected on the economic crisis of the Great Depression and the sociopolitical crisis that he feared would follow.[2] Adams observed that the United States had lost its way in valuing material success above collective moral character and well-being. He wrote of the American Dream: "It is not a dream of motor cars and high wages merely, but a dream of a social order in which each man and each woman shall be able to attain to the fullest stature of which they are innately capable, and be recognized by others for what they are, regardless of the fortuitous circumstances of birth or position."[3]

This is the conception of the American Dream—one encompassing not only economic security but also equal opportunity—that President Barack Obama invokes in his memoir *The Audacity of Hope*. Addressing the Democratic National Convention in 2004, then-senator Obama invoked the values of tolerance and generosity that he saw as central to the promise of America:

> My parents shared not only an improbable love, they shared an abiding faith in the possibilities of this nation. They would give me an African name, Barack, or "blessed," believing that in a tolerant America your name is no barrier to success. They imagined me going to the best schools in the land, even though they weren't rich, because in a generous America you don't have to be rich to achieve your potential.

In what would become a signature part of his stump speech while campaigning for president, Obama stated, "I stand here knowing that my story is part of the larger American story, that I owe a debt to all of those who came before me, and that, in no other country on earth, is my story even possible."[4]

What does the American Dream mean now? At this moment, our political institutions feel broken and our economy feels stuck. In the 2020 presidential campaign, President Donald Trump weaponized calls to "Make America Great Again" with a more explicit discourse of racial resentment and xenophobia than Americans had seen in the mainstream for a generation, and then President Joe Biden waged a campaign in 2021 calling on Americans to "Build Back Better" with social and economic infrastructure investments at a level not seen since the New Deal. Both campaigns appealed to the American Dream to convey the sense that something good has been lost, but the two presidents presented drastically different visions of how to move toward it.

For the Black and White men and women we spoke with in the summer of 2015, the American Dream was a value system that emphasizes personal responsibility and hard work in the form of educational attainment. What about the white picket fence, the happy family, and the economic security of the good life? Those cultural components of the Dream are alive and well, but they remain more dream than reality for many Americans, and even those who own homes and have high incomes feel insecure.

Those in the vanishing middle—middle-aged workers, like our participants, whose income and investments in education would probably have
made them solidly middle class in the postwar period—today cling to the
promise of education as a key to success, not because they are certain that
it will unlock the American Dream, but because they see it as the only way
to hedge their bets in an unpredictable and uncertain world.

For White Americans, education is their best tool for recapturing the
opportunities they recall being available to their parents. Even without the
same historical access to opportunity in their families, Black Americans
nevertheless turn to education as the best way to get ahead and navigate
the enduring racial inequalities they confront in the workplace. For both
groups, the postindustrial period is filled with frustration and pessimism.
Pessimism runs at somewhat higher levels, however, among White
workers, whose current economic insecurity stems from the paradigm
shift driving the racial futures paradox: despite their comparatively more
stable economic circumstances than those of Black Americans, White
Americans tend to be more tentative about the potential for improvement
in the future, while Black Americans, who are in much more objectively
challenging economic straits, tend to be more optimistic that brighter
days lie ahead.

We wish to interject a provocative, and perhaps counterintuitive, observa-
tion into the ongoing debate over opportunity, security, and the American
Dream. Among policymakers and the public alike, *Americans talk too
much about education*. Conceiving of success and failure mainly in terms of
educational attainment puts all of the burden on the individual. Besides
implicating people in their own failures, this conception also encourages
them, when they fall short, to direct their blame toward less deserving
others. At a societal level, conceiving of success and failure mainly in
terms of educational attainment simply asks too much of our schools,
which we expect to fix a wide array of problems that are fundamentally
rooted in our workplaces, labor markets, and political institutions. In short,
resources are directed only at education, which has become an arena
for determining moral worth and deservingness and in which existing
inequalities are legitimated.

What would it take to restore some measure of security to the promise of
the American Dream? Americans, including the vanishing middle, want
the game of life to be fair. Our participants provided plenty of ideas for
what a just society could look like. They articulated a clear role for the
government in ensuring that all Americans can realistically aspire to the
American Dream, even as they emphasized the importance of personal
responsibility. They all found common ground on the ideal of a meritocratic America, but opinions about how to get ahead in a meritocracy
continued to diverge along racial lines, depending on how each participant understood their current and past access to opportunity. Black

participants emphasized the need for more to be done to address the problems of unequal access, while White participants emphasized the need for more opportunities for all Americans, skirting the question of ongoing racial imbalance.

In this final chapter, we discuss some ways to address the insecurity that both Black and White workers experience in the current economic context, including ways to reduce the unequal access that continues to fall along racial and gender lines. We explain that focusing less on education as the key to opening the door to the Dream would allow greater attention to the mechanisms that actually create economic opportunity and security. As the people we spoke to for this book made clear, the current structures are not working for most Americans, and it is time to rethink ways to achieve the American Dream. The institutions that created economic security after the Great Depression were established to meet the threat of systemic crisis, both political and economic. Today the foundations of our capitalist democracy are no less at risk than they were in the 1930s. Now, as then, making change requires an acknowledgment of what is at stake and a willingness to tackle head-on the politics of racial resentment that fuels division.

Toward a Just Society: Different Ideas about How to Achieve a Common Ideal

This book has outlined how people's access to opportunity in the United States has shaped their understanding of current economic insecurity and of the American Dream as a guiding economic and cultural myth. Although both Black and White workers put significant emphasis on meritocracy to explain success, there remain notable differences between them in their understanding of the American meritocracy when faced with the realities of unequal access, both historic and present-day. This pattern—sharing the ideal but diverging in their understanding of what the broader society needs to do to make the ideal more obtainable—is also present in middle-aged workers' vision for a "just society." Both Black and White workers point to the importance of meritocracy in their estimation of a just society, but they diverge in their conceptualizations of how systems should change to actually be meritocratic. These differences follow the patterns of racial divergence already discussed, and they highlight the complex influence of race and historic access to the American Dream on people's understanding of their struggles today.

Black workers' emphasis on meritocracy for achieving a just society was evident in the responses of both men and women. For example, Tanesha, the Black teacher introduced in chapter 3 who said that with determination anyone can escape the projects, described her "utopia" as simply one that enables "everyone to be on an equal playing field." Tony, the Black bus driver and paraprofessional educator we met in chapter 4, agreed with this idea, but added that the meritocratic ideal is achievable in the United States only if Black Americans' historical lack of access is also addressed. A just society should "be what the promise of America was set up to be," he explained, "an equal opportunity for every individual. Unfortunately, when they wrote that, every individual meant White and male. We have to broaden that scope to include everybody. Realistically speaking, an equal opportunity will be our reparations."

We asked Tony to expand on what he meant by "equal opportunity will be our reparations." He explained that he was not optimistic that other kinds of reparations will happen, and he discussed at length the obstacles to tracing one's line of descent to legitimately lay claim to such reparations. Then he clarified what he meant by equal opportunity in the context of reparations: "So, equal opportunity, or fair opportunity, and it doesn't mean close the economic divide even. It just means if I put myself in position, then I deserve to be judged on my merits, not where I come from and who I know."

Tony here sounded much more like Tanesha and many of our other Black participants who described a just society as America simply living up to its ideals. They did not condemn the idea of meritocracy, but in reflecting on what a just society requires, they acknowledged that the United States is not there yet. They critiqued specifically the pervasive racial inequality that they recognized as limiting their own and others' access to occupational opportunities.

Many of our White participants agreed with our Black participants' assessments of what America as a just society could or should look like, but they frequently avoided the issue of unequal access due to race or historical inequality and insisted that taking advantage of opportunity is up to the individual. Some also felt that the inequalities that Black American workers felt need to be addressed are likely to remain as part of the general "unfairness" that will always be part of an American meritocracy. For instance Blake, the White fitness trainer, felt that hard work pays off regardless of personal background. When reflecting on what it would take for America to be a just society, he said outright, "I don't know if there ever really could be one." He continued:

> I just feel like there are so many underlying issues that are always preventing us from really being a just society, you know what I mean? You know with the, I mean, sh—t, look at the media right now. I mean, Donald Trump is all over the place throwing his remarks about immigration and immigration issues. We have the old Black-White racial issues. You got economic inequality issues. So it's always, I just feel like somebody is always going to have something to say that it's just not fair.

Blake could name the societal issues America faces, but he saw them as structural rather than interpersonal, or as he put it, "Somebody always hav[ing] something to say." He went a step further when asked what advice he would give the president (who, in 2015, was Barack Obama). Pushing on the ideals of meritocracy once again, he said bluntly, "To tell people to stop f—king whining. I don't know. I don't—you know, I just, I don't know. It's just try to find a way to inspire people to want more for themselves, you know?"

Whereas Blake suggested crassly that people should "stop whining" and "want more for themselves," Claire, the White nurse, took a circular approach, saying that she didn't know what to do to create a just society.

This country, it's so big and so diverse. Again, being White, I feel like I have such an imperfect understanding of what it is to be not White in this country. I know what my—the small number of Black friends that I do have, I know what they tell me. I know what I read online. I know what I observe, like at the hospital or just in day-to-day life. But I feel like I don't have a good understanding of what it means—what the lived experience of somebody who's Hispanic or Asian or African American [is]. I only know what I've experienced. And so, yeah, I don't know. I do know enough to know that we still have huge racial problems in this country and that I don't know enough about them to try to fix them. But I also know enough to trust that people in these communities of color are smart and motivated and that they would like to find solutions to make their communities better. And if I'm told what I need to do, I'm willing to do it. I have very limited power, and I sort of feel like—I don't know. I feel very helpless and very ignorant and very—I'm happy to help. I just don't know what to do, and I sort of feel like an asshole for being White. Sorry.

Claire was confident that "people in these communities of color are smart and motivated" to create solutions for a just society, though she herself felt paralyzed and unable to participate in this effort. Yet the change she imagined will come from individuals, and only from people of color and others whose lived experience gives them insights into injustice. Her conclusion that she needed to be "told what to do" and was "helpless" is particularly striking given that she described herself as "incredibly privileged" as a result of her educational background and family resources. Although Claire was quite opinionated throughout the interview when discussing the challenges of insecure workers—like her husband's inability, despite holding a PhD, to "[earn] more than like $20,000 in a calendar year"—she was silent on broader inequality. After engaging throughout the interview with the reality of profound racial inequality, these silences of both Claire and Blake were striking. Although they could articulate racial disparities in need of remedy, they could not envision what those remedies would look like.

Instead of engaging with the issue of racial inequality, Claire turned the magnifying glass inward, ending in guilt sharing: "I feel like an asshole for being White." Most of our White participants, however, simply focused on the familiar narratives of individualism for achieving a more just society. For instance, Peter, a fifty-three-year-old White business owner, argued that a just American society would take not only time but also more ideological and political change. He was fairly certain that the United States would never turn toward socialism, because that would not be in alignment with American identity and would "be just giving up too much of what America is about from the American Dream and the opportunity." Rather, like Blake, he said that it comes down to the individual, not the government. "Become a little bit more informed, have an opinion, let your opinion be heard, vote. I think there are too many people that are just disengaged. 'Well, our government did this to me. Well, the government did that to me.' It's like, 'Oh, did you vote in the last election?' 'No.' Stop complaining!" Spencer, the White marketer, also advised against putting the onus on officials, saying, "It's not going to be just me pointing a finger at the government because it takes everyone."

Although many of our White participants, like Spencer, believed that all Americans must play their role to make the country fair, some of our White participants observed that not everyone who takes advantage of opportunity sees the same results. Take the attempt of Susan, the White clinical psychologist we met earlier, to explain the relationship between opportunity and outcome:

> If the input is the same and the outcome is different, then that doesn't feel just. So I guess outcome is a part of it. But the opportunity and outcome. Like, there's a part of me that still values, like, you have to do your part too. It's the individual responsibility. I'm not saying that part is not part of opportunity. It's just, if everyone has the same opportunities, [then] two people who kind of do the same work [should] have the same outcome.

For Susan, individual responsibility would always be the catalyst for opportunity, but she struggled to explain what happens when the outcomes are different. Like the other White participants quoted here, she put little to no emphasis on the structural forces that produce vulnerability.

Callie, the White truancy officer, outreach worker, and freelancer we met earlier, began to see that structures like education can be inherently inequitable by focusing on a comparison between two different areas of the neighboring city—Greenwood, which is urban and largely poor, and Brenton, which is suburban and wealthy. As she observed:

> There would have to be universal education and day care, and our public schools would have to have some uniformity if you go into Greenwood. It's not the same public school that you're seeing in Brenton, because then,

all things equal, your five-year-old and my five-year-old would be starting with the same level. So race then would become not an important, not significant, not attributing factors, because all those things would still take place. You still have for generations your grandfather was a slave, but at least today in this moment you'd have equal opportunity.

Once equal opportunity has been established, Callie maintained, America will be a just society because people can act on their personal responsibility to take advantage of that opportunity.

In the context of existing structural inequality in the United States for many Black participants, however, a "just society" is impossible. For Shantelle, the Black tutor we met in chapter 4, the unequal distribution of wealth in America makes a just society a pipe dream.

There's never going to be equality like that because it depends who's looking at it and who has the quote-unquote money, power, and decision-making ability. You know, if I'm struggling, working hard, and the neighbor's struggling hard and working hard, and the person upstairs is struggling hard and working hard, and you got so many millions to send to all these other places, there's something wrong with the picture, you know? And I guess, according to the Bible, the poor will always be among us, but they ain't got to be so dirt poor that they die, you know?

In Shantelle's view, becoming a just society requires wrestling with power imbalances and economic inequality to create a system in which the wealthy can "help."

Many of our Black and White participants endorsed meritocracy and personal responsibility as ideals for American society. But because of their divergent experiences along racial lines in accessing the fruits of meritocracy and personal responsibility, they had different ideas about how to address inequality. To create a just society, our Black participants pointed to the need for structural change that would disrupt contemporary inequality by intentionally addressing the history of unequal access by race. But even as they focused on the need for structural change, their emphasis on meritocracy continued to lead them into a complex contradiction. As discussed in earlier chapters, educated workers in particular increasingly find that their credentials do not provide security, and non-White educated workers also find that racial inequality remains an obstacle to accessing work. And yet, as this book also shows, these same workers still believed in the basic logic of the American Dream: hard work and education are the keys to future success. The contradiction between this still widely held belief and Americans' lived experience is one that meritocracy by itself is unlikely to resolve.

Although some White participants, in emphasizing personal responsibility, eschewed a role for the government and pushed for a "free market" solution, even Adam Smith's 1776 classic formulation of the benefits of a "free market" identified a government responsibility to maintain public institutions, including education.[5] Some White participants, however, did articulate a clear role for the government in ensuring that all Americans can realistically aspire to the American Dream, even as they more frequently emphasized personal responsibility and avoided discussions of inequality as a barrier to a meritocratic society. The commonalities between White and Black participants' ideas point to several potential policy solutions, from wealth redistribution and enforcement of equal opportunity law to a shift in our economic system that would establish an economic floor and ensure minimum standards of well-being for all workers. Like the larger American public, our participants did not all see eye to eye on these measures. But they did agree that *the game of life should be fair*. Let's take a moment to consider what that might mean.

"The Game of Life," the classic American board game, was developed by Milton Bradley in the 1860s. Generations of Americans have played one version of this game or another. While the challenges and opportunities the game offers have changed over time, its basic structure has remained the same: players spin the dial to learn what spaces they will land on as they progress through "life." The game's subtext is essentially that life is composed of choices and luck, and while we cannot control the spaces where we land, we can control the choices we make about what comes next. That message resonates with Americans' distinctly individualistic frames of merit and opportunity. "Life" is also a game with a clear moral perspective on right and wrong: Bradley designed the game to teach players that the right choices can lead to success and the wrong choices will lead to despair.

"The Game of Life" brings players to one fork in the road that represents the single most important decision they will make: Do you want to take the college path, or do you want to step right into a job?[6] Compared with the job track, choosing the college path entails taking on debt, but also gaining access to higher-paying jobs. College is no guarantee of success, since the number a player spins with each turn most directly shapes what spaces they land on, but the game leaves little doubt that the college path is better than the alternative. In the board game as in real life, the focus on education is located within an invisible and unpredictable set of larger circumstances. Education is the key because it is a way to hedge one's bets in what is fundamentally seen as a game of chance.

But what if it were possible to make success in the labor market predictable, and not just a game of chance? To make work actually pay? In reality, where we land is not only about the luck of the draw. The real game of life in the United States is set up to favor the few at the expense of the many. For decades Americans have looked almost exclusively to educational institutions to solve a wide range of social problems, at the expense of maintaining other civic institutions that are necessary to ensure not just equal opportunity but also shared security and the sense that hard work is rewarded.[7] In this time of increasing vulnerability to economic insecurity across the educational spectrum, and even among White men, coupled with relative advantages across racial and gender lines remaining unchanged, ensuring equal opportunity and nondiscrimination will not be enough.

Although Black and White workers point to similar visions of the just society, economic insecurities and enduring racial inequalities push people to imagine solutions through divergent lenses, depending on how they interpret their overall access to opportunity. Because both groups remain firm believers in the American Dream overall, they emphasize similar meritocratic ideas. But as educational attainment becomes increasingly unattached to economic security and structural inequalities in income and occupational opportunity persist across both race and gender groups, our participants encounter significant obstacles to actually achieving their vision of a just society.

The full promise of the American Dream cannot be realized without ensuring dignity in working conditions, decent pay, and a program for household income security.[8] But strong resistance to this idea, a foundation of which is the idea of a living wage, has always been America's challenge. Overcoming this challenge will require engaging with the public's desire for security while ensuring both fairness and freedom, and without reproducing racialized and gendered myths about who deserves to be a part of the Dream.

Disrupting Black Vulnerability: Moving beyond Nondiscrimination as Economic Fairness

In 1938, the price of a gallon of milk was higher than the minimum wage. At twenty-five cents an hour, the minimum wage had been set by the Fair Labor Standards Act during the Great Depression to ensure that workers could achieve a basic standard of living. As the impact of the Black Tuesday stock market crash in 1929 caused companies to make harsh labor decisions, like reducing salaries and workweeks, workers felt the pressure at home as they struggled to make even harder decisions, such as what would end up on the dinner table.

The federal minimum wage, initially created to give average wage workers a buffer against the realities of insecurity during dark and uncertain economic times, reached its peak in 1968, when it was able to support a family of three well above the poverty line. By the 1980s, according to the Economic Policy Institute, the minimum wage could barely support a family of two.[9] Since that time, grassroots mobilizing around the idea of a living wage—one that actually meets the cost of living to ensure a minimum standard of living—has gained traction in the Fight for $15 campaign and in a series of recent state and local measures to increase minimum wage levels.[10] Let's take a closer look at the arguments that have been leveraged against these measures.

Classically, economists have objected to raising the minimum wage because employers would cut jobs in response. Employers are motivated by sales and profit, they argue, and labor is a cost to be managed and minimized, so increasing wage rates requires employers either to increase the cost of goods or to reduce the labor needed to produce them. In 1966, the Nobel Prize–winning economist Milton Friedman opened an op-ed he penned for *Newsweek* on minimum wage rates with the following statement: "Congress has just acted to increase unemployment. It did so by raising the legal minimum-wage rate from $1.25 to $1.60 an hour. . . . The result will be and must be to add to the ranks of the unemployed." Although the intent of the minimum wage laws was to create and sustain a universal economic living standard for all workers, Friedman argued that "the intended beneficiaries" (low-paid and unskilled workers) would probably end up "not employed at all."[11]

In 1966, those workers were overwhelmingly Black and overwhelmingly women and teenagers—young entrants into the labor market. This intersection, and the expected impact on Black teenagers in particular, led Friedman to label the federal minimum wage as the most "anti-Negro law on our statute books—in its effect not its intent." He continues:

> It is a tragic but undoubted legacy of the past—and one we must try to correct—that on the average Negroes have lower skills than Whites. Similarly, teenagers are less skilled than older workers. Both Negroes and teenagers are only made worse off by discouraging employers from hiring them. On-the-job training—the main route whereby the unskilled have become skilled—is thus denied them.[12]

It is telling that Friedman focused his critique on teenagers; one of the key changes in the U.S. labor market from the time of his writing to today is the increasing share of adults who rely on minimum wage work.[13] At the root of Friedman's critique, however, is the distinction between wage rates and income. Support for wage rates is grounded in the mistaken belief, he argues, that raising the wage rate will help the poor. Friedman firmly believed, given the prevailing capitalist economic system and employer motivations, that it would not. Pointing to the idea that the root problem is not the wage rate but employment itself, Friedman explains:

> It has always been a mystery to me to understand why a youngster is better off unemployed at $1.60 an hour than employed at $1.25. Moreover, many workers in low wage brackets are supplementary earners—that is, youngsters

who are just getting started or elderly folk who are adding to the main source of family income. *I favor governmental measures that are designed to set a floor under family income.* Legal minimum-wage rates only make this task more difficult.[14]

Friedman concluded that the federal minimum wage, which was intentionally created to serve as a safety net for the economically vulnerable, in effect only deepened the divide between the haves and have-nots as unemployment rose. The conservative economist Mark Perry revisited Friedman's 1966 claims in 2016 and found that his predictions were "pretty accurate": the excess teenage jobless rate had risen to nearly 12 percent by June 1971, compared to 8 percent in early 1967.[15] Tracking trends in jobless rates by race from when they are first available in January 1972 is revealing and devastating. Perry found that the average jobless rate for Black male teens over the previous forty-five years was 36.7 percent and was as high as 58.1 percent in June 1982.

For the Black and White middle-aged participants in our study, born between 1960 and 1980, the labor market that emerged out of these policy changes was the one they faced as teenagers. Between the 1970s and 1990s, the labor market was at a critical juncture, as it was transforming from the manufacturing model of the postwar economy to the service economy of the postindustrial era. Despite the job gains for women and Black workers, during this period the economy was moving rapidly toward less secure employment structures. Our participants lived through that transformation and bore its scars, both in their employment histories and in their fears for their children and the future. Although the impact of race on equal employment opportunity in the postindustrial era may have been disputed by our White participants, its decisive impact on unemployment is beyond refute. Looking again at Black male teens, since 1972 through November 2016, Perry found, their jobless rate "has been above 30% in 468 out of 539 months, or 86.8% of the time. . . . It's exceeded 50% in 13 months." We do not need to accept Friedman's argument on the relationship between the minimum wage and unemployment—indeed, this is a source of ongoing debate among economists—to appreciate his point about family income and the deep and enduring disparate impact of unemployment on Black Americans. Building a broad coalition for higher minimum wage rates will require attending to such arguments about the disproportionate burden of unemployment faced by Black Americans of all ages and tackling arguments about teen unemployment head-on.

Friedman laid the blame for the "shockingly high" rate of unemployment among Black teens squarely at the feet of the federal minimum wage. Yet it was not until 1966 that the federal minimum wage applied to the occupations and industries where nearly one-third of Black workers were employed, such as agriculture, restaurants, nursing homes, laundries, construction, and other services.[16] Despite Friedman's belief that it is against employers' interest to discriminate, since it narrows the labor pool and raises the cost of labor (a belief that many other economists share), employers are not neutral actors in pursuit of profit; they have in the past and continue now to act on racialized and gendered preferences, though they are often either unaware of those preferences or unwilling to acknowledge them.[17] Even today, many economists treat Black unemployment as a puzzle, noting that "lower levels of education cannot account for the size of the racial gap."[18] This confounding reality is leading the economic mainstream increasingly to acknowledge the role of discrimination as it catches up to what sociologists and some economists have long documented: race- and gender-based discrimination is a defining feature of the American labor market.[19]

In their cleverly titled 2015 report, "Umbrellas Don't Make It Rain: Why Studying and Working Hard Isn't Enough for Black Americans," the economists Darrick Hamilton, William Darity Jr., Anne Price, Vishnu Sridharan, and Rebecca Tippet chronicle the persistent legacy of Black unemployment beyond youth.

> Data from the U.S. Department of Labor shows that blacks are systemically denied access to employment. Over the past 40 years there has been only one year, 2000, in which the black unemployment rate fell below 8 percent, in contrast, there have only been four years in which the white rate has exceeded 8.0 percent. The March 2015 unemployment rate for whites is 4.7 percent, while the 10.1 percent unemployment rate for blacks is consistent with a double-digit unemployment trend that has persisted since the onset of the Great Recession. Moreover, it continues a structural trend where blacks are kept from employment roughly twice as often as whites.[20]

Such trends highlight the normalcy of vulnerability, the absence of economic security for Black Americans, and the soundness of Friedman's call for a focus on setting a floor for family income alongside the minimum wage rate. These measures, which are often described as unrealistic or pejoratively labeled "socialist," encounter deep resistance at least in part because they would disrupt purposefully produced racial inequality.[21] It is no accident that women and people of color, especially Black women, are disproportionately exposed to economic insecurity characterized by low wages and unstable access to employment. Working conditions, such as pay levels and access to benefits or steady work, are not set through race- and gender-neutral market mechanisms. Rather, they reflect historical and continuing inequalities in how society values different types of work and workers. Critical to making the game fair, making work pay, and moving toward the kind of just society that our participants discussed, one in which meritocracy can truly function, must be a renewed commitment to nondiscrimination.[22] But simply committing to nondiscrimination is not enough.

Like most Americans, our participants did not think much about who is paid what, and why, when they talked about economic security or evaluated their earnings. The public, policymakers, and many scholars see individual skills and hard work as the keys to unlocking good pay for a job well done. But the reality of who earns what and why is much more complicated, and enforcement of antidiscrimination legislation alone will not address it.[23] A vast body of scholarship shows that all human societies distribute scarce resources—such as food, status, money, and power—unequally. But how unequally those resources are distributed, and what processes or criteria are used to decide who gets what, vary enormously across places and over time. In short, societies choose the amount and type of inequality that they will have. They choose them with the institutions they create, the laws they adopt, and the policies they enforce. In the United States, the American Dream was premised on a very specific set of inequalities that amounted to cumulative advantages for White workers and cumulative disadvantages for Black workers. Although the law now forbids discrimination, much more work is needed to reach a more level playing field.

Today some people question whether national laws and policies can still impact inequality as much as they might have been able to in the past. In an increasingly global economy, one in which new workplace technologies are changing the way work is done, can societies still reduce inequalities and remain prosperous? Is rising inequality the cost that must be paid for economic growth? The sociologist Lane Kenworthy has extensively studied the relationship between inequality, economic growth, and public policy across nations.[24] In providing very clear answers to these questions, his research shows that there is no necessary trade-off between economic growth and greater equality. Further, it is possible to use public policy to maximize employment while also reducing poverty and maintaining high living standards. Measures that make work pay, support workers during periods of unemployment, offer a minimum basic income for those unable to work, and share the costs of health and childcare offer the possibility of more economic growth and less inequality. Industry-specific strategies for making work pay can generate better job opportunities for workers as well as sustainable profit levels in sectors with relatively thin margins.[25]

Labor and employment law represents another important area for action to make work pay.[26] Updated protections that reflect the organizational and technological realities of work in the twenty-first-century economy are critical, as is efficient enforcement of existing standards for union organizing, collective bargaining, and other employment rights. Large, highly profitable employers can often avoid legal compliance by paying fees and tying up claims of employment rights violations in the courts, as recent high-profile organizing efforts at Amazon well illustrate.[27] Such enforcement and compliance measures may not grab headlines, but they are a key frontier of good governance with very real material consequences for American workers.

In short, there is nothing inevitable about the historically high levels of economic inequality that we currently see in the United States. And far from driving growth, historically high levels of inequality in the United States actually serve as a drag on prosperity. Too much economic inequality is bad for democracy too. The same is true of individual health and well-being, opportunities for upward mobility, community engagement, and household stability. Viewed from any angle, high levels of inequality are bad for society.[28]

To begin to address economic inequality in the United States, and to deliver on the promise of the American Dream, we need to focus on the workplace. Sociologists who study inequality emphasize the workplace as the key site for earnings determination, and they emphasize the use of power in workplace relationships as key for understanding who gets what. At the heart of this research is the concept of exploitation: the use of power in the transfer of income from one party to another.[29] Many of the institutional features of the American labor market that produce poor working conditions have their origins in slavery and, in its aftermath, employers' desire to exploit Black labor.[30] The historian Caitlin Rosenthal, in her 2018 book *Accounting for Slavery*, details the organizational practices used on plantations to manage output and compliance among the enslaved.[31] Such practices for measuring and rewarding productivity, the sociologist Matthew Desmond argues, are recognizable in today's "low-road" American capitalism.[32]

Public policy and law set boundaries for action in the workplace, establishing pay practices that are deemed legitimate and sanctioning practices that are out of step with legislated provisions. Yet, as we discussed in chapter 1, the cornerstone of American employment policy, the Fair Labor Standards Act of 1937, reflects the racial and gender power imbalances of its time. It was written during the New Deal era to be race- and gender-neutral in theory, but in effect—and by design—its provisions have had a differential impact for women and people of color owing to persistent industrial and occupational segregation. Today we have a term for supposedly race-neutral policies and practices that differentially impact racial minorities: "systemic racism" (or "institutional racism"). If the American Dream and its promise of economic security deriving from hard work are to survive, then the rules of the game that determine fair pay need to be updated to remove racist and sexist exemptions from minimum wage and other employment standards.

The low pay and poor working conditions that we see today in the restaurant and hospitality industries and among agricultural and domestic workers are a direct result of the exclusion of classes of work based on the racial and gender composition of those industries. Low wages in occupations traditionally dominated by women, such as childcare, teaching, and retail service, derive from a process known as "devaluation": some categories of work are systematically paid less because the people who perform that work are valued less within society.[33] Throughout the labor market, the Black/White binary has served as an organizing principle of inequality through its historical impact on who is placed in which occupations and the rewards associated with favorable occupational placement. Two core workplace processes—"opportunity hoarding" and "exploitation"—were mobilized historically to generate inequalities, and they continue to do so today. These underexamined organizational practices have been naturalized over time, making the profound inequality we have observed over time durable. At the same time, however, achieving parity with the labor market experiences of White men is not a recipe for economic justice, since insecurity for all workers has increased. Measures that reduce racial and gender disparities, provide for the dignity of work, and ensure a baseline of household income security are all needed to ensure access to the American Dream for this generation and beyond.

Unpacking Insecurity: Covid-19 and the American Worker

Economic vulnerability is the new normal. Nothing has made that clearer in recent years than the impact of Covid-19 on the middle class. Prior to the pandemic, the middle class was viewed as an economic group with a meaningful degree of economic security, while the working class and the working poor were recognized as struggling and barely holding on long before the pandemic. The struggles of the working class and the working poor were normalized, and their vulnerability was served up as a cautionary tale to others: their fate awaited those who did not work hard and invest in education. As a society, we did not see those struggling economically as being among the deserving, as people who had simply fallen on hard times and were legitimately in need of help. The pandemic, however, shifted the face of economic insecurity overnight.

We conducted our interviews with the seventy-nine middle-aged workers in 2015, several years prior to the pandemic. In many ways the pandemic brought to life the fears of our participants, but on a scale they could not have imagined. Headline after headline spoke to the difficulties and financial ruin resulting from unprecedented rates of unemployment. On August 6, 2020, the American labor market struck a devastating note: the first week of August marked the "20th straight week," the Labor Department reported, "that at least 1 million people sought jobless aid."[34] Even during the Great Recession from 2007 to 2009, jobless claims did not exceed 700,000 a week. The pandemic had led to an unmatched crisis in joblessness. Traditionally, to qualify for federal benefits, an applicant had to be looking for work. Obviously, the Covid-19 pandemic was different: as one economist pointed out, "there are many people that are not actually looking because they're taking the advice of health experts in this country. . . . Maybe they're caring for children right now, whose schools are closed."[35] In recognition, the Cares Act, passed in March 2020, required only that applicants for supplemental unemployment and rental assistance show that they had lost income or employment due to the pandemic, and it extended onetime stimulus payments that aimed relief toward those most in need.[36]

Covid-19's radical upset of the American economy prompted officials to summon the political will for intervention. As millions of Americans faced the prospect of job loss and the high possibility of furloughs, the government unveiled a $484 billion stimulus package that gave small businesses as well as ordinary Americans temporary relief that would soften the economic blow from the pandemic. For most Americans, the stimulus check enabled them to pay rent. In Chicago, for instance, the $1,200 stimulus check enabled more than 70 percent of tenants to pay their rent in full, though, on average, just under $100 was left for anything else.[37] The average grocery bill alone for Chicagoans is $397 per month.[38]

Struggling to meet these basic needs has increased dependence on food stamps, locally run food pantries, and thrift stores across a growing cross-section of the United States for years. But prior to the pandemic, people's struggle to meet basic needs was not a subject of serious policy discussion, much less on the list for direct intervention. In fact, in 2019, funding for the Supplemental Nutrition Assistance Program (SNAP, or food stamps) was on the table to be cut.[39] We had accepted and normalized the suffering and uncertainty experienced by vast numbers of women and children living in poverty and written off able-bodied adults who were unable, for a wide variety of reasons, to make ends meet. State-sponsored pandemic relief provided a lifeboat in an ongoing sea of uncertainty for working-class Americans. But the pandemic hit below the economic belt of the income spectrum, causing people across economic classes to recognize the scope of their own insecurity and providing a window into the challenges that had plagued the long-term unemployed long before the pandemic.

Highly skilled laborers in esteemed white-collar jobs discovered their vulnerability during the pandemic. Jobs that were once thought impossible to perform remotely were nevertheless done remotely. Though low-income and working-class jobs in service industries were immediately impacted in March 2020, layoffs in thousands of white-collar workers were announced as the pandemic and the resultant economic slump dragged on.[40] Those who were fortunate enough to keep their jobs had to adjust to telecommuting becoming the new normal. They recognized that unemployment might be just a phone call or an email away, since short-term labor strategies to enable work continuity during the pandemic were accelerating changes in work itself.

Speculation has already begun about the long-term impacts of Covid-19 on the organization of work. For instance, observers are considering whether the disruptions of the pandemic will accelerate automation or signal permanent labor market shifts.[41] The turn toward insecure work as corporations have adopted flexible organizational strategies, such as outsourcing, temporary or contract employment, and layoffs, has already reminded all workers of the uncertainty of their fate.[42] Insecurity, which has spread among everyone in a workplace, benefits a mostly absent, invisible owner class (including shareholders) whose wealth skyrocketed, by as much as 54 percent, during the pandemic.[43]

As we start to imagine recovery from the pandemic, the fault lines of racial and gender inequality continue to haunt us. As President John F. Kennedy signed the Equal Pay Act of 1963, he observed,

> The lower the family income, the higher the probability that the mother must work, I believe they bear the heaviest burden of any group in our nation. Where the mother is the sole support of the family, she must often face the hard choice of either accepting public assistance or taking a position at a pay rate which averages less than two thirds of the pay rate for men.

When Kennedy spoke these words, women who worked full-time and year-round earned fifty-nine cents for every dollar a man made.[44] In 2009, when President Obama signed the Lilly Ledbetter Fair Pay Act with bipartisan support, the pay gap for women working full-time and year-round stood at seventy-eight cents.[45] In 2021, nearly six decades after the 1963 legislation was signed, the gap has yet to be closed; women now make only eighty-two cents for each dollar a man earns.[46] Black women have been particularly affected: because they earned only sixty-three cents for each dollar a man earned in 2019, it would take them nineteen months to match the twelve-month earnings of the average White man. This was the pre-pandemic economic reality for Black women—hard work and fewer rewards.[47]

The pandemic illuminated that, like the disparities in deaths resulting from Covid-19, economic vulnerability is universal, but impact is not. Women found themselves once again "bearing the heaviest burden of any group" in the nation as job shortages and childcare demands from school closures forced them to cut their losses. A census survey revealed stark inequalities between men and women: 28 percent of unemployed mothers said that they had stopped working owing to lack of childcare, whereas fewer than half that number of fathers (12 percent) were out of work for the same reason.[48] Overall, more than 2.3 million women experienced job loss as a result of the pandemic, and women lost more jobs than men in 2020. In fact, in December 2020, when the economy lost 140,000 jobs, all of them were held by women.[49]

Prior to the pandemic, women's labor market experiences were racially disparate. Black women had experienced unemployment rates that were double or nearly double those of White women for decades. The disparities in the employment experiences of Black and White women had shaped their vulnerability prior to the pandemic, and recent data show that these disparities are now shaping an uneven recovery. Jobs were added in 2021, but the recovery has been slower for minority women compared to their White counterparts. The March 2021 jobs report found contradictory trends by race: the unemployment rate for White women declined, while the unemployment rate for Black women increased.[50] Examining these trends by gender shows that the pandemic has been tougher on Black women, whose total employment was 9.7 percent lower in March 2021 than it was in February 2020 (before Covid-19), compared to White women, whose employment was reduced by 5.4 percent; moreover, Black women's decrease in employment was the highest of all the racial-ethnic and gender groups observed. Kate Bahn, an economist at the Washington Center for Equitable Growth, commented on these trends: "Whoever was hit the hardest takes the longest to recover. . . . Once we are long into the recovery, employment levels and income levels may not fully recover for years."[51]

Black women entered the pandemic at a distinct economic and labor market disadvantage compared with other groups. They are more likely to be unmarried and less likely to own their own home. Though highly educated comparatively, they are unlikely to receive rewards commensurate with their education. For Black women, the labor market has never been "good." They have labored and sustained themselves and their families through both boom periods and recessions, and financial instability is a way of life. The deterioration of the social safety net and the reliance on the language of personal responsibility—as if not taking responsibility is the obstacle to the financial independence of Black women—belie this fact.

The Path Forward: Policy Prescriptions for the United States

In his January 2021 inauguration speech, President Biden affirmed his commitment to supporting access to the American Dream by working to "put people to work in good jobs . . . reward work, rebuild the middle class . . . and deliver on racial justice." Yet he acknowledged the real fears fueling divisiveness in this moment: "I understand," he said, "that many Americans view the future with some fear and trepidation. I understand they worry about their jobs, and taking care of their families, about what comes next."[52] This understanding of the depth of the need, coupled with recognition that his election win was fueled by the broadest and most diverse coalition in history, set in motion an ambitious and historic policy agenda to "Build Back Better" by naming the structural weaknesses and inequalities of old that limited full participation in economic and social life and investing in a "three-part agenda to rescue, recover, and rebuild the country."[53]

In 2021, policymakers grappled with the racism and sexism inscribed in our nation's labor market policies and considered legislation to improve economic security and access to the American Dream. The Raise the Wage Act, which would increase the federal minimum wage to $15 an hour, would increase pay for approximately 32 million American workers, 59 percent of whom are women, including 3.4 million Black women and 4 million Latinas.[54] The Protecting the Right to Organize (PRO) Act, also under consideration before Congress, would make it easier for workers to form labor unions by, among other provisions, imposing monetary penalties on employers that violate workers' rights, forbidding employer interference in union organizing campaigns, neutralizing the negative effects of state right-to-work laws on organizing efforts, and preventing employers from using employees' immigration status against them in determining the terms of their employment.[55] At the close of 2021, the Build Back Better legislation appeared to be stalled by divisions among Democratic senators, even though failing to pass the bill into law was projected to negatively affect GDP.[56]

Although Congress continues to debate these and other measures to advance racial-ethnic, gender, and economic justice in the American labor market, some observers have noted that substantial progress can be made through presidential executive orders and administrative regulations. Executive orders that set higher pay, better working conditions, and antidiscrimination requirements for federal government contractors have historically produced enduring and widespread changes in the regulation of work. Heidi Shierholz, a senior economist at the Economic Policy Institute, estimates that if President Biden were to exercise his authority to set conditions for federal contractors by raising their wage floor to $15 an hour, at least 250,000 Americans would be affected.[57]

Janelle Jones, the top economist in the Biden administration's Labor Department and the first Black woman to ever hold her position, coined the phrase "Black Women Best" early in her career "as a way to gauge the health of the economy through the lens of whether Black women and other marginalized groups are thriving."[58] Speaking with National Public Radio's Ayesha Rascoe, Jones explained that "this philosophy is not about putting one group above another, but instead about making sure that people are not left behind."[59] This approach has the potential to address multiple and intersecting vulnerabilities in ways that advance economic security more broadly.

The pandemic has exposed racialized and gendered fault lines in access to good jobs, as well as the centrality of care work to the overall economic and social health of the nation. There are signs that the Biden administration's economic proposals appreciate the policy interconnections between economic security, racial justice, and gender equity. The American Jobs Plan, which includes provisions to use federal dollars to support home- and community-based services for older adults and people with disabilities, conceptualizes care work as part of a nation's critical infrastructure in ways that will improve wages, benefits, and stability for workers in those fields.[60] The journalist Emily Peck notes that this is a departure for policymakers, who have ignored childcare issues in the past. "The Biden administration and its allies are pushing the notion that caring for children—and the sick and the elderly—is just as crucial to a functioning economy as any road, electric grid or building. It's human infrastructure, they argue, echoing a line of thought long articulated by feminist economists (and often ignored)."[61]

Insecurity is not new, but its ubiquity across the income spectrum is. Addressing it requires a renewed focus on individuals (embedded in families) who are insecure along multiple dimensions. The policy interventions offered by the Biden administration, which offer a multipronged approach to addressing compounding insecurity and the acute challenges it presents, could have a transformative impact on individuals and families.

How can policymakers move forward with an ambitious and potentially transformative legislative agenda in a period of partisan gridlock, intraparty divisions, and a polarized electorate? Here we think the perspectives shared by our participants are instructive. Like many Americans, when the educated middle-aged workers we spoke with in 2015—the "vanishing middle"—thought about inequality and opportunity, no matter whether they were Black or White, they focused on schools. Public education plays a vital role in democracy. As school closures and remote learning showed during much of 2020 and the spring of 2021, schools are among the most important institutions that keep our families, communities, and workplaces running smoothly. As a society, we turn to our schools to keep our children safe, to ensure that kids get the nutrition and exercise they need to stay healthy, and to keep them busy while parents are doing other things, including working. But most importantly, we expect our schools to give kids access to the skills and knowledge they need to build a good life, which starts with preparation for college.

Today, as we discussed in chapter 3, there is a large and growing earnings gap between those with at least a four-year college education and everyone else (figure 3.1). It's no wonder that education is front and center in the minds of the vanishing middle and for Americans in general: the stakes of being on the wrong side of the educational divide have never been greater. Yet as our participants' experiences made plain, educational attainment does not guarantee high wages or secure employment. As important as education is to personal growth and fulfillment, democratic citizenship, and economic productivity, ensuring universal access to high-quality education will not reduce economic insecurity because there are not enough good jobs or sources of stable income to go around. Schools provide tools that individuals use in the competition for access to good jobs, but they do not determine how many good jobs are available, or what kinds of social supports exist outside of paid employment. Though schools are perhaps our most visible institution that impacts inequality, schools cannot do it all. A society's invisible policy choices—such as labor and housing market regulation, financial support for higher education, and state welfare programs—play a more direct role, as Claude Fischer and his colleagues argue in *Inequality by Design: Cracking the Bell Curve Myth*.[62] To advance structural changes that will increase security, we need a public discourse on opportunity and fairness that underscores the role of these core institutions, starting with the workplace.

There are multiple reasons to center the workplace in efforts to build a good society and shore up the foundations of our economic and political systems. As sociologists of work have long observed, work represents an important source of identity creation and meaning-making in people's lives. The workplace is a key site for developing social relationships, including those that reach across the class, racial-ethnic, and other boundaries of social difference that increasingly organize our communities outside of work. In addition to being the focus of our efforts to achieve economic security, the workplace is where we evaluate the efficacy and basic fairness of our economic institutions. Building workplaces that can deliver on the American Dream's promise of both security and fairness is critical for social stability, and doing so may even create the space for renewed individual investments in our civic institutions and community life outside of work.

The perspectives of the vanishing middle also remind us that the American Dream is about more than getting a good job, owning a home, and having a happy family. It is more than the promise of fairness and equal opportunity. Our participants' views of a just society also centered the values of self-reliance and personal independence. As the historian Steven Gillon has argued, however, these ideals that draw on a Jeffersonian version of the American Dream—"owning enough land to guarantee economic self-sufficiency and personal independence"—are fueling partisanship.[63] This Jeffersonian vision of the American Dream centers freedom and choice, not simply the economic and cultural aspirations with which most Americans are familiar, as objects of desire. A focus on economic and cultural aspirations is critical to the progressive policy agenda, which aims to secure economic stability for individuals, as opposed to merely enabling them to have the freedom to determine their own life course.

Today, however, this agenda, as reflected in Build Back Better, is alienating Republicans and independents as well as some Democrats.

Yet, as we discussed in chapter 1, President Franklin D. Roosevelt, in promoting his Economic Bill of Rights in 1944, argued that personal freedom rests on economic security. Democratic politicians and policymakers who do not consider the interconnectedness of Roosevelt's "Four Freedoms"—freedom of speech, freedom of worship, freedom from want, and freedom from fear—in the discourse they build around progressive legislation are not likely to be successful.[64] Take, for instance, Senator Joe Manchin's stated opposition, on September 30, 2021, to President Biden's Build Back Better legislation: "I'm just not . . . I cannot accept our economy or basically our society moving toward an entitlement mentality . . . because I can help those who are going to need help if those who can help themselves do so."[65]

Framing policies that aim to create economic stability for families as an entitlement that disincentivizes those who can "help themselves"—as Manchin does in his comment—reemphasizes self-sufficiency as a cultural anchor for the American Dream in a way that has long been at odds with the labor market realities for low-skill workers. Today even individuals who have invested in higher education and worked hard, attempting to "help themselves," increasingly find that it is not enough. The reference to an "entitlement mentality" instead produces shame and recalls the welfare arguments of the 1990s that ended in a rejection of the role of government in creating a safety net and emphasized instead personal responsibility. Our participants at times exemplified this perspective and used deservingness as a thread to distinguish between themselves and others. Yet what is missing from the ideal of self-reliance is the necessity of having the means to accomplish it—to ensure that hard work will succeed in gaining economic security. The anxiety our participants expressed arose from their commitment to striving for the American Dream amid rising insecurity and their uncertainty that the Dream could be reached. They had bought into the cultural ideal of self-reliance but in their lived experience the connection between effort and outcome had become unpredictable.

Finally, the experiences of the vanishing middle illustrate well the complicated realities of race, gender, and class in the contemporary United States. In this book we have shown that what are often viewed as competing narratives—increasing economic insecurity among White men, on the one hand, and their enduring economic advantage relative to women and people of color, on the other hand—are both true. Our aim in this book has been to provide clear documentation and explanation of these complicated truths and to leverage the lived experiences of Black and White men and women to add nuance and context to the numbers. An effective political discourse to restore the promise of the American Dream—and support the creation of real economic security—must attend to these facts.

A Final Word

Amid continuing shifts in the structures of the U.S. labor market and economy, Americans' commitment to meritocracy has them working harder and harder to stay afloat. Recent studies have linked health complications to trends of overworking. According to a report conducted by the World Health Organization, workers who were middle-aged or older, like the participants in our study, who work over fifty-five hours per week are facing conditions like heart disease and stroke.[66] While the pandemic has exacerbated these trends, the study found that this pattern was present as early as 2016. In that year alone, more than 745,000 people died from stroke and heart disease triggered by overwork.

The promise of the American Dream is that hard work leads not only to opportunity but also to security. Yet as insecurity rises and workers, holding tight to the cultural mythology, push themselves to work harder, they end up fueling an invisible, but highly consequential, form of insecurity. The Kaiser Commission on Medicaid and the Uninsured found that the quality of health care is inextricably linked to equal opportunity. One key finding was that health-care accessibility improves workplace performance and efforts to pursue higher education. The commission's 2002 report concluded, "Better health would improve annual earnings by about 10–30 percent (depending on measures and specific health condition) and would increase educational attainment."[67] In 2014, the implementation of the Affordable Care Act (or "Obamacare") attempted to address health-care inaccessibility. During that year, uninsured rates for Blacks went down significantly, despite the persistence of structural disparities that impeded health-care access.[68]

The tension between health care and equal opportunity reveals another salient dimension of the imperceptible rise in vulnerability, particularly for our Black participants. As health researchers have documented, persistent stress has negative effects on the body (so-called weathering), including the stress of navigating systemic racism. A 2020 ProPublica report on the intersections of racial health disparities and Covid-19 mortality discusses the determination and strength required to succeed in a system that is stacked against Black men and the negative effect of this struggle on their health and well-being:

> "Typically when you study resilience in any group, and [subjects are] doing well by our typical metrics" — going to college, getting a good job, not taking drugs — "we say, 'Woo-hoo,'" University of Georgia researcher Gene Brody said. "Logically, we thought this would transfer to have health benefits." But for Black young adults trying to climb the economic ladder, they found just the opposite. "When you look under the skin, doing blood draws and using other kinds of measures, they look like their health is starting to suffer."[69]

This devastating reality has equally devastating implications. As Black Americans cling to the assurances of the American Dream and grapple with the host of impediments to achieving it, they are literally dying in the process. There is no structural accountability built into the Dream—just an assumption of individual responsibility to work for it.

As economic vulnerability defines our new normal, perhaps we can now realize the critical role of social supports for Americans going through tough times and find the political will to make the invisible policy choices that create structures of opportunity. Such structures are necessary not just during a profound and disruptive crisis like the Covid-19 pandemic, but also during the ordinary and now routine labor force disruptions that characterize modern work in the United States. Because as long as individuals are chasing job security, hustling to demonstrate deservingness, and internalizing failure, the broad coalition needed to push for change and sustain it cannot be formed. Instead, Black and White Americans will keep chasing the elusive American Dream while bemoaning the fact that it is not working for them. The reality is this: unless we redefine the American Dream to be inclusive and create not only the aspirational opportunity to achieve true economic freedom but also the means to do so, we will not live up to the ideal, the promise, or the possibility of America.

= Appendix A =

Methodological Appendix

We use a mixed-methods approach to unpack the shifting associations between economic insecurity, belief in the American Dream, and race and gender. We argue that rising insecurity has reformulated but not erased underlying racial and gender inequality, and we show how Black and White Americans on the front lines of contemporary economic restructuring are making sense of these changes.

This project was supported by a grant from the National Science Foundation (1424140), "The Rise of Insecure Work and Changes in Durable Inequality." We collected data for this project in the summer of 2015.

Qualitative Data

The postindustrial employment restructuring that began in the 1970s has unfolded at an uneven pace, targeting different types of workers at different times. In the 1980s, unionized blue-collar workers were the first to feel deep cracks in the foundations of their economic security. In the 1990s, white-collar workers became more widely affected, but higher education remained a powerful insurance policy against the effects of changing employment relations. In the 2000s, and especially following the Great Recession, neither occupational nor educational attainment effectively insulated American workers from economic risk.

This narrative of economic restructuring, while accurate, most closely captures White Americans' experiences. Black Americans' economic fortunes have been shaped by a parallel timeline of shifting occupational and educational opportunities.

Our qualitative data center the experiences of a pivotal generation born between 1960 and 1980. These workers were on a path to middle-class economic security, given their educational investments, before the structure of opportunity changed. These White and Black Americans who entered the labor force between 1980 and 2000 were ideally positioned to report from the front lines of shifting opportunities to achieve economic security and the American Dream in the post–civil rights era. We interviewed them in a medium-sized, diverse city in New England with a diversified economy anchored in health care and education, as well as manufacturing. Although it experienced a decline in manufacturing jobs in the 1980s and thereafter, the city also had job sectors that experienced growth.

We focused our attention on men and women between the ages of thirty-five and fifty-five. Having been of working age for at least a full decade, and being at least a decade away from retirement, our interviewees had witnessed changes in the rise of insecure work. Unlike those in their twenties and early thirties, middle-aged Americans are generally expected to have attained stable jobs. An absence of such stability is likely to elicit concern as well as reflection. Our middle-aged interviewees were also more likely to be married, remarried, or divorced, as well as better able to reflect on how experiences with stable and unstable employment had affected their identities and intimate relationships.

Here we focus on women's idealized expectations because they limit the possibilities of men, shaping the consequences for failing to meet the ideal in heterosexual relationships. Insomuch as women insist on adherence to the male breadwinner role, the cost to men for their inability to fill that role remains high. The majority of White women were married (twelve), divorced and cohabitating (two), or otherwise partnered (one); only four out of nineteen were single and never married.[1] The majority of Black women were single and never married (eleven), although a substantial number were married (six), partnered (four), or divorced (two).

Participants were recruited to take part in our Changing Economy Research Study, which we described as a one-on-one conversation to discuss the changes in the economy and how those changes had affected them personally, on the job and at home. Potential participants were told that they would receive $30 as compensation for completing an interview lasting one and a half to two hours, at the location of their choice. We developed paper flyers and circulated Facebook ads that featured the question, "Is it easy or difficult to get ahead?" We invited respondents to participate in our study if they answered "yes" to the following questions: (1) Are you between the ages of thirty-five and fifty-five? (2) Do you have at least some college education? (3) Is your household income $30,000 or more? and (4) Are you Black/African American or White?

Given the specificity in terms of educational background and income mix that we hoped to reach in our participants, we utilized a varied and targeted approach. In our initial recruitment phase, we mailed letters (followed by phone calls) to recipients whom we identified from registered voter lists within census tracts, with enhancements that included information on race and household income. We expanded our recruitment strategy to include direct recruitment of participants through organizations that were likely to draw men and women of these ages and class and racial backgrounds, including churches, professional organizations, volunteer organizations, and social clubs. We also visited typical hangout spots, such as coffee shops. We utilized snowball sampling, asking each interviewee to provide names of one or two men and/or women whom they saw as a person like themselves but who was at the periphery of their social network. Further, we incentivized the recommendation by offering participants an additional $5 for each person they recommended if they completed the interview.

Since we were targeting a narrow slice of the middle-aged population—individuals who had at least some college education and family incomes above the poverty line—we used a screening questionnaire that was available online but could also be used in person when recruiting participants in public places, like Panera Bread. The screening questions confirmed that the individual worked outside of the home and asked about their education level and household income. Most individuals who did not meet our targets were excluded. However, because we used a direct solicitation method of recruitment and wanted to have a specific race and gender mix of participants, we included a few participants who were younger than thirty-five as well as a few who were unemployed or underemployed. In the analysis, we looked to see if their narratives differed in important ways from those of the participants who fell squarely within our target population, and they did not.

Our emphasis on race as an important lens of change and the charged racial atmosphere of the summer of 2015—which followed the Charleston massacre and featured the racial rhetoric of Donald Trump, then running for president—led us to prioritize race-matching during the interviews. Matching was particularly important if we were to have candid discussions on the impact of race with our White participants; the pressure of social desirability might have made them less likely in a conversation with a Black interviewer to share their honest views on the impact of changes in the economy on Black and White individuals. We successfully race-matched in the vast majority of interviews, but in a few cases this was not possible. The resulting qualitative sample of seventy-nine in-depth interviews with twenty-three Black women, nineteen White women, twenty Black men, and seventeen White men were conducted by a mixed-race interviewing team comprising three White interviewers (all women) and three Black interviewers (two women and one man). All interviews were conducted between June and August 2015 and ranged from one and a half to three and a half hours.

We focused on the middle-aged to investigate the extent to which the rise of insecure work has disrupted or strengthened narratives of privilege and disadvantage in access to work and we targeted the vanishing middle—those workers who are on the fault line of economic restructuring. Our participants had a minimum annual household income of $30,000, although most were much higher and some exceeded $200,000.

To explore perceptions of insecurity among those whose access to the economic stability at the heart of the American Dream had been most upended by recent restructuring trends, we were especially interested in educated workers—those whose education ranged from a minimum of some college to a terminal degree (JD, PhD, MD). People with just a high school education had long been economically insecure. The importance placed on a college education culturally and institutionally makes this distinction especially important. The vanishing middle includes those who thought their education would insulate them against market changes, and who entered a labor market in the post–civil rights era that promised de jure equality of opportunity. This is the group of largely lower-middle-class and middle-class families for whom the notion and negotiation of insecurity are most prominent.

The education levels of the participants in our qualitative sample far outpaced those of middle-aged Americans more generally (see figure 3.2; for summaries of Americans' economic and educational characteristics, see table 1.3). The vast majority—fifty-two out of the seventy-nine participants—held a college degree or higher (see table 3.2). In fact, more than one-third had a master's degree or higher. This was a highly educated group across race and gender, and as is true of the national trend, the women had higher education levels than the men. Fifty-two percent of Black women held a master's degree or higher, compared to 31 percent of Black men, while 42 percent of White women held a master's degree or higher, compared to 30 percent of White men.

We devised interview questions aimed at soliciting information about individuals' economic and emotional experiences and the narratives they used to understand them. The interviews moved across a number of topics but were anchored around four main ideas: (1) work and the meaning of a good job and a good life; (2) inequality in the United States and the impact of race on who gets what; (3) finding a job and navigating economic instability and hardship; and (4) what it means to be a good man or a good woman today. Following typical qualitative interview protocol, we began with questions we expected would be easier to answer and moved gradually into more emotional and controversial topics once rapport had been built. The interview aimed to build a complete picture of each individual's work and family background, as well as their present and expected future economic circumstances, so that in the analytical phase we could understand what produced or undergirded their perspectives on the economy, racial inequality, and whether or not they saw potential for change.

Our line of interview questioning purposefully elicited a longitudinal perspective; asking questions about experiences and aspirations over time moved us beyond naturalized cultural differences between groups and enabled us to get a better view of how previous experiences had affected the participants' present perspectives and worldviews. The resulting transcripts provide a wealth of rich data from which we interrogated the implications of economic insecurity for the family, access to work, racial inequality, and perceptions of a just society.

Our sample of middle-aged and middle-class Black and White men and women with at least some college education was well suited to our questions, in that the data from their interviews enabled us to explore the role of race and gender in shaping expectations of economic security, experiences of employment insecurity, and explanations for success and failure. Participants' lived experiences demonstrated that contemporary employment restructuring rests on racial, gender, and class narratives that legitimize insecurity and maintain inequality.

Quantitative Data

Our quantitative data allowed us to put the experiences of our qualitative sample into a larger historical context. First, we used the U.S. Census Integrated Public-Use Microdata Series (IPUMS) from 1960 to 2000 to provide a historical perspective on the period of "secure" employment that was lost as waves of postindustrial restructuring unfolded, starting in the 1970s.[2] Using an explicit race-gender lens, we showed that access to a job in the primary labor market, once a reliable marker of security, corresponded with a strict racial and gender division of labor in the postwar period, and that the recent "rise" of insecurity is better understood as a redistribution of insecurity to occupations, sectors, and workers formerly insulated from insecure work.

Second, we drew on the 2016 American Community Survey (ACS) to locate the qualitative sample of middle-class, middle-aged workers within a larger national context.[3] We sought to understand how representative our qualitative sample was of the national vanishing middle, and how the experiences of the vanishing middle compared with the experiences of those at the top and bottom of the economic distribution. Third, to clarify the nature of change over time in race, gender, work, and security we developed a cohort analysis—comparing the experiences of employment and economic security among today's postindustrial cohort (2015) with the experiences of the postwar cohort (1980), who were middle-aged during the postindustrial transition.

The detailed job histories that our qualitative interviewees gave us underscored the dynamic nature of employment insecurity. Our fourth data source was ACS data from 2001 to 2016, which we utilized to trace national trends in employment and economic security for this cohort by race and gender, seeking to contextualize the unfolding of group differences in security at different stages of the employment life cycle (that is, as people transitioned from new labor market entrants to middle-aged workers). This analysis allowed us to reflect on variations in the Great Recession's impact by race and gender.

Finally, we used the General Social Survey (GSS) to document Americans' rising perceptions of economic insecurity over time, analyzing the shifting trends by race and gender group.

= Appendix B =

Figures and Tables

Figure B.1   Annual Earnings Percentiles for Full- and Part-time Earners, by Race and Gender and by Year (2015 Dollars)

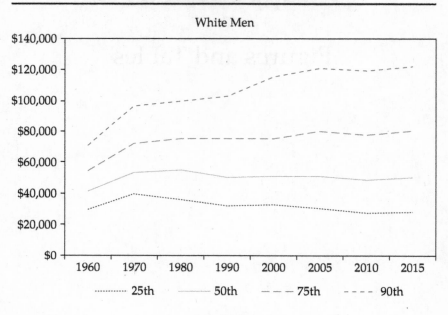

White Men

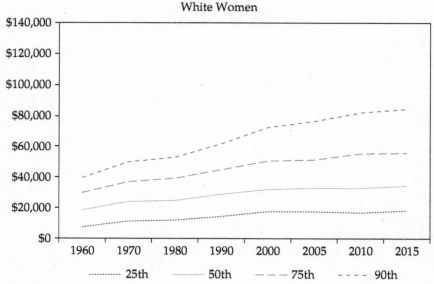

White Women

Figure B.1   Annual Earnings Percentiles for Full- and Part-time Earners, by Race and Gender and by Year (2015 Dollars) (*Continued*)

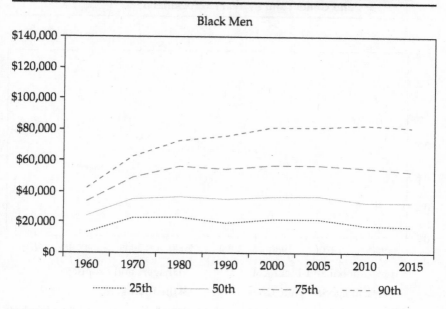

Black Men

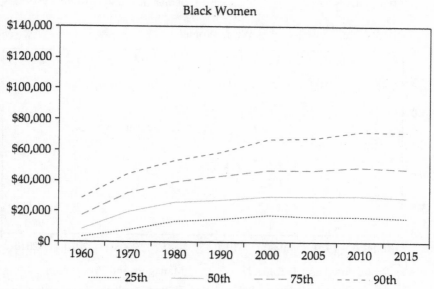

Black Women

Source: Authors' analysis of data from Integrated Public Use Microdata Series, version 7.0.

Figure B.2   Coefficient of Variation in Annual Earnings within Occupations for Full- and Part-time Earners, by Race and Gender and by Year (2015 Dollars)

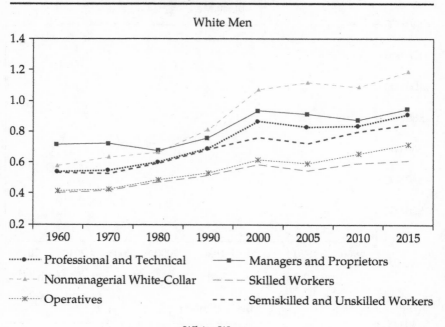

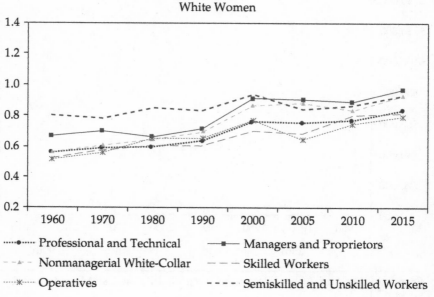

Figure B.2   Coefficient of Variation in Annual Earnings within Occupations for Full- and Part-time Earners, by Race and Gender and by Year (2015 Dollars) (*Continued*)

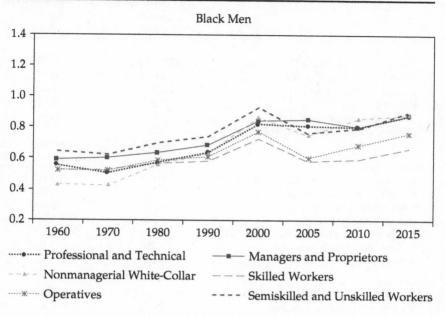

Black Men

Professional and Technical · · · · ●· · · · ·   *Managers and Proprietors* ——■——
Nonmanagerial White-Collar – – ▲ – –   *Skilled Workers* – – –
Operatives · · · ✳· · ·   *Semiskilled and Unskilled Workers* – – – –

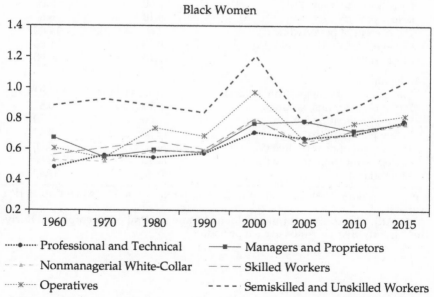

Black Women

Professional and Technical · · · · ●· · · · ·   *Managers and Proprietors* ——■——
Nonmanagerial White-Collar – – ▲ – –   *Skilled Workers* – – –
Operatives · · · ✳· · ·   *Semiskilled and Unskilled Workers* – – – –

Source: Authors' analysis of data from Integrated Public Use Microdata Series, version 7.0.

Table B.1   Postwar and Postindustrial Economic Security at Middle Age, by Race and Gender

	Postwar Cohort 1980	Postindustrial Cohort 2015
White men		
Mean annual earnings (2015 dollars)	$72,053.81	$79,809.82
Variation in annual earnings	0.614	0.987
Unemployment rate (%)	3.50	4.00
Below poverty line (%)	3.20	3.10
150 percent of poverty line (%)	6.50	6.50
College education or more (%)	25.50	38.40
Married (%)	86.10	69.40
White women		
Mean annual earnings (2015 dollars)	$30,955.83	$50,841.61
Variation in annual earnings	0.721	0.991
Unemployment rate (%)	4.30	4.00
Below poverty line (%)	3.60	4.10
150 percent of poverty line (%)	7.50	8.30
College education or more (%)	16.20	43.10
Married (%)	74.00	65.70
Black men		
Mean annual earnings (2015 dollars)	$48,171.86	$49,425.63
Variation in annual earnings	0.604	0.909
Unemployment rate (%)	7.60	9.00
Below poverty line (%)	9.10	6.60
150 percent of poverty line (%)	17.60	14.00
College education or more (%)	10.50	21.80
Married (%)	72.10	51.90
Black women		
Mean annual earnings (2015 dollars)	$31,302.41	$41,025.91
Variation in annual earnings	0.714	0.871
Unemployment rate (%)	6.60	7.50
Below poverty line (%)	13.00	10.60
150 percent of poverty line (%)	24.00	20.60
College education or more (%)	11.70	30.60
Married (%)	52.40	37.80

Source: Authors' analysis of data from Integrated Public Use Microdata Series, version 7.0.
Note: All indicators except unemployment rate are limited to employed thirty-five- to fifty-five-year-olds in each period.

Table B.2   Economic Security, Marital Status, and Educational Attainment among the Vanishing Middle, by Race and Gender, 2015

	White Men	White Women	Black Men	Black Women
Occupational attainment				
Professional and technical	35.3%	49.3%	29.3%	41.1%
Managers and proprietors	27.9	16.9	17.6	13.9
Nonmanagerial white-collar	13.3	23.7	13.9	25.8
Skilled workers	9.3	0.8	9.7	1.0
Operatives	5.3	1.5	13.5	3.2
Semiskilled and unskilled workers	8.9	7.9	16.0	14.9
Economic security measures				
Nonstandard employment	9.7%	22.9%	10.7%	12.6%
Mean annual earnings (2015 dollars)	$44,701.81	$27,911.78	$28,991.69	$26,667.15
Variation in annual earnings (coefficient of variation)	1.55	1.14	1.13	1.13
Usual hours worked per week (mean)	37.18	25.72	32.25	27.68
Standard employment	90.3%	77.1%	89.3%	87.4%
Mean annual earnings (2015 dollars)	$101,965.00	$67,457.92	$66,598.80	$54,776.75
Variation in annual earnings (coefficient of variation)	0.91	0.86	0.82	0.72
Usual hours worked per week (mean)	46.60	43.37	44.64	42.23
Unemployment rate	2.2%	2.4%	4.1%	3.6%
Household characteristics				
Mean total family income (2015 dollars)	$151,065.62	$131,036.87	$115,501.23	$97,795.63
Variation in total family income (coefficient of variation)	2.25	1.58	3.61	3.62
Homeownership	80.8%	81.4%	59.0%	57.4%
Marital status				
Married, spouse present	72.70%	67.80%	54.90%	39.30%
Married, spouse absent	1.30	1.20	3.10	2.90
Separated	1.40	1.90	3.30	5.00
Divorced	10.80	15.70	14.20	18.90
Widowed	0.50	1.30	0.70	1.90
Never married/single	13.40	12.10	23.70	31.90

Source: Authors' analysis of data from Integrated Public Use Microdata Series, version 7.0.

Table B.3   Economic Security among the Vanishing Middle, by Education, Race, and Gender, 2015

	White Men	White Women	Black Men	Black Women
Some college				
Unemployment rate	2.67%	2.77%	4.97%	4.40%
Nonstandard employment	11.41%	25.24%	11.84%	15.15%
Usual hours worked per week (mean)	44.99	38.26	42.97	39.57
Mean annual earnings (2015 dollars)	$65,890.22	$42,093.24	$49,211.38	$39,731.33
Mean total family income (2015 dollars)	$101,520.20	$97,159.33	$83,370.28	$71,078.15
Homeownership	81.24%	81.06%	59.17%	55.57%
Married	72.42%	68.89%	56.94%	40.10%
Bachelor's degree				
Unemployment rate	1.85%	2.31%	3.68%	3.33%
Nonstandard employment	9.23%	24.31%	10.07%	11.65%
Usual hours worked per week (mean)	45.62	38.93	43.41	40.59
Mean annual earnings (2015 dollars)	$107,372.50	$62,942.45	$69,986.81	$56,351.43
Mean total family income (2015 dollars)	$152,398.80	$138,046	$112,304.90	$97,270.73
Homeownership	85.34%	86.19%	67.66%	66.46%
Married	78.10%	73.26%	64.52%	46.46%
Master's degree				
Unemployment rate	1.64%	1.70%	3.06%	2.83%
Nonstandard employment	6.64%	17.99%	7.78%	8.96%
Usual hours worked per week (mean)	46.18	40.81	43.67	41.43
Mean annual earnings (2015 dollars)	$125,055.80	$73,059.14	$87,538.62	$65,865.03
Mean total family income (2015 dollars)	$176,846.50	$152,199.90	$134,547.30	$108,346.50
Homeownership	84.18%	86.54%	70.99%	72.50%
Married	81.97%	74.20%	69.62%	48.32%
Doctoral or professional degree				
Unemployment rate	1.07%	1.53%	3.30%	2.25%
Nonstandard employment	10.58%	21.27%	10.25%	11.99%
Usual hours worked per week (mean)	48.21	42.42	45.87	43.1
Mean annual earnings (2015 dollars)	$173,162.70	$113,489.90	$128,363.90	$97,344.38
Mean total family income (2015 dollars)	$235,144.80	$214,333.10	$184,449.50	$152,564.40
Homeownership	85.07%	86.38%	72.87%	74.21%
Married	82.83%	75.23%	73.24%	54.96%

Source: Authors' analysis of data from Integrated Public Use Microdata Series, version 7.0.

= Notes =

Introduction

1. Gould and Shierholz 2020. For an extended analysis of the racial and gender dimensions of essential work, see McNicholas and Poydock 2020 and Powell 2021.
2. WABC-TV 2020.
3. Mays and Newman 2020. See also CDC 2020, the analysis of the Centers for Disease Control and Prevention of Covid-19 mortality in New York City in the spring of 2020.
4. These numbers reflect the Black proportions of death when race was known (American Public Media Research Lab 2020).
5. Columbia University 2020.
6. Branch 2011.
7. Cooper 2014.
8. Hacker 2008, 20; see also Kalleberg and Vallas 2017.
9. Tilly 1998, 6.
10. Jones 1998; Glenn 2004.
11. Tilly 1998, 7.
12. Frederickson 2003; Wooten and Branch 2012.
13. See the sociologist Ruth Milkman's recent book *Immigrant Labor and the New Precariat* (2020) for a detailed and compelling account of how the influx of low-wage immigrants since the 1970s is not a cause of rising economic precarity and inequality, but rather a consequence of American employers' concerted efforts to weaken labor unions. Although our book focuses on the Black/White binary, we share her perspective on class mobilization as a proximate cause of rising inequality, including the class-based mobilization of racist and xenophobic tropes as a means of legitimizing neoliberal policies. We think it vital to build broad and inclusive coalitions for change.
14. Kaufman 1986, 310.
15. Ibid., 321.
16. In *Opportunity Denied*, Branch (2011) uses quantitative data drawn from the U.S. census from 1860 to 2008 to demonstrate that the labor market restriction experienced by Black women was distinct from that of either Black men or White women. She argues that a focus on both race and gender is necessary to more fully understand labor market inequality. Such a focus is especially important for understanding how race and gender have been combined to limit Black women's occupational opportunities, from constructions of womanhood that excluded Black women to the role of racial ideology in allowing Whites

to reconcile their ideas about race and gender in such a way as to leave Black women ever vulnerable to exploitation. The chapters in *Opportunity Denied* on farm labor, domestic service, and industrial fringe jobs show how Black women were restricted to devalued work.

17. Wooten and Branch 2012.
18. The General Social Survey is an annual assessment of the attitudes of Americans on a range of topics.
19. Yen and Agiesta 2013.
20. Branch and Couloute, n.d.
21. Hochschild 1995, 18.
22. Further, conceptions of Black and White femininity were historically defined in opposition to one other: Black women were expected to work, and White women were expected to care for the family (Landry 2000).
23. Ibid.
24. Although scholars have explored the cultural and subjective impacts of the rise of insecurity on individuals' sense of self and the family (Cooper 2014; Pugh 2014), less is known about how insecurity is reshaping race relations and the understanding of occupational opportunity itself.
25. Raley, Sweeney, and Wondra 2015.
26. Because marriage rates in the United States are increasingly stratified by education (Wang 2015), our focus in this book on educationally advantaged Americans may understate the extent to which the decline in marriage rates causes White women to experience rising economic insecurity.
27. We also included a few participants who were younger than thirty-five to capture this perspective, as well as a few who were unemployed or underemployed.
28. Proctor, Semega, and Kollar 2016.
29. Kalleberg 2011.
30. Silverstein 2015.
31. DiTomaso 2013.
32. Kaufman 2002.

Chapter 1: The Power of the Illusion: The Way We Never Were

1. Coontz 2016.
2. Rosenfeld 2014; Rubin 1986.
3. Kalleberg, Reskin, and Hudson 2000, 258.
4. Dixon 2021. For an extended discussion of the role of gender in New Deal policymaking, see Mettler 1998.
5. Katznelson 2005; Palmer 1995.
6. Alexander 2021; Jayaraman 2016.
7. Quadagno 1994.
8. Kessler-Harris 1989.
9. Landry 2000.
10. Glenn 2004.
11. Roosevelt 1950.

12. The Full Employment Bill of 1945, introduced by Democrats in Congress, declared, "All Americans able to work and seeking work have the right to useful, remunerative, regular, and full-time employment" (Bailey 1950, 243). Yet the United States never implemented the idea of a *right* to employment, as the language in the original bill was revised in the legislative process (Weir 1992). While a full employment policy remained in the platform of the Democratic Party until the 1980s, the Employment Act of 1946 signed by President Harry S. Truman merely committed the federal government to *promoting* employment opportunity. It stated: "The Congress hereby declares that it is the continuing policy and responsibility of the federal government to use all practicable means consistent with its needs and obligations and other essential considerations of national policy with the assistance and cooperation of industry, agriculture, labor, and state and local governments, to coordinate and utilize all its plans, functions, and resources for the purpose of creating and maintaining, in a manner calculated to foster and promote free and competitive enterprise and the general welfare, conditions under which there will be afforded useful employment for those able, willing, and seeking work, and to promote maximum employment, production, and purchasing power" (Steelman 2013).
13. Bonacich 1972.
14. Branch 2011.
15. Bonacich 1976.
16. Reid and Rubin 2003. We draw on the research categorizing core versus peripheral industries and primary versus secondary occupations created by the sociologists Lesley Williams Reid and Beth Rubin (2003, 412–13).
17. We use census data on race, gender, and occupational position drawn from the IPUMS. Census data provide the most comprehensive set of quantitative information on long-term changes in the U.S. population. IPUMS integrates the census data samples across years to allow for uniformity in concepts and measures, permitting an analysis of historical change. Census survey questions on earnings refer to the previous calendar year, so the 1960 figures give a snapshot of employment conditions in 1959, 1970 figures depict conditions in 1969, and so on (see Ruggles et al. 2010).
18. In this analysis nonstandard work includes work that is either part-time, in the temporary service industry, or unincorporated self-employment. Additional types of nonstandard employment relations not examined in this book include part-year or seasonal work, multiple job holding, or outsourced employment in which on-site management is legally separate from the de jure employer. Given the limited ability of U.S. Census data to identify the full range of nonstandard employment relations, our analysis likely underestimates its prevalence.
19. By definition, unemployment rates characterize the labor force, so unlike previous figures, figure 1.3 is not confined to the population of employed Black and White adults.
20. Tomaskovic-Devey 1993, 4.
21. Stainback and Tomaskovic-Devey 2012.
22. Moss and Tilly 2001.
23. Branch 2011.

24. Ibid.
25. The regulatory race to the bottom that we associate with globalization has deep historical roots, as American companies have long used the threat of relocation—and have often followed through on that treat—to undermine union organizing (Hanley 2021) and escape certain types of government regulation, but the process accelerated in the 1980s and 1990s. For a detailed analysis of the causes and consequences of capital mobility in the United States, see Cowie 1999. The embrace of free trade agreements, including the North American Free Trade Agreement (NAFTA), probably contributed to a loss of American jobs and forced remaining workers to accept lower wages and benefits. See Faux 2013.
26. While economists have often emphasized the process known as skill-biased technological change (SBTC) as an explanation for rising earnings inequality (for example, Acemoglu and Autor 2011; Autor, Levy, and Murnane 2003; Autor, Katz, and Kearney 2008; Goldin and Katz 2010; but see Card and DiNardo 2002), sociologists have emphasized the institutionally contingent and class-biased nature of technological change (for example, Fernandez 2001; Hanley 2014; Kristal 2020).
27. The sociologist Jake Rosenfeld shows in *What Unions No Longer Do* (2014) that union decline was a political outcome with far-reaching consequences. As we discuss in more detail in chapter 6, deunionization and rising inequality were particularly pronounced in the United States after 1980 compared with other nations, owing to its political economic policy choices: American employment and labor law is relatively weak, and federal enforcement of existing statutes after 1980 was weak and uneven, tipping the balance of workplace power further in the direction of employers at the expense of employees. For a comprehensive account of the sources of rising inequality in the United States, see Tomaskovic-Devey and Avent-Holt 2019.
28. See, for example, Centre for Public Impact 2017. For more detail on welfare reform and its impact, see Hays 2003.
29. After 1980, changes in the composition of the American labor market and in the measurement of industrial and occupational characteristics reduce the utility of the classification of core or peripheral industry by primary or secondary occupation. The rise of a large and highly variegated service sector makes the more manufacturing-centric postwar classification system less useful, as the characteristics of core industries increasingly resembled those of peripheral industries; primary and secondary occupations become more difficult to distinguish; and new occupational categories to match new forms of work were introduced. For more details on changes in the U.S. Census Bureau's measurement of industry and occupation groups, see U.S. Census Bureau 1989.
30. Exceptions in manufacturing included products related to lumber and furniture.
31. Bluestone and Harrison 1982; Cowie 1999.
32. Rampell 2012.
33. The coefficient of variation was 0.94 in 1970 and rose to 1.26 in 2015; values over 1 indicate that the standard deviation in earnings variation in that year was greater than the mean earnings level.

34. The coefficient of variation was 0.85 in 1970, compared with 1.11 in 2015.
35. See figure B.1 in the appendix for annual earnings percentiles for full- and part-time earners disaggregated by race and gender group and by year. Comparing the level of each percentile across each group and over time illustrates well our argument that from 1960 to the present White men were advantaged relative to other groups (as evidenced by higher values for each within-group percentile). Over time within-group inequality also grew most sharply for White men. For example, the ratio of White men's seventy-fifth to twenty-fifth earnings percentile increased by 54.7 percent from 1960 to 2015, compared with a decline of between 20 and 40 percent for other racial gender groups (not shown). Note that these earnings percentiles are not restricted to full-time workers, so they reflect inequalities in compensation and hours worked.
36. Figure B.2 in the appendix disaggregates earnings variation within occupations for full- and part-time earners by race and gender group. It shows that earnings variation, along with inter-occupations differences in earnings variation, was greatest for White men.
37. For professional and technical workers, the coefficient of variation rose from 0.69 in 1970 to 0.96 in 2015; for managers and proprietors it rose from 0.79 to 1.02. The coefficient of variation rose from 0.47 in 1970 to 0.69 in 2015 for skilled blue-collar workers. For nonmanagerial white-collar workers, the coefficient of variation rose from 0.84 in 1970 to 1.21 in 2015, and for semiskilled and unskilled blue-collar workers, it rose from 0.84 in 1970 to 1.03 in 2015.
38. Pettit and Ewert 2009.
39. Plunkert 1990.
40. To better understand the nuances in the measurement of economic security, see Olsthoorn 2014 and Vosko 2006.
41. The U.S. Census Bureau's IPUMS database provides information on each individual's personal earnings as well as their household income. They also use individuals' household size to calculate a variable ("POVERTY") indicating how each individual's household income relates to the poverty line (expressed as a percentage of the poverty line). To generate our variables for "working poverty" and being "at risk of poverty," we identify employed individuals whose household incomes relative to the poverty line place them in each defined category. In 2015 the federal poverty line was $11,770 for a single individual, $20,090 for a family of three, and $24,250 for a family of four (see U.S. Office of the Assistant Secretary for Planning and Evaluation, "2015 Federal Poverty Guidelines," https://aspe.hhs.gov/2015-poverty-guidelines [accessed May 21, 2021]). Absolute poverty measures attempt to identify the level of income necessary to obtain basic human necessities, whereas measures of relative poverty seek to identify the minimum income necessary for social inclusion. As such, and owing to the near-universal acknowledgment that the official poverty rate in the United States significantly underestimates exposure to material hardship, our measure of "at risk of poverty" is particularly important for assessing economic barriers to social inclusion.
42. Hout and Hanley 2003.

Chapter 2: The Dream Interrupted: Insecurity among the Middle-Aged

1. Temin 2017.
2. Edin and Kefalas 2011.
3. See, for example, DeParle and Tavernise 2012.
4. Clark 2020.
5. The AP-NORC survey questions gauging economic security and optimism differ somewhat from the comparable items on the GSS, and other elements of the data collection differ across the two surveys as well. See National Opinion Research Center 2013 and Tompson and Benz 2013.
6. The responses here are limited to middle-aged members of the labor force. They sum to 100 percent of valid responses within racial and gender groups.
7. Black women's labor market attachments were never characterized by security. Instead, they were purposefully employed as a reserve labor force that employers drew in or cast out, based on their needs (Beale 1970; Branch 2007; Glenn 1992). Their occupational segregation facilitated their exploitation before 1960, at which time "more than 60 percent of all employed Black women were in service work and the vast majority, nearly 63 percent, worked in private households" (Branch 2011, 127). It was not until 1970 that Black women's occupational opportunities mirrored White women's admittedly limited occupational opportunities, yet even this progress was tenuous. As clerical work, the primary occupation of employed women in the 1970s and 1980s, grew, Black women gained access, but they were overrepresented in poorly paid clerical occupations and "ghettoized within office work" (Branch 2011; Glenn and Tolbert 1987, 318). Black women's labor market history suggests that they were only conditionally accepted in the primary labor market and continued to be marginalized in contemporary workplaces (Stainback and Tomaskovic-Devey 2009).
8. Lamont 2002.
9. Hunt 2007.
10. See table B.3 in the appendix for the variation in mean annual earnings among employed adults, by education, 1960 to 2015.
11. Economists have emphasized the centrality of educational policy in countering rising inequality in an age of new technologies, as expressed in Goldin and Katz 2010, but paying too much attention to education obscures other critical policy areas. For a comprehensive account of how education has supplanted welfare state and labor market policy, see Kantor and Lowe 2013.

Chapter 3: Privileged Expectations and Insecure Realities

1. Abrams 2018, xv.
2. Ibid.
3. Frank 2017.
4. Budig and Hodges 2010.

5. Both the public and policymakers are very interested in clarifying the returns to increasingly steep investments in higher education (see, for example, Carrns 2021). Those who assume that racial and gender differences in the choice of a college major or degree field explain the patterns of unequal returns described here should consider the data on earnings means and variation across college majors in Selingo 2017. The choice of college is at least as important as the choice of major for predicting lifetime earnings. Although this analysis does not disaggregate by race, it is reasonable to expect that race and gender earnings differences among those who studied in the same degree fields contribute to the large earnings variation we see here.

6. Branch and Hanley 2017.

7. On White families' focus on education, see DiTomaso 2013.

8. Branch 2011.

9. To learn more about the impact of college debt on declining marriage and birth rates, see Nau, Dwyer, and Hodson 2015. To learn more about declining homeownership among young people, see Houle and Berger 2015 and Noguchi 2019.

10. Clarke 2011.

11. Pelletier 2020.

12. Carnevale, Jaysundera, and Gulish 2016.

Chapter 4: The Myth of Equal Opportunity

1. Cooper 2014.

2. Fisher 2019.

3. Kanter 1977, 62.

4. Elliott and Smith 2004, 365.

5. Stainback and Tomaskovic-Devey (2009, 800) found that a racial management-subordinate status hierarchy emerged, such that "the presence of similar others in nonmanagerial jobs" increasingly drove the identity of the manager.

6. Branch 2011, 148.

7. Bertrand and Mullainathan 2004.

8. Pager 2003.

9. Kang et al. 2016.

10. Ibid., 478.

11. Ibid., 479.

12. Ibid., 491.

13. Stainback and Tomaskovic-Devey 2012.

14. 30 FR 12319, 12935, 3 CFR, 1964–1965 Comp., 339.

15. Leonard 1990, 49.

16. DiTomaso 2013, 99.

17. Ibid.

18. Parks-Yancy 2010.

19. DiTomaso 2013, 81. Both were college graduates who were exceptional in other ways.

20. Ibid., 8.

21. Harris 2018.

22. In this national moment of racial reckoning, more and more organizations are stating their diversity goals and being clear about how they intend to work toward them in ways that will not run afoul of the law (Werner 2020).
23. Obama 2006, 247.
24. Ibid.
25. Ibid.
26. Slatton 2015, 1.

Chapter 5: Negotiating Uncertainty

1. Quoted in DiTomaso 2013, 1.
2. Branch and Jackson 2020.
3. Oliver and Shapiro 1995.
4. The sociologists Enobong Hannah Branch and Christina Jackson argue in *Black in America: The Paradox of the Color Line* (2020) that we must take a critical approach to the claim made by many people today that they do not "see" race and therefore believe that they cannot be "racist." This logic misses a fundamental truth: one can claim not to be "racist" and yet reproduce a racial hierarchy (6). The sociologist Robert Blauner (2001, 19) argues that "prejudiced attitudes are not the essence of racism." While intense prejudice is often expressed via "overt racism" —explicit mistreatment or denigration of a racial minority group—a "racist social structure" does not require individual "bad" actors to maintain racial inequality (Bonilla-Silva 1996). Blauner (2001, 20) argues that racism in America is institutionalized, such that "the processes that maintain domination—control of Whites over non-Whites—are built into the major social institutions."
5. See in the appendix table B.1, which compares postwar and postindustrial middle-aged cohorts along economic security indicators, including educational attainment and marriage rates. For all groups there was a notable decline in rates of marriage between the postwar (1980) cohort and the postindustrial (2015) cohort.
6. The sociologist Lane Kenworthy (2004, 2008) examines cross-national patterns of inequality, economic growth, labor market regulation, and welfare state policies. He argues that despite a pervasive belief in the "inevitability thesis"—the idea that high levels of inequality are inevitable in the face of globalization and technological change, such that societies face a trade-off between inequality and economic growth—the evidence contradicts it.
7. Sharone 2014.
8. Lewis 1978.
9. DiTomaso 2013; Lamont 2002.
10. Hunt 2007.
11. Jones 1986.
12. Landry 2000, 73.
13. Although evidence of such disruption was obvious before 2008, with the 1980s decline of manufacturing, the sudden jump in stay-at-home dads led some to label the Great Recession the "mancession," owing to the disproportionate loss of men's jobs in the construction and manufacturing sectors of the economy (Bukszpan 2012).

14. Livingston 2014.
15. Maxine Baca Zinn (1990) critiques the normative focus on the arrangements of the traditional White family and argues that what appears new for Whites now (for example, a rise in female breadwinners and egalitarian relationships) has been common among Blacks for years. Differences in "family lifestyles," Baca Zinn argues, reflect differences in "structural patterns ... because social and economic conditions produce and may even require diverse family arrangements" (73).
16. Wang, Parker, and Taylor 2013.
17. Married Black women would take on laundry work that could be done in their home to supplement their household income, enabling the image of their husband as a male breadwinner (Landry 2000).
18. Two of the White women we interviewed were lesbian, one married and the other partnered.
19. Branch 2016.

Chapter 6: Economic Vulnerability as the New Normal

1. For "Prouder, Stronger, Better," Ronald Reagan's 1984 presidential campaign ad, see *Time* magazine's "Top 10 Campaign Ads," http://content.time.com/time/specials/packages/article/0,28804,1842516_1842514_1842575,00.html.
2. Churchwell 2018, 160–67.
3. Adams 1931, 404.
4. Obama 2004.
5. Smith 1776.
6. The object of "The Game of Life" is to "count your cash. . . . Life's most important squares are its red-letter [paydays]. What you earn on those paydays depends, in large part, on a crucial choice you make on your very first move: will you go to college, or take a job? If you start work, you can collect paychecks right away; if you go to college, you have to pay tuition, but you earn more when you eventually do start getting paychecks" (Lepore 2007).
7. Kantor and Lowe 2013.
8. Coleman 2018.
9. Cooper 2013.
10. To learn more about living wages, including the wage rate required to meet basic needs in local communities across the country, see the Massachusetts Institute of Technology's "Living Wage Calculator" at https://livingwage.mit.edu/. See also Rushe 2021.
11. Friedman 1966/1972, 144.
12. Ibid.
13. Newman 2000.
14. Friedman 1966/1972, 145 (emphasis added).
15. See Perry 2016 or Neumark and Wascher 2010. For an alternative perspective, consider Card and Kruger 2016 or Luce 2004.
16. Derenoncourt and Montialoux 2021.
17. See, for example, Pager and Quillian 2005 and a wide array of other experimental audit studies that definitively document the persistence of discrimination in the American labor market (see chapter 4).

18. See *Economist* 2017, highlighting research by Cajner et al. 2017.
19. The economists William Darity and Patrick Mason note that prior to the passage of the Civil Rights Act, race- and gender-based discrimination was rampant in the American labor market. Utilizing newspaper help-wanted advertisements from 1945 to 1965, Darity and Mason illustrate that, far more often than not, employers' preference for applicants of a particular race was for White applicants. Further, they note that help-wanted ads listed jobs for men and women separately, categorizing them according to stereotypical gendered notions of labor. For example, men were solicited for managerial, sales, and labor-intensive jobs, whereas women were solicited for domestic service, clerical work, and waitressing. The degree of segregation by race and gender was clear in this advertisement for a switchboard operator posted by Nancy Lee's employment service: "all women applying be White" (Darity and Mason 1998, 65).
20. Hamilton et al. 2015, 6.
21. When 2020 Democratic presidential candidate Bernie Sanders introduced a "Twenty-First-Century Bill of Rights" that called for raising the minimum wage in the United States to $15, among other measures intended to stabilize family income, such as expanding Social Security, he was labeled by his Republican and Democratic opponents as unrealistic or "socialist" (see Epstein and Ember 2019).
22. A greater federal commitment to identifying instances of discrimination and enforcing existing equal opportunity statutes advanced desegregation in the decade following the civil rights movement, and progress in occupational opportunity declined when that federal commitment was reduced (Stainback and Tomaskovic-Devey 2012).
23. See, for example, Rosenfeld 2021.
24. See Kenworthy 2004, 2008, 2019.
25. For a detailed analysis of "high road" versus "low road" employment in retail, see Carré and Tilly 2017. See also Osterman 2020.
26. The Economic Policy Institute (https://www.epi.org/) and the National Employment Law Project (https://www.nelp.org/) are good sources of data and analysis.
27. See, for example, Kantor and Weise 2022 and Streitfeld 2021. At the federal level, interpretation and enforcement of existing statutes that govern franchise and supplier relationships are also critical, as those rules of the game can put smaller firms with thinner profit margins in a vulnerable position vis-à-vis the major retailers who set prices for their goods in the marketplace and make it difficult for smaller employers to pay their employees a living wage. For a nice discussion of exploitation in relations between firms, see Tomaskovic-Devey and Avent-Holt 2019.
28. For an overview of scholarly research on the individual and societal consequences of economic inequality, see Boushey 2019; Chetty et al. 2017; DiPrete 2006; Iceland 2014; Kruger 2011; and Neckerman and Torche 2007.
29. Tomaskovic-Devey and Avent-Holt 2019.
30. Alexander 2021.

31. Rosenthal 2018.
32. Desmond 2019.
33. See Levanon, England, and Allison 2009; Mandel 2013; and Tomaskovic-Devey and Stainback 2007.
34. Rosenberg 2020; Associated Press 2020.
35. Hartman 2020.
36. See the U.S. Department of Labor guidance on "Unemployment Insurance Relief during Covid-19 Outbreak," https://www.dol.gov/coronavirus/unemployment-insurance.
37. Smith 2020.
38. Loudenback and Knueven 2020.
39. See Schnell and Hughes 2019 and Fadulu 2019.
40. Egan 2020.
41. Rosenbaum 2021.
42. Pugh 2014.
43. Picchi 2021.
44. Kennedy 1963. Learn more about the origins of Equal Pay Day at National Women's History Museum 2013.
45. See The White House 2009.
46. See Morad 2021. The gender gap in pay was part of the highly gendered employment dynamics driving the "Great Resignation" of 2021 (Parker and Horowitz 2022). See also Donegan 2021.
47. As Joya Misra and Marta Murray-Close (2014) show, the gender wage gap points to how much room there is for the United States to utilize policy levers to reduce inequalities.
48. Miller and Robinson 2021.
49. Kurtz 2021.
50. Rattner and Franck 2021.
51. Ibid.
52. The White House 2021a.
53. The White House 2021b.
54. Boesch, Bleiweis, and Haider 2021.
55. Gonyea 2021.
56. Cochran and Edmundson 2021.
57. Covert 2021.
58. Rascoe 2021.
59. Ibid.
60. Schulte and Robertson 2021.
61. Peck 2021.
62. Fischer et al. 1996.
63. Gillon 2020.
64. Roosevelt 1941.
65. Hains 2021.
66. Chappell 2021.
67. See Kaiser Commission on Medicaid and the Uninsured 2002.
68. Buchmueller et al. 2016.
69. Johnson and Martin 2020.

Appendix A: Methodological Appendix

1. Two of the White participants were lesbian, one married and the other partnered.
2. The specific IPUMS samples we used were the 5% samples in 1960, 1980, 1990, and 2000; the Form 2 Metro samples in 1970; and the American Community Survey (ACS) samples for 2001 onward.
3. Most ACS work and income questions ask about the previous year, so the 2016 sample best captured conditions in 2015, when the interviews took place.

═ References ═

Abrams, Stacey. 2018. *Minority Leader: How to Lead from the Outside and Make Real Change.* New York: Henry Holt and Co.

Acemoglu, Daron, and David Autor. 2011. "Skills, Tasks and Technologies: Implications for Employment and Earnings." In *Handbook of Labor Economics,* edited by David Card and Orley Ashenfelter, vol. 4, part B: 1043–1171. Amsterdam: Elsevier.

Adams, James Truslow. 1931. *The Epic of America.* Boston: Little, Brown, and Co.

Alexander, Michelle. 2021. "Tipping Is a Legacy of Slavery: Abolish the Racist, Sexist Subminimum Wage Now." *New York Times,* February 5. https://www.nytimes.com/2021/02/05/opinion/minimum-wage-racism.html.

American Public Media Research Lab. 2020. "The Color of the Coronavirus: Covid-19 Deaths by Race and Ethnicity in the U.S." American Public Media Group, September 16. https://www.apmresearchlab.org/covid/deaths-by-race#black.

Associated Press. 2020. "1.2 Million Seek Unemployment Benefits after $600 Federal Check Ends." *Marketplace,* August 6. https://www.marketplace.org/2020/08/06/weekly-jobless-claims-unemployment-benefits-600-federal-payment/.

Autor, David, Lawrence F. Katz, and Melissa S. Kearney. 2008. "Trends in U.S. Wage Inequality: Revising the Revisionists." *Review of Economics and Statistics* 90(2): 300–323.

Autor, David, Frank Levy, and Richard J. Murnane. 2003. "The Skill Content of Recent Technological Change: An Empirical Exploration." *Quarterly Journal of Economics* 18(4): 1279–1334.

Baca Zinn, Maxine. 1990. "Family, Feminism, and Race in America." *Gender and Society* 4(1): 68–82.

Bailey, Stephen Kemp. 1950. *Congress Makes a Law: The Story behind the Employment Act of 1946.* New York: Columbia University Press.

Beale, Frances. 1970. "Double Jeopardy: To Be Black and Female." In *The Black Woman: An Anthology,* edited by Toni Cade Bambara, 90–100. New York: Signet.

Bertrand, Marianne, and Sendhil Mullainathan. 2004. "Are Emily and Greg More Employable than Lakisha and Jamal? A Field Experiment on Labor Market Discrimination." *American Economic Review* 94(4): 991–1013.

Blauner, Robert. 2001. *Still the Big News: Racial Oppression in America.* Philadelphia: Temple University Press.

Bluestone, Barry, and Bennett Harrison. 1982. *The Deindustrialization of America: Plant Closings, Community Abandonment, and the Dismantling of Basic Industry.* New York: Basic Books.

Boesch, Diana, Robin Bleiweis, and Areeba Haider. 2021. "Raising the Minimum Wage Would Be Transformative for Women." Center for American Progress,

February 23. https://www.americanprogress.org/issues/women/news/2021/02/23/496221/raising-minimum-wage-transformative-women/.

Bonacich, Edna. 1972. "A Theory of Ethnic Antagonism: The Split Labor Market." *American Sociological Review* 37(5): 547–59.

———. 1976. "Advanced Capitalism and Black/White Race Relations in the United States: A Split Labor Market Interpretation." *American Sociological Review* 41(1): 34–51.

Bonilla-Silva, Eduardo. 1996. "Rethinking Racism: Toward a Structural Interpretation." *American Sociological Review* 62(3): 465–80.

Boushey, Heather. 2019. *Unbound: How Inequality Constricts Our Economy and What We Can Do about It*. Cambridge, Mass.: Harvard University Press.

Branch, Enobong Hannah. 2007. "The Creation of Restricted Opportunity due to the Intersection of Race and Sex: Black Women in the Bottom Class." *Race, Gender and Class* 14(3–4): 247–64.

———. 2011. *Opportunity Denied: Limiting Black Women to Devalued Work*. New Brunswick, N.J.: Rutgers University Press.

———. 2016. "Racialized Family Ideals: Breadwinning, Domesticity, and the Negotiation of Insecurity." In *Beyond the Cubicle: Insecurity Culture and the Flexible Self*, edited by Allison Pugh. New York: Oxford University Press.

Branch, Enobong Hannah, and Lucius Couloute. n.d. "Gaming the Racialized Social System: How Blacks Talk about Navigating Inequality." Unpublished paper. University of Massachusetts–Amherst.

Branch, Enobong Hannah, and Caroline Hanley. 2017. "A Racial-Gender Lens on Precarious Nonstandard Employment." In *Precarious Work*, edited by Arne L. Kalleberg and Steven P. Vallas. Bingley, U.K.: Emerald Publishing.

Branch, Enobong Hannah, and Christina Jackson. 2020. *Black in America: The Paradox of the Color Line*. London: Polity Press.

Buchmueller, Thomas C., Zachary M. Levinson, Helen G. Levy, and Barbara L. Wolfe. 2016. "Effect of the Affordable Care Act on Racial and Ethnic Disparities in Health Insurance Coverage." *American Journal of Public Health* 106(8): 1416–21.

Budig, Michelle J., and Melissa J. Hodges. 2010. "Differences in Disadvantage: Variation in the Motherhood Penalty across White Women's Earnings Distribution." *American Sociological Review* 75(5): 705–28.

Bukszpan, Daniel. 2012. "Economy: The Man-cession and the He-covery." CNBC, January 29. https://abcnews.go.com/Business/economy-man-cession-covery/story?id=15467590.

Cajner, Tomaz, Tyler Radler, David Ratner, and Ivan Vidangos. 2017. "Racial Gaps in Labor Market Outcomes in the Last Four Decades and over the Business Cycle." Finance and Economics Discussion Series 2017–071. Board of Governors of the Federal Reserve System, June. DOI: https://doi.org/10.17016/FEDS.2017.071.

Card, David, and John E. DiNardo. 2002. "Skill-Biased Technological Change and Rising Wage Inequality: Some Problems and Puzzles." *Journal of Labor Economics* 20(4):733–83.

Card, David, and Alan B. Kruger. 2016. *Myth and Measurement*. Princeton, N.J.: Princeton University Press.

Carnevale, Anthony, Tamara Jaysundera, and Artem Gulish. 2016. "America's Divided Recovery: College Haves and Have-Nots." Georgetown University,

Center on Education and the Workforce. https://1gyhoq479ufd3yna29x7ubjn
-wpengine.netdna-ssl.com/wp-content/uploads/Americas-Divided-Recovery
-web.pdf.

Carré, Françoise, and Chris Tilly. 2017. *Where Bad Jobs Are Better: Retail Jobs across Countries and Companies.* New York: Russell Sage Foundation.

Carrns, Ann. 2021. "Will That College Degree Pay Off?" *New York Times,* August 13. https://www.nytimes.com/2021/08/13/your-money/college-degree-investment-return.html.

Centers for Disease Control and Prevention (CDC). 2020. "COVID-19 Outbreak — New York City, February 29–June 1, 2020." *Morbidity and Mortality Weekly Report* 69(46): 1725–29. https://www.cdc.gov/mmwr/volumes/69/wr/mm6946a2.htm.

Centre for Public Impact. 2017. "The 1996 Personal Responsibility and Work Opportunity Reconciliation Act in the U.S." October 30. https://www.centrefor publicimpact.org/case-study/personal-responsibility-and-work-opportunity-reconciliation-act-the-clinton-welfare-reform.

Chappell, Bill. 2021. "Overwork Killed More than 745,000 People in a Year, WHO Study Finds." NPR, May 17. https://www.npr.org/2021/05/17/997462169/thousands-of-people-are-dying-from-working-long-hours-a-new-who-study-finds.

Chetty, Raj, David Grusky, Maximillian Hell, Nathaniel Hendren, Robert Manduca, and Jimmy Narang. 2017. "'The Fading American Dream': Trends in Absolute Income Mobility since 1940." *Science* 356(6336): 398–406.

Churchwell, Sarah. 2018. *Behold, America: The Entangled History of "America First" and "the American Dream."* New York: Basic Books.

Clark, Alexis. 2020. "Returning from War, Returning to Racism." *New York Times,* July 30. https://www.nytimes.com/2020/07/30/magazine/black-soldiers-wwii-racism.html.

Clarke, Averil Y. 2011. *Inequalities of Love: College-Educated Black Women and the Barriers to Romance and Family.* Durham, N.C.: Duke University Press.

Cochran, Emily, and Catie Edmundson. 2021. "Manchin Pulls Support from Biden's Social Policy Bill, Imperiling Its Passage." *New York Times,* December 19. https://www.nytimes.com/2021/12/19/us/politics/manchin-build-back-better.html.

Coleman, Llezlie Green. 2018. "Disrupting the Discrimination Narrative: An Argument for Wage and Hour Laws' Inclusion in Antisubordination Advocacy." *Stanford Journal of Civil Rights and Civil Liberties* 14(1): 49–87.

Columbia University, Mailman School of Public Health. 2020. "NYC Subway Data Reveals Communities of Color Carry the Burden of Essential Work and COVID-19." *Newswise,* June 4. https://www.newswise.com/coronavirus/nyc-subway-data-reveals-communities-of-color-carry-the-burden-of-essential-work-and-covid-19.

Coontz, Stephanie. 2016. *The Way We Never Were: American Families and the Nostalgia Trap.* New York: Basic Books.

Cooper, David. 2013. "The Minimum Wage Used to Be Enough to Keep Workers Out of Poverty — It's Not Anymore." Economic Policy Institute, December 4. https://www.epi.org/publication/minimum-wage-workers-poverty-anymore-raising/.

Cooper, Marianne. 2014. *Cut Adrift: Families in Insecure Times.* Berkeley: University of California Press.

Covert, Bryce. 2021. "The Exponential Power of a $15 Wage Floor." *New York Times,* February 5. https://www.nytimes.com/2021/02/05/opinion/minimum-wage-fight-for-15.html.

Cowie, Jefferson. 1999. *Capital Moves: RCA's Seventy-Year Quest for Cheap Labor.* New York: New Press.

Darity, William A., Jr., and Patrick L. Mason. 1998. "Evidence of Discrimination in Employment: Codes of Color, Codes of Gender." *Journal of Economic Perspectives* 12(2): 63–90.

DeParle, Jason, and Sabrina Tavernise. 2012. "For Women under 30 Most Births Occur Outside Marriage." *New York Times,* February 17. https://www.nytimes.com/2012/02/18/us/for-women-under-30-most-births-occur-outside-marriage.html.

Derenoncourt, Ellora, and Claire Montialoux. 2021. "Minimum Wages and Racial Inequality." *Quarterly Journal of Economics* 136(1): 169–228.

Desmond, Matthew. 2019. "In Order to Understand the Brutality of American Capitalism, You Have to Start on the Plantation." *New York Times,* August 14, 2019.

DiPrete, Thomas A. 2006. "Is This a Great Country? Upward Mobility and the Chance for Riches in Contemporary America." *Research in Social Stratification and Mobility* 25(1): 89–95.

DiTomaso, Nancy. 2013. *The American Non-Dilemma: Racial Inequality without Racism.* New York: Russell Sage Foundation.

Dixon, Rebecca (National Employment Law Project). 2021. "From Excluded to Essential: Tracing the Racist Exclusion of Farmworkers, Domestic Workers, and Tipped Workers from the Fair Labor Standards Act." Testimony before U.S. House of Representatives Education and Labor Committee, Workforce Protections Subcommittee, May 3. https://www.nelp.org/wp-content/uploads/NELP-Testimony-FLSA-May-2021.pdf.

Donegan, Moira. 2021. "Part of the 'Great Resignation' Is Actually Just Mothers Forced to Leave Their Jobs." *Guardian,* November 19.

Economist. 2017. "Daily Chart: The Mystery of High Unemployment Rates for Black Americans." *Economist,* August 3. https://www.economist.com/graphic-detail/2017/08/03/the-mystery-of-high-unemployment-rates-for-black-americans.

Edin, Kathryn, and Maria Kefalas. 2011. *Promises I Can Keep: Why Poor Women Put Motherhood before Marriage.* Berkeley: University of California Press.

Egan, Matt. 2020. "From Exxon to Charles Schwab, White-Collar Job Cuts Are Mounting." *CNN Business,* October 30. https://www.cnn.com/2020/10/30/business/jobs-white-collar-layoffs/index.html.

Elliott, James R., and Ryan A. Smith. 2004. "Race, Gender, and Workplace Power." *American Sociological Review* 69(3): 365–86.

Epstein, Reid J., and Sydney Ember. 2019. "Bernie Sanders Calls His Brand of Socialism a Pathway to Beating Trump." *New York Times,* June 12. https://www.nytimes.com/2019/06/12/us/politics/bernie-sanders-socialism.html.

Fadulu, Lola. 2019. "Trump Administration Unveils More Cuts to Food Stamp Program." *New York Times,* October 4.

Faux, Jeff. 2013. "NAFTA's Impact on U.S. Workers." Economic Policy Institute, December 9. https://www.epi.org/blog/naftas-impact-workers.

Fernandez, Roberto. 2001. "Skill-Biased Technological Change and Wage Inequality: Evidence from a Plant Retooling." *American Journal of Sociology* 107(2): 273–320.

Fischer, Claude S., Michael Hout, Martín Sánchez Jankowski, Samuel R. Lucas, Ann R. Lucas, Ann Swidler, and Kim Voss. 1996. *Inequality by Design: Cracking the Bell Curve Myth*. Princeton, N.J.: Princeton University Press.

Fisher, Julia Freeland. 2019. "Opinion: How to Get a Job Often Comes Down to One Elite Personal Asset, and Many People Still Don't Realize It." CNBC, December 27. https://www.cnbc.com/2019/12/27/how-to-get-a-job-often-comes-down-to-one-elite-personal-asset.html.

Frank, Robert H. 2017. *Success and Luck: Good Fortune and the Myth of Meritocracy*. Princeton, N.J.: Princeton University Press.

Frederickson, George M. 2003. *Racism: A Short History*. Princeton, N.J.: Princeton University Press.

Friedman, Milton. 1966/1972. "Minimum Wage Rates," *Newsweek*, September 26, 1966. https://miltonfriedman.hoover.org/internal/media/dispatcher/213993/full. Reprinted in Milton Friedman, *An Economist's Protest: Columns on Political Economy* (Glen Ridge, NJ: Thomas Horton & Daughters, 1972).

Gillon, Steven M. 2020. "Competing Visions of the American Dream Are Driving Democrats and Republicans Apart." *Washington Post*, September 3. https://www.washingtonpost.com/outlook/2020/09/03/competing-visions-american-dream-are-driving-democrats-republicans-apart/.

Glenn, Evelyn Nakano. 1992. "From Servitude to Service Work: Historical Continuities in the Racial Division of Paid Reproductive Labor." *Signs* 18(1):1–43.

———. 2004. *Unequal Freedom: How Race and Gender Shaped American Citizenship and Labor*. Cambridge, Mass.: Harvard University Press.

Glenn, Evelyn Nakano, and Charles M. Tolbert II. 1987. "Stratification for Women of Color: Race and Gender." In *Women, Work, and Technology: Transformations*, edited by Barbara Drygulski Wright et al. Ann Arbor: University of Michigan Press.

Goldin, Claudia and Lawrence F. Katz. 2010. *The Race between Education and Technology*. Cambridge, Mass.: Harvard University Press.

Gonyea, Don. 2021. "House Democrats Pass Bill That Would Protect Worker Organizing Efforts." National Public Radio, March 9. https://www.npr.org/2021/03/09/975259434/house-democrats-pass-bill-that-would-protect-workerorganizing-efforts.

Gould, Elise, and Heidi Shierholz. 2020. "Working Economics Blog: Not Everybody Can Work from Home." Economic Policy Institute, March 19. https://www.epi.org/blog/black-and-hispanic-workers-are-much-less-likely-to-be-able-to-work-from-home/.

Hacker, Jacob S. 2008. *The Great Risk Shift: The New Economic Insecurity and the Decline of the American Dream*. New York: Oxford University Press.

Hains, Tim. 2021. "Sen. Joe Manchin Explains Opposition to Democratic Budget: 'Moving towards an Entitlement Mentality.'" *Real Clear Politics*, September 30. https://www.realclearpolitics.com/video/2021/09/30/sen_joe_manchin

_explains_opposition_to_democratic_budget_moving_towards_an_entitlement
_mentality.html.

Hamilton, Darrick, William Darity Jr., Anne E. Price, Vishnu Sridharan, and
Rebecca Tippet. 2015. "Umbrellas Don't Make It Rain: Why Studying and
Working Hard Isn't Enough for Black Americans." New School, Duke Center
for Social Equity, and Insight Center for Community Economic Development,
April. http://insightcced.org/wp-content/uploads/2015/08/Umbrellas_Dont
_Make_It_Rain_Final.pdf.

Hanley, Caroline. 2014. "Putting the Bias in Skill-Biased Technological Change?
Postwar White Collar Automation Technologies at General Electric." *American
Behavioral Scientist* 58(3): 400–415.

———. 2021. "Institutionalized Insecurity: Post-War Employment Restructuring
and the Politics of the Local Business Climate." *Socio-Economic Review* (May 29):
mwab017. DOI: https://doi.org/10.1093/ser/mwab017.

Harris, Adam. 2018. "The Supreme Court Justice Who Forever Changed
Affirmative Action." *Atlantic*, October 13. https://www.theatlantic.com/education
/archive/2018/10/how-lewis-powell-changed-affirmative-action/572938/.

Hartman, Mitchell. 2020. "30 Million? 18 Million? How Many Americans Are Out
of Work Right Now?" *Marketplace*, August 6. https://www.marketplace.org
/2020/08/06/how-many-americans-unemployed-right-now/.

Hays, Sharon. 2003. *Flat Broke with Children: Women in the Age of Welfare Reform.*
New York: Oxford University Press.

Hochschild, Jennifer. 1995. *Facing Up to the American Dream: Race, Class, and the
Soul of the Nation.* Princeton, N.J.: Princeton University Press.

Houle, Jason N., and Lawrence Berger. 2015. "The End of the American Dream?
Student Loan Debt and Homeownership among Young Adults." Third Way
Next, June 2. https://www.thirdway.org/report/the-end-of-the-american
-dream-student-loan-debt-and-homeownership-among-young-adults.

Hout, Michael, and Caroline Hanley. 2003. "Working Hours and Inequality,
1968–2001: A Family Perspective on Recent Controversies." Russell Sage
Foundation Working Paper Series. Survey Research Center, University of
California, Berkeley, March. https://www.russellsage.org/sites/all/files/u4
/Hout%20%26%20Hanley.pdf.

Hunt, Matthew O. 2007. "African American, Hispanic, and White Beliefs about
Black/White Inequality, 1977–2004." *American Sociological Review* 72(3): 390–415.

Iceland, John. 2014. *A Portrait of America: The Demographic Perspective.* Berkeley:
University of California Press.

Jayaraman, Sarumathi. 2016. *Forked: A New Standard for American Dining.* Oxford:
Oxford University Press.

Johnson, Akilah, and Nina Martin. 2020. "How Covid-19 Hollowed Out a
Generation of Young Black Men." *ProPublica*, December 22. https://www
.propublica.org/article/how-covid-19-hollowed-out-a-generation-of-young
-black-men.

Jones, Jacqueline. 1986. *Labor of Love, Labor of Sorrow: Black Women, Work, and the
Family from Slavery to the Present.* New York: Vintage Books.

———. 1998. *American Work: Four Centuries of Black and White Labor.* New York:
W. W. Norton & Co.

Kaiser Commission on Medicaid and the Uninsured. 2002. "Sicker and Poorer: The Consequences of Being Uninsured," Kaiser Family Foundation, April 30. https://www.kff.org/uninsured/report/sicker-and-poorer-the-consequences -of-being/.

Kalleberg, Arne L. 2011. *Good Jobs, Bad Jobs: The Rise of Polarized and Precarious Employment Systems in the United States, 1970s to 2000s*. New York: Russell Sage Foundation.

Kalleberg, Arne L., Barbara F. Reskin, and Ken Hudson. 2000. "Bad Jobs in America: Standard and Nonstandard Employment Relations and Job Quality in the United States." *American Sociological Review* 65(2): 256–78.

Kalleberg, Arne L., and Steven P. Vallas, eds. 2017. *Precarious Work*. Bingley, U.K.: Emerald Group Publishing.

Kang, Sonia K., Katherine DeCelles, András Tilcsika, and Sora Jun. 2016. "Whitened Résumés: Race and Self-Presentation in the Labor Market." *Administrative Science Quarterly* 61(3): 469–502.

Kanter, Rosabeth Moss. 1977. *Men and Women of the Corporation*. New York: Basic Books.

Kantor, Harvey, and Robert Lowe. 2013. "Educationalizing the Welfare State and Privatizing Education: The Evolution of Social Policy since the New Deal." In *Closing the Opportunity Gap: What America Must Do to Give Every Child an Even Chance*, edited by Prudence Carter. New York: Oxford University Press.

Kantor, Jodi, and Karen Weise. 2022. "How Two Best Friends Beat Amazon." *New York Times*, April 14. https://www.nytimes.com/2022/04/02/business/amazon -union-christian-smalls.html.

Katznelson, Ira. 2005. *When Affirmative Action Was White: An Untold History of Racial Inequality in Twentieth-Century America*. New York: W. W. Norton & Co.

Kaufman, Robert L. 1986. "The Impact of Industrial and Occupational Structure of Black-White Employment Allocation." *American Sociological Review* 51(3): 310–23.

———. 2002. "Assessing Alternative Perspectives on Race and Sex Employment Segregation." *American Sociological Review* 67(4): 547–72.

Kennedy, John F. 1963. "Remarks on Signing Equal Pay Act of 1963, 10 June 1963." Papers of John F. Kennedy, Presidential Papers, John F. Kennedy Presidential Library and Museum. https://www.jfklibrary.org/asset-viewer/archives /JFKPOF/045/JFKPOF-045-001.

Kenworthy, Lane. 2004. *Egalitarian Capitalism: Jobs, Income, and Growth in Affluent Countries*. New York: Russell Sage Foundation.

———. 2008. *Jobs with Equality*. New York: Oxford University Press.

———. 2019. *Social Democratic Capitalism*. New York: Oxford University Press.

Kessler-Harris, Alice. 1989. "A New Agenda for American Labor History: A Gendered Analysis and the Question of Class." In *Perspectives on American Labor History: The Problems of Synthesis*, edited by J. Carroll Moody and Alice Kessler-Harris. DeKalb: Northern Illinois University Press.

Kristal, Tali. 2020. "Why Has Computerization Increased Wage Inequality? Information, Occupational Structural Power, and Wage Inequality." *Work and Occupations* 47(4): 466–503.

Kruger, Alan B. 2011. "Inequality, Too Much of a Good Thing." In *The Inequality Reader*, 2nd ed., edited by David B. Grusky and Szonia Szelenyi. Boulder, Colo.: Westview Press.

Kurtz, Annalyn. 2021. "The U.S. Economy Lost 140,000 Jobs in December. All of Them Were Held by Women." *CNN Business*, January 8. https://www.cnn.com/2021/01/08/economy/women-job-losses-pandemic/index.html?utm_term=link&utm_content=2021-01-08T22%3A29%3A01&utm_source=twCNN&utm_medium=social.

Lamont, Michèle. 2002. *The Dignity of Working Men: Morality and the Boundaries of Race, Class, and Immigration*. Cambridge, Mass.: Harvard University Press.

Landry, Bart. 2000. *Black Working Wives: Pioneers of the American Family Revolution*. Berkeley: University of California Press.

Leonard, Johnathan S. 1990. "The Impact of Affirmative Action Regulation and Equal Employment Law on Black Employment." *Journal of Economic Perspectives* 4(4): 47–63.

Lepore, Jill. 2007. "The Meaning of Life." *New Yorker*, May 21. https://www.newyorker.com/magazine/2007/05/21/the-meaning-of-life.

Levanon, Asaf, Paula England, and Paul Allison. 2009. "Occupational Feminization and Pay: Assessing Causal Dynamics Using 1950–2000 U.S. Census Data." *Social Forces* 88(2): 865–91.

Lewis, Michael. 1978. *The Culture of Inequality*. Amherst: University of Massachusetts Press.

Livingston, Gretchen. 2014. "Growing Number of Dads Home with the Kids." Pew Research Center, June 5. https://www.pewresearch.org/social-trends/2014/06/05/growing-number-of-dads-home-with-the-kids/.

Loudenback, Tanza, and Liz Knueven. 2020. "What Average Americans Spend on Groceries Every Month in 22 Major Cities." *Business Insider*, March 5. https://www.businessinsider.com/personal-finance/what-americans-spend-on-groceries-every-month-2019-4#12-chicago-11.

Luce, Stephanie. 2004. *Fighting for a Living Wage*. Ithaca, N.Y.: Cornell University Press.

Mandel, Hadas. 2013. "Up the Down Staircase: Women's Upward Mobility and the Wage Penalty for Occupational Feminization, 1970–2007." *Social Forces* 91(4): 1183–1207.

Mays, Jeffrey C., and Andy Newman. 2020. "Virus Is Twice as Deadly for Black and Latino People than Whites in NYC." *New York Times*, April 8. https://www.nytimes.com/2020/04/08/nyregion/coronavirus-race-deaths.html.

McNicholas, Celine, and Margaret Poydock. 2020. "Working Economic Blog: Who Are Essential Workers? A Comprehensive Look at Their Wages, Demographics, and Unionization Rates." Economic Policy Institute, May 19. https://www.epi.org/blog/who-are-essential-workers-a-comprehensive-look-at-their-wages-demographics-and-unionization-rates/.

Mettler, Suzanne. 1998. *Dividing Citizens: Gender and Federalism in New Deal Public Policy*. Ithaca, N.Y.: Cornell University Press.

Milkman, Ruth. 2020. *Immigrant Labor and the New Precariat*. New York: Polity Press.

Miller, Jane, and Jennifer Robison. 2021. "7 Ways to Save Your Working Moms before It's Too Late." Gallup, March 5. https://www.gallup.com/workplace/333185/ways-save-working-moms-late.aspx?elqTrackId=72afffe7afa94dc8b11

86a2a0cbd5f0e&elq=792449cd1d164bb2b0febfdf2b6f6508&elqaid=6133&elqat
=1&elqCampaignId=1283.

Misra, Joya, and Marta Murray-Close. 2014. "The Gender Wage Gap in the United States and Cross Nationally." *Sociology Compass* 8(11): 1281–95.

Morad, Renee. 2021. "It's 2021 and Women STILL Make 82 Cents for Every Dollar Earned by a Man." MSNBC, March 23. https://www.msnbc.com/know-your -value/feature/it-s-2021-women-still-make-82-cents-every-dollar-ncna1261755.

Moss, Philip, and Chris Tilly. 2001. *Stories Employers Tell: Race, Skill, and Hiring in America.* New York: Russell Sage Foundation.

National Opinion Research Center (NORC). 2013. "U.S. Public Mood: Significant Differences in Optimism Broken Down by Race." NORC, August 1. https:// www.norc.org/NewsEventsPublications/PressReleases/Pages/u-s-public -mood-significant-differences-in-optimism-broken-down-by-race.aspx.

National Women's History Museum. 2013. "Equal Pay Day." National Women's History Museum, April 9. https://www.womenshistory.org/articles/equal -pay-day.

Nau, Michael, Rachel Dwyer, and Randy Hodson. 2015. "Can't Afford a Baby? Debt and Young Americans." *Research in Social Stratification and Mobility* 42(December): 114–22.

Neckerman, Kathryn M., and Florencia Torche. 2007. "Inequality: Causes and Consequences." *Annual Review of Sociology* 33: 335–57.

Neumark, David, and William L. Wascher. 2008. *Minimum Wages.* Cambridge, Mass.: MIT Press.

Newman, Katherine. 2000. *No Shame in My Game: The Working Poor in the Inner City.* New York: Russell Sage Foundation.

Noguchi, Yuki. 2019. "Heavy Student Loan Debt Forces Many Millennials to Delay Buying Homes." NPR, *All Things Considered*, February 1. https://www.npr .org/2019/02/01/689660957/heavy-student-loan-debt-forces-many-millennials -to-delay-buying-homes.

Obama, Barack. 2004. "Remarks to the Democratic National Convention." *New York Times*, July 27. https://www.nytimes.com/2004/07/27/politics/campaign /barack-obamas-remarks-to-the-democratic-national.html.

———. 2006. *The Audacity of Hope: Thoughts on Reclaiming the American Dream.* New York: Crown Publishers.

Oliver, Melvin L., and Thomas M. Shapiro. 1995. *Black Wealth/White Wealth: A New Perspective on Racial Inequality.* New York: Routledge.

Olsthoorn, Martin. 2014. "Measuring Precarious Employment: A Proposal for Two Indicators of Precarious Employment Based on Set-Theory and Tested with Dutch Labor Market-Data." *Social Indicators Research* 119(1): 421–41.

Osterman, Paul, ed. 2020. *Creating Good Jobs: An Industry-Based Strategy.* Cambridge, Mass.: MIT Press.

Pager, Devah. 2003. "The Mark of a Criminal Record." *American Journal of Sociology* 108(5): 937–75.

Pager, Devah, and Lincoln Quillian. 2005. "Walking the Talk? What Employers Say Versus What They Do." *American Sociological Review* 70(3): 355–80.

Palmer, Phyllis. 1995. "Outside the Law: Agricultural and Domestic Workers under the Fair Labor Standards Act." *Journal of Policy History* 7(4): 416–40.

Parker, Kim, and Juliana Menasce Horowitz. 2022. "Majority of Workers Who Quit a Job in 2021 Cite Low Pay, No Opportunities for Advancement, Feeling Disrespected." Pew Research Center, March 9. https://www.pewresearch.org /fact-tank/2022/03/09/majority-of-workers-who-quit-a-job-in-2021-cite-low-pay -no-opportunities-for-advancement-feeling-disrespected/.

Parks-Yancy, Rochelle. 2010. *Equal Work, Unequal Careers: African Americans in the Workforce.* Boulder, Colo.: First Forum Press.

Peck, Emily. 2021. "Policymakers Used to Ignore Child Care. Then Came the Pandemic." *New York Times,* May 9.

Pelletier, John. 2020. "Opinion: This Isn't the College Experience You Were Expecting—but Get a Degree Anyway." *MarketWatch,* September 1. https:// www.marketwatch.com/story/this-isnt-the-college-experience-you-were -expecting-but-get-a-degree-anyway-2020-09-01.

Perry, Mark J. 2016. "Milton Friedman in a 1966 *Newsweek* Op-ed: The Minimum-Wage Law Is a 'Monument to the Power of Superficial Thinking.'" American Enterprise Institute, December 5. https://www.aei.org/carpe-diem/milton -friedman-in-a-1966-newsweek-op-ed-the-minimum-wage-law-is-a-monument -to-the-power-of-superficial-thinking/.

Pettit, Becky, and Stephanie Ewert. 2009. "Employment Gains and Wage Declines: The Erosion of Black Women's Relative Wages since 1980." *Demography* 46(3): 469–92.

Picchi, Aimee. 2021. "Billionaires Got 54% Richer during Pandemic, Sparking Calls for 'Wealth Tax.'" *CBS News,* March 31. https://www.cbsnews.com/news /billionaire-wealth-covid-pandemic-12-trillion-jeff-bezos-wealth-tax/.

Plunkert, Lois M. 1990. "The 1980's: A Decade of Job Growth and Industry Shifts." *Monthly Labor Review* (September): 3–16. https://www.bls.gov/opub /mlr/1990/09/Art1full.pdf.

Powell, Catherine. 2021. "Color of Covid and Gender of Covid: Essential Workers, Not Disposable People." *Yale Journal of Law and Feminism* 33(1): 1–44.

Proctor, Bernadette D., Jessica L. Semega, and Melissa A. Kollar. 2016. "Income and Poverty in the United States: 2015." U.S. Census Bureau, September 13. https://www.census.gov/library/publications/2016/demo/p60-256.html.

Pugh, Allison J. 2014. *The Tumbleweed Society: Working and Caring in an Age of Insecurity.* New York: Oxford University Press.

Quadagno, Jill. 1994. *The Color of Welfare: How Racism Undermined the War on Poverty.* New York: Oxford University Press.

Raley, R. Kelly, Megan M. Sweeney, and Danielle Wondra. 2015. "The Growing Racial and Ethnic Divide in U.S. Marriage Patterns." *Future Child* 25(2): 89–109.

Rampell, Catherine. 2012. "Majority of New Jobs Pay Low Wages, Study Finds." *New York Times,* August 31.

Rascoe, Ayesha. 2021. "This Top Biden Economist Has a Plan: Create Jobs, Address Inequality, Ignore Trolls." NPR, April 11. https://www.npr.org/2021 /04/11/985122570/this-top-biden-economist-has-a-plan-create-jobs-address -inequality-ignore-trolls.

Rattner, Nate, and Thomas Franck. 2021. "Black and Hispanic Women Aren't Sharing in the Job Market Recovery." CNBC, March 5. https://www.cnbc .com/2021/03/05/black-and-hispanic-women-arent-sharing-in-the-job-market -recovery.html.

Reid, Lesley Williams, and Beth A. Rubin. 2003. "Integrating Economic Dualism and Labor Market Segmentation: The Effects of Race, Gender, and Structural Location on Earnings, 1974–2000." *Sociological Quarterly* 44(3): 405–32.

Roosevelt, Franklin D. 1941. "FDR and the Four Freedoms Speech." Presented in the Annual Message to Congress, January 6, 1941. Franklin D. Roosevelt Presidential Library and Museum. https://www.fdrlibrary.org/four-freedoms.

———. 1950. "Economic Bill of Rights." Presented in the Annual Message to Congress, January 11, 1944. Reprinted in *The Public Papers and Addresses of Franklin D. Roosevelt*, edited by Samuel I. Rosenman. New York: Harper and Bros.

Rosenbaum, Eric. 2021. "How Low-Wage Work Could Get Even Worse in a Post-Pandemic Future." CNBC, March 22. https://www.cnbc.com/2021/03/22/how-low-wage-work-could-get-even-worse-in-post-pandemic-future.html.

Rosenberg, Eli. 2020. "For the 20th Straight Week, More than 1 Million Americans Filed Jobless Claims Even as Enhanced Benefits Expired." *Washington Post*, August 6. https://www.washingtonpost.com/business/2020/08/06/20th-straight-week-more-than-1-million-americans-filed-jobless-claims-even-enhanced-benefits-expired/.

Rosenfeld, Jake. 2014. *What Unions No Longer Do*. Cambridge, Mass.: Harvard University Press.

———. 2021. *You're Paid What You're Worth: And Other Myths of the Modern Economy*. Cambridge, Mass.: Belknap Press of Harvard University Press.

Rosenthal, Caitlin. 2018. *Accounting for Slavery: Masters and Management*. Cambridge, Mass.: Harvard University Press.

Rubin, Beth. 1986. "Class Struggle American Style: Unions, Strikes and Wages." *American Sociological Review* 51(5, October): 618–33.

Ruggles, Steven, J. Trent Alexander, Katie Genadek, Ronald Goeken, Matthew B. Schroeder, and Matthew Sobek. 2010. *Integrated Public Use Microdata Series: Version 5.0* (machine-readable database). Minneapolis: University of Minnesota. https://usa.ipums.org/usa/.

Rushe, Dominic. 2021. "'Hopefully It Makes History': Fight for $15 Closes In on Mighty Win for U.S. Workers." *Guardian*, February 13. https://www.theguardian.com/us-news/2021/feb/13/fight-for-15-minimum-wage-workers-labor-rights.

Schnell, Lindsay, and Trevor Hughes. 2019. "'A Terrible Time to Be Poor': Cuts to SNAP Benefits Will Hit 700,000 Hungry Americans." *USA Today*, December 21 .https://www.usatoday.com/story/news/nation/2019/12/21/trump-food-stamps-cut-snap-benefits-more-hungry-americans/2710146001/.

Schulte, Brigid, and Cassandra Robertson 2021. "Mother and Daughter Do the Same Job. Why Does One Make $9 More an Hour?" *New York Times*, May 10.

Selingo, Jeffrey. 2017. "Six Myths about Choosing a College Major." *New York Times*, November 3. https://www.nytimes.com/2017/11/03/education/edlife/choosing-a-college-major.html.

Sharone, Ofer. 2014. *Flawed System/Flawed Self: Job Searching and Unemployment Experiences*. Chicago: University of Chicago Press.

Silverstein, Jason. 2015. "Dylann Roof was Obsessed with Trayvon Martin, Wanted to Save the 'White Race': Friend." *New York Daily News*, June 20. https://www.nydailynews.com/news/national/dylann-roof-obsessed-trayvon-martin-white-race-article-1.2263647.

Slatton, Brittany C. 2015. "Book Review: The American Non-Dilemma: Racial Inequality without Racism." *Social Forces* 94(2): 1–3.

Smith, Adam. 1776. *An Inquiry into the Nature and Causes of the Wealth of Nations*, vol. 1. London: W. Strahan.

Smith, Ryan. 2020. "Your Stimulus Check Will Cover May Rent, and That's about It." *Chicago*, April 23. https://www.chicagomag.com/real-estate/April -2020/Coronavirus-Stimulus-Check-Pay-Rent/.

Stainback, Kevin, and Donald Tomaskovic-Devey. 2009. "Intersections of Power and Privilege: Long-Term Trends in Managerial Representation." *American Sociological Review* 74(5): 800–820.

———. 2012. *Documenting Desegregation: Racial and Gender Segregation in Private-Sector Employment since the Civil Rights Act*. New York: Russell Sage Foundation.

Steelman, Aaron. 2013. "Employment Act of 1946." Federal Reserve History, November 22. https://www.federalreservehistory.org/essays/employment -act-of-1946.

Streitfeld, David. 2021. "How Amazon Crushes Unions." *New York Times*, March 16. https://www.nytimes.com/2021/03/16/technology/amazon-unions-virginia.html.

Temin, Peter. 2017. *The Vanishing Middle Class: Prejudice and Power in a Dual Economy*. Cambridge, Mass.: MIT Press.

Tilly, Charles. 1998. *Durable Inequality*. Berkeley: University of California Press.

Tomaskovic-Devey, Donald. 1993. *Gender and Racial Inequality at Work: The Sources and Consequences of Job Segregation*. Ithaca, N.Y.: ILR Press.

Tomaskovic-Devey, Donald, and Dustin Avent-Holt. 2019. *Relational Inequalities: An Organizational Approach*. New York: Oxford University Press.

Tomaskovic-Devey, Donald, and Kevin Stainback. 2007. "Discrimination and Desegregation: Equal Opportunity Progress in U.S. Private Sector Workplaces since the Civil Rights Act." *Annals of the American Academy of Political and Social Science* 609(1): 49–84.

Tompson, Trevor, and Jennifer Benz. 2013. "The Public Mood: White Malaise but Optimism among Blacks, Hispanics." Associated Press–National Opinion Research Center, July 13. https://apnorc.org/wp-content/uploads/2020/02/AP -NORC_PublicMoodWhiteMalaiseButOptimismAmongBlacksandHispanics.pdf.

U.S. Census Bureau. 1989. "The Relationship between the 1970 and 1980 Industry and Occupation Classification Systems." Technical Paper 59. U.S. Census Bureau, February. https://www.census.gov/library/publications/1989/demo /tp-59.html.

Vosko, Leah. 2006. *Precarious Employment: Understanding Labour Market Insecurity in Canada*. Montreal: McGill-Queen's University Press.

WABC-TV. 2020. "Coronavirus News: Social Distancing Is Not Happening on the NYC Subway." WABC-TV, *Eyewitness News*, April 1. https://abc7ny.com /overcrowded-subway-train-nyc-social-distancing-coronavirus/6068366/.

Wang, Wendy. 2015. "The Link between a College Education and a Lasting Marriage." Pew Research Center, December 4. https://www.pewresearch.org /fact-tank/2015/12/04/education-and-marriage/.

Wang, Wendy, Kim Parker, and Paul Taylor. 2013. "Breadwinner Moms." Pew Research Center, May 29. https://www.pewresearch.org/social-trends/2013/05/29 /breadwinner-moms/.

Weir, Margaret. 1992. *Politics and Jobs: The Boundaries of Employment Policy in the United States*. Princeton, N.J.: Princeton University Press.

Werner, Julie Levinson. 2020. "Workplace Diversity—Getting It Right with Goals, Not Quotas." *Bloomberg Law*, November 10. https://news.bloomberglaw.com /us-law-week/workplace-diversity-getting-it-right-with-goals-not-quotas.

The White House. 2009. "Remarks of President Barack Obama on the Lilly Ledbetter Fair Pay Restoration Act Bill Signing." The White House Briefing Room, January 29. https://obamawhitehouse.archives.gov/the-press-office /remarks-president-barack-obama-lilly-ledbetter-fair-pay-restoration-act-bill -signin.

———. 2021a. "Inaugural Address by President Joseph R. Biden, Jr." The White House Briefing Room, January 20. https://www.whitehouse.gov/briefing -room/speeches-remarks/2021/01/20/inaugural-address-by-president-joseph -r-biden-jr/.

———. 2021b. "The Build Back Better Framework: President Biden's Plan to Rebuild the Middle Class." The White House, October 28. https://www .whitehouse.gov/build-back-better/.

Wooten, Melissa E., and Enobong Hannah Branch. 2012. "Defining Appropriate Labor: Race, Gender, and Idealization of Black Women in Domestic Service." *Race, Gender, and Class* 19(3/4): 292–308.

Yen, Hope, and Jennifer Agiesta. 2013. "Blacks, Hispanics More Optimistic than Whites." *PBS Newshour*, August 1. https://www.pbs.org/newshour/politics /blacks-hispanics-more-optimistic-than-whites.

= Index =

Tables and figures are listed in **boldface**.

and, 2, 8–9, 12–13, 83–85; GI
Bill and, 52; homeownership
rates and, 75, **77**, 80–81; income
levels and, 69–70, **69**, 75, **76**, **78**,
80, 187n5; as insurance for hard
times, 74–81, 144, 150; marriage
rates and, 75, 78, **79**, 182n26;
personal responsibility and, 73,
144; returns on investment in,
81–85, **84–85**; unemployment and,
75, **77**, 80, 97; upward mobility
and, 2–3; vanishing middle and,
45–46, 62–66, 69–70, 84, **85**, 170;
White American employment
and, 91–96, 101–2; worker cohorts
compared, 39, **40**, 42
EEOC (Equal Employment Opportunity
Commission), 28
Elliot, James, 99
employment, 16–17, 98–119. *See also*
postindustrial employment;
postwar employment; affirmative action and, 108–12, 115, 117,
188n22; American Dream and,
7–8; Covid-19 pandemic and, 159;
differential treatment based on
race, 101–4, 130; discrimination
in, 6, 99–101, 103–5, 130, 154–55,
187n5, 190n19, 190n22; diversity
goals in, 114–15; economic anxiety
and, 126–31; economic inequality and, 156–57; education and,
2, 8–9, 12–13, 83–85; gender disparities in, 1–2, 11, 23–28, 46–48,
47, 78–80, **79**, 99, 187n5; gender
roles and, 11, 21–22, 57, 131–37,
182n22, 182n24, 189n16; historical
restrictions of, 2, 6, 156–57,
181–82n16, 190n19; job screenings
for, 99–101, 103–5; job security
and, 7–9, 11–13, 19–20; marriage
rates and, 75, 78, **79**, 182n26;
minimum wage increases and,
152–54; nonstandard jobs by race
and gender, 78–80, **79**; offshoring
and outsourcing, 33, 128, 184n25;
organizational practices and

unequal access to, 99–101; public
policy on, 160–65; racial discrimination and, 104–8; racial disparities in, 1, 23–28, 46–48, **47**, 78–80,
79, 85–91; racial diversity in, 5,
6; social networks and, 101–2,
110–18, 121; standard employment relationship and, 20–23, 25,
48; technological changes and, 33,
126, 129, 184n26, 188n6; unions,
weakening of, 181n13; of vanishing middle, 46–50, **47**
Employment Act (1946), 22, 183n12
Equal Employment Opportunity Act
(1972), 2
Equal Employment Opportunity
Commission (EEOC), 28
Equal Pay Act (1963), 159

Facing Up to the American Dream
(Hochschild), 10
Fair Labor Standards Act (1937), 20,
151, 156
fairness, 138–41, 144, 151–57
femininity, 11, 21–22, 182n22
Fischer, Claude, 163
Flawed System/Flawed Self (Sharone), 130
Friedman, Milton, 152–54

gender disparities: in economic
outlook and security, 4, 19–28,
37–42, **39–41**, 42, 53–56, **55–56**,
178–80; in education, 39, **40**, **180**;
in employment, 1–2, 11, 23–28,
46–48, **47**, 78–80, **79**, 99, 187n5;
in homeownership, 51–52, 75, **77**,
80–81; in income, 48–49, **49**, 75,
76, **78**, 80, 159, **174–77**, 191n47;
occupational restrictions based
on race and gender, 2, 6, 156–57,
181–82n16; in opportunity and
reward, 32–37, **34**, **36–37**; in postindustrial labor market, 29–32,
30–31; in postwar labor market,
19–28, **24**, **26–27**; in unemployment,
75, **77**, 78, 80, 154, 159–60; in vanishing middle occupations, 46–48, **47**